THE PRINCIPAL

ABOUT THE AUTHOR

Arbitrator — American Arbitration Association, New York, New York
Professor — East Stroudsburg University, East Stroudsburg, Pennsylvania
Superintendent — East Stroudsburg Area School District, East Stroudsburg, Pennsylvania
Assistant Superintendent for Personnel and Administration, Director of Curriculum, Secondary School Principal, Elementary School Principal, Assistant Elementary School Principal, Elementary/Physical Education/Health/Science Teacher — Harborfields Central School District, Greenlawn, New York
University of Kentucky, Teacher College Columbia University, Hofstra University, Yeshiva University, East Coast University, Wilkes University, Appalachian State University

"THE PRINCIPAL"
LEADERSHIP FOR THE EFFECTIVE AND PRODUCTIVE SCHOOL

By

ROBERT M. BOOKBINDER, ED.D.

CHARLES C THOMAS • PUBLISHER
Springfield • Illinois • U.S.A.

Published and Distributed Throughout the World by

CHARLES C THOMAS • PUBLISHER
2600 South First Street
Springfield, Illinois 62794-9265

© *1992 by* CHARLES C THOMAS • PUBLISHER

ISBN 0-398-05785-0

Library of Congress Catalog Card Number: 91-44816

With **THOMAS BOOKS** *careful attention is given to all details of manufacturing
and design. It is the Publisher's desire to present books that are satisfactory as to
their physical qualities and artistic possibilities and appropriate for their particular
use.* **THOMAS BOOKS** *will be true to those laws of quality that assure a good
name and good will.*

Printed in the United States of America
SC-R-3

Library of Congress Cataloging-in-Publication Data

Bookbinder, Robert M.
    The principal : leadership for the effective and productive school
/ by Robert M. Bookbinder.
       p.   cm.
    Includes bibliographical references (p.   ) and index.
    ISBN 0-398-05785-0
    1. School principals — United States.   2. School management and
organization — United States.   I. Title.
LB2831.92.B66   1991
371.2'012 — dc20
                                            91-44816
                                            CIP

This book is dedicated to my three grandchildren:
David, Emily and Rachel

A piece appeared in a book, *Principles of Education*, written by two Columbia University Professors, J. C. Chapman and George Counts (one of this author's earlier professors) during the early 1940s. It went like this:

Greeting his pupils, the master asked, What would you learn of me?
And the reply came: How shall we care for our bodies?
How shall we rear our children? How shall we work together?
How shall we live with our fellow men? How shall we play?
For what ends shall we live?
And the teacher pondered these words, and sorrow was in his heart, for his own learning touched not these things.

PREFACE

Would you tell me, please, said Alice, *which way I ought to walk from here?*
That depends a good deal on where you want to get to, said the Cat.
I don't much care where . . . , said Alice.
Then it doesn't matter which way you walk, said the Cat.
. . . so long as I get somewhere, Alice added as an explanation.
Oh, you're sure to do that, said the Cat. *If you only walk long enough.*
Lewis Carroll: *Alice's Adventures in Wonderland* New York, 1941, p. 85.

Every author has a public in mind when he or she embarks on a manuscript for a graduate school textbook. Insights contributing to such undertakings are generated by experiences that bring with them an awareness of a need in a particular area. The author of this book has spent more than four decades as a public school teacher, an educational administrator and a professor of graduate courses in educational administration and he has had these experiences.

This book is addressed to educational administrators, particularly school principals and those responsible for their preparation. It is influenced by and designed to contribute to the effectiveness of the school principalship by underscoring significant trends, new knowledge, insights and understandings. It presents the principal as an educational leader who confidently and optimistically takes on unfamiliar problems, issues, and conflicts arising from the social revolution which has overtaken this nation's school community. This principal, as a proactive risk taker, seeks new understandings and creative solutions to the school's organization management, instruction, and human resources, and creatively addresses its internal and external environments.

The principal is viewed as a key factor in assuring the effectiveness and productivity of the school. As a direct-line action administrator, the principal: is the first and continuing contact with parents and the local community; responds to teachers and support staff needs and resources, and their development and inservicing; anticipates students' learning and the educational environment; and communicates with the central administrative staff, outside agencies and institutions. All of these impact upon the individual school unit.

Although many earlier educational developments and concepts are still pertinent today, this book introduces much needed new thought and ideas which have surfaced from: (1) the new information, changes in value systems, attitudes, perspectives, and expectations of the school's clientele; (2) a recognition that schools are failing to adequately respond to the needs of today's dynamic society; and (3) that school improvement, restructuring, renewal, and effectiveness are more likely to occur when everyone involved, directly or indirectly in the educational process, is a stakeholder. They have all experienced a democratization, a decentralization, and an empowerment in those areas of the educational scene which directly affect them personally.

The book is concerned with modeling the principal who views the school from a larger perspective, he or she sees the school as having a mission.

It is from these viewpoints that this book is directed to principals, their university professors of educational administration, superintendents, prospective principals, and those community lay persons who are grasping for some understandings of what may be needed to make their schools more effective and productive.

The motivation for writing this book grew out of the basic conviction that the principalship represents, and will increasingly represent, a powerful position for effecting change in the schools. Hopefully, this text will make an important contribution toward improving the technical, human, and conceptual competencies of the school principal, and in turn contribute significantly to the effectiveness and productivity of the school.

R.M.B.

INTRODUCTION

Excellence is an art won by training and habituation. We do not act rightly because we have virtue or excellence, but we rather have those because we have acted rightly. We are what we repeatedly do. Excellence, then, is not an act but a habit.

Aristotle

Today's business and management journals, publications and other such resources are replete with an emphasis upon excellence, productivity and attempt to discern the key characteristics of successful organizations. With very little exception, they concentrate on the pivotal role played by the organization's executive.

These effective and productive business and management leaders are seen as possessing common characteristics and performing practices that distinguish them, and their organizations. Although these leaders are not similar in their approaches and leadership styles, there appears to be a number of common elements and characteristics among the leaders who occupy these posts. Similarly, educational studies, professional publications dealing with excellence, effectiveness and productivity are commonplace.

Each and every national, state or local meeting, or discussion of educational reform, renewal or restructuring is replete with the terms effective schools and instructional leadership. The literature abounds with reports of research and strategies directed toward the improvement of schools. These resources, while analyzing the multitude of problems facing the nation's educational systems, conclude with urgings, proposals and recommendations for school improvements and an increased responsiveness to current societal expectations.

Much like the literature from business and management in the private sector, the focus is upon the leader's role in achieving excellence and productivity in the public sector. Also, numerous books rely heavily on theoretical models and on research findings regarding leadership and organization from the social and management sciences; they seek to apply these ideas to problems that principals face. Others, follow the same format but rely more on the available theory and research regarding teaching effectiveness and learning. In each case, the purpose is to discover the best ways to administer, organize, teach, and evaluate, and to prescribe them as universal treatments for school problems. Still others follow a different path by relying heavily on the anecdotes of experienced administrators who relate what worked for them. This information is arranged in the form of principles of administration, systematically organized according to tasks, roles, and responsibilities, and is prescribed to readers as the best way to practice. This book seeks to incorporate the best elements of each of these approaches, and hopefully approaches the matter of improving practice for principals from flexible and creative mindscapes of schooling and educational administration.

According to a synthesis of research on effective schools several characteristics bring the various dichotomies into sharper focus. These distinctions, supported by numerous research investigations are: (1) high expectations for student achievement, (2) strong organizational, managerial and instructional leadership, (3) well-defined school mission, goals and emphases, (4) staff training and development, (5) staff involvement and ownership in instructional decision making and practices, (6) a sense of order and purpose, (7) an effective and purposeful system of monitoring student progress, and (8) good discipline and student self-direction.

Research, studies, plus the personal and professional experiences of the author abound with the recommendation that it is the principal of the school who is most likely to meaningfully impact upon the characteristics noted above. It is the principal who occupies the best position to influence school norms, the climate of the school, and the outcomes of productivity and satisfactions for students and staff alike. It is generally believed, that these respond, directly or indirectly, to what the principal does or does not do.

In this book, the author presents the principal as the school leader in six chapters: (1) Foundations and the Principalship. (2) The Principal and Instructional Leadership. (3) Effective School Management. (4) Effecting a Productive School Organization. (5) Leadership and the School's Human Resources. (6) The Environments of the Proactive Principal. The emphasis is upon the nature of principal needed to respond, in the affirmative to this nation's demand for a renewal, reform and restructuring of its schools, and insure effective and productive school experiences for their clients, the students.

Included, are proposals for the redirection and improvement of principal development programs sponsored through school, community and university partnerships. Among these are the reform of university educational administration programs, improvements in the student selection process, the provision for more and richer clinical administrative experiences, and the broadening of students' professional and political contacts and consciousnesses. Recruitment efforts are directed toward attracting potential principals from the best and brightest resources who aspire to develop those proficiencies needed to function within organizations that cannot rely solely on traditional views of how they should operate, to understand both the rational and non-rational models of thinking about organizations and reality.

The principal appears as being in the best position to influence the school's norms, most responsible for the outcomes and satisfactions obtained by students and staff members through his or her leadership in school organization, management, human resource development and instruction, and affirmatively responsive to current internal and external factors impacting upon the school's success potential.

The overall theme of the book centers on an absolute commitment to the improvement, restructuring, reform and renewal of the school, all encouraged and advanced through the efforts of the effective and productive principal. It is his or her leadership style, skills and training, that affects within today's irrational school-community setting such change as is required to produce the effective and productive school. Methodology includes an extensive literature review, participation and observation grounded in theory, and pragmatic responses to conditions and issues as they now exist and appear, and how they are anticipated to affect the schools of the future.

The author views the expanded organizational, managerial, instructional and human productivity knowledge base as functional means by which the principal can effectively introduce an increased self-effectiveness, introduce meaningful and purposeful change, and bring improved student achievement patterns to the school.

The sociological challenge is one of empowering groups to address educational productivity. Building organizational linkages require numerous levels of support, trust, volunteered efforts, communications, and understandings of social realities. The congruent belief systems and role identities that result, clarify instructional messages, facilitate improved home-community-school relations, instructional leadership. They effect, create, produce and produce distinguished schools.

Drawing upon documented accounts and the author's personal and professional experiences, this book presents understandings of interactive partnerships, identifies barriers to school improvement and acknowledges the culture of schools concepts.

This book is the work of an educational professional who for a period of four decades succeeded as a: teacher, assistant elementary school principal, elementary school principal, secondary school principal, director of curriculum and instruction, assistant superintendent for personnel and administration, superintendent, professor of educational administration and arbitrator.

ACKNOWLEDGMENTS

Without the assistance of many people, this book never could have been written. I am most grateful to Michael Thomas of Charles C Thomas, Publisher for his advice, patience, and encouragement. He helped me find my way through the maze of material.

Many institutions, organizations, school administrators, and teachers assisted me in gathering materials for the book. I do wish to express my gratitude to Executive Director Dr. John Abbruzzese, Assistant Executive Director Dr. Charles Miller, Superintendents John Lambert and Dr. Edward Coyle, Assistant Superintendent Russell Treible, Secondary School Principals Dr. James Bonner and Karl Dickl, Middle School Principal Maurice Beaulieu, Assistant High School Principal Horace Cole, and Professor Dr. Michael Kelly who shared with me research, studies and professional journals that helped me insure that the book would be responsive to current issues and concerns. Also, Howard Wood, Bill Broad, and my daughter, Pamela Spears, who not only helped me more fully understand the workings of my personal computer, but also helped me with the reproduction of this manuscript on lazer printers.

Particular thanks are due Superintendent Thomas J. Lahey who was my *mentor*, long before this term gained its current popularity. He encouraged me, put a hand on my shoulder when that was needed, and was a role model as I served in almost every administrative post of the Harborfields Central School District. Also, Elementary School Teacher Harold (Hesh) Vilinsky, a *friend* and truly *professional educator*, whose classroom I visited more frequently than any other to observe exciting, motivating, creative teaching at its best. These *vissionaries* are now gone and are missed.

Secondary School Teacher Joseph Zeichner, a *risk taker* and *model* for his fellow teachers, who helped me understand and value the merits of *empowerment* long before that term was given its current meaning and purpose.

Thanks to the thousands of students who passed me by during these four decades, from whom I have learned and continue to learn so very much.

CONTENTS

xv

THE PRINCIPAL

Chapter I

FOUNDATIONS AND THE PRINCIPALSHIP

INTRODUCTION

Conductors of great symphony orchestras do not play every musical instrument; through leadership the ultimate production is an expressive and unified combination of tones.

Thomas D. Bailey

There is a resurgence of public concern about the effectiveness of the schools and a renewed appreciation of the importance of the principal in the educational process. This attention has been matched by research on principals' behavior (Boyon, 1988), school effectiveness (Levine and Lezotte, 1990), and popular work outside of education focusing on leadership and organizational excellence in general (Peters and Waterman, 1982; Peters and Austin, 1985).

There is an abundance of research in today's literature citing the principal as perhaps the most important factor in an effective school. Effective schools research consistently cites strong instructional leadership as one of the correlates for success. (Shoemaker and Fraser, 1981) conclude in their study that principals can provide schools with assertive, achievement oriented leadership; an orderly, and purposeful climate; high expectations for staff and pupils, and well-designed goals, objectives and evaluation systems. This view is furthered by the National Association of Secondary Principals (NASSP) when it concluded that almost *everyone agrees that the principal is the key to a good school* (McCurdy, 1983).

This is not to suggest that the principal alone can make a school good. However, researchers, observers and practitioners generally conclude that a capable principal is necessary in the establishment and maintenance of the *effective* and productive school, and it is their implicit and explicit considered opinions that principals have the necessary decision-making autonomy and authority to exercise this strong leadership. The Southern Regional Educational Board noted that the success or failure of a public school depends more on the principal than any other single person (Southern Regional Education Board, 1986).

3

Also, in an acclaimed presentation, Weick (1976) argued that educational organizations are *loosely coupled systems* and that individual units (schools) do maintain considerable operating autonomy. This view was furthered in the Morris, Crowson, Hurwitz, Porter-Gehrie (1982) comprehensive study of building principals. They found that principals exercised considerable decision-making authority in the implementation of school district policy. Generally, most of the research does suggest that principals ordinarily have the authority and autonomy to exercise leadership in their schools if they choose to do so.

For the most part, the various commission reports of the 1980s, calling for a return to excellence in the public schools, and the numerous state mandates and reforms, that followed these reports, have been promulgated among the educational bureaucracy. There are those who view many of the changes in educational administration practices which followed the reports and reform movements as threatening to the principal's authority and decision-making autonomy. Such terms and conditions as: strategic planning, collaborative management, empowerment, decentralization, distributive leadership, shared decision-making, horizontal compatibility, organizational culture, site-based management, and synergy do bring with them new challenges and change. However, the creative and effective school leader sees these as new challenges and does not view this role as having been eroded because of these changes in the means for providing school leadership.

HISTORICAL OVERVIEW

Ever since the colonization of the United States educational reform has been proposed and appeared in various forms. The early Puritan leaders (1642), stressed salvation as the school reform that they would encourage with the introduction of the *New England Primer.* Later, educational reform appeared in the curriculum of Benjamin Franklin's Philadelphia Academy (1751), when the emphasis was directed towards practical needs with the introduction of surveying and navigational studies in addition to the classics. Monitorial schools appeared in the early 1880s, schools designed to aid the poor by teaching discipline, morality, and reducing delinquency. Horace Mann provided the leadership with the common school movement which lead to tax supported compulsory schools, schools intended to unify and sustain the American culture, perpetuate the American form of representative governments, promote free enterprise, and instill morality. The Smith-Hughes Act of 1917 advanced home economics and vocational courses of study.

The United States saw the need for a more global education following World War I, and the *Cardinal Principals of Secondary Education* (1918) provided for the introduction of a variety of programs in high schools to respond to these newly recognized needs. The child-centered progressive education movement lasted until the 1930s, and it is often thought, particularly by those who opposed this movement, that this reform led to a lowering of school standards. Other reforms that followed included:

1. social reconstruction in the 1930's (Counts, Rugg)
2. essential subjects in 1938, called *basics* since 1950
3. area studies: Asia, Africa, Latin America, following World War II
4. inquiry learning after 1950: new math, etc. (Jerome Bruner)
5. Black studies, women's studies, since 1960s
6. alternative schools since 1970s
7. behavioral objectives (B. F. Skinner)

The *Effective Schools* movement is rooted in the reform studies, reports and programs of the 1980s and 1990s. One of the first such reports, *A Nation At Risk* (1983), stirred things up at the national level with its statement that the nation's schools are being eroded by a rising tide of mediocrity that threatens its very future. These reports all focus upon the oft reported *decline of student achievement.* Accordingly, the credibility of the nation's educational system is again under attack, and a number of changes were proposed or made with the supposition that these would make the schools more effective and competitive. Following the publication and distribution of *A Nation At Risk,* almost all of the states raised their high school graduation requirements, more than 37 states assessed student achievement, more than half of the states raised teacher certification requirements (including competency tests), and more than 300 state level education study groups adopted key national report recommendations, while adding recommendations of their own.

Educational reform, renewal, and restructuring is politically fashionable today. Schools are highly visible, involve many people, and are central to our very way of life. Reasons for these reforms are many and varied. Some blame the loss of world markets, others, the lower skilled jobs going abroad, increasing dropouts, functional illiterates, and unemployable youth. Most of the reform reports were prepared by persons or groups that are supportive of the schools, while a number do urge the dismantling of the nation's public education program as we now view it with: tuition tax credits, vouchers, and schools of choice.

The *Effective Schools* movement seeks to isolate and deal with some of the problems of the 1980s. Much of the literature focuses on the various aspects of current educational problems, while most offer help to the schools with their efforts to effectively respond to students' and society's needs. *Effective Schools* research looks to supplying answers to the question, What is different about the successful school?

In spite of these reform efforts, public education skeptics and critics continue to voice their doubts. On the November 7, 1990, the following appeared in the editorials of that day's newspapers:

> American education has been described as everything from a national wasteland to a derelict institution which is failing miserably in its mission. Television documentaries, news magazines, and newspapers have been decrying the short-comings of those who have gone through the nation's classrooms only to be found inadequately prepared for life in the real world. Pleas for improvement have been heard from nearly every quarter of society. Overall, a grim picture of the education structure has been painted. However, there is hope, there are oases in *this wasteland.*

Griffith (1988) made the following statement at an assemblage of school administrators. *I am thoroughly and completely convinced that, unless a radical reform movement gets underway, and is successful, most of us in this room will live to see the end of educational administration as a profession.*

This author proposes that one such oasis is the school principal and the principalship. In study after study, and personal observations, it has been shown that one key determinant of excellence in public schooling is the leadership of the individual school principal (Educational Commission of the States, 1983, p. 29). This resurgence of public concern about the effectiveness of the schools has brought with it a renewed appreciation of the importance of the principal in the educational process. This attention has been matched by research on principal's behavior (Boyon 1988), school effectiveness (Levine and Lezotte 1990), and popular work outside of education focusing on leadership and organizational excellence in general (Peters and Waterman 1982 and Peters and Austin 1985). Concurrent with this interest in describing characteristics of effective schools numerous states and school systems have mandated formal evaluation procedures for school administrators. More than 30 states now have in place such evaluation procedures and school systems reporting such procedures have increased from 40% in 1968 to 86% in 1984 (ERS 1985).

Throughout research on the effective and productive school, the principal appears again and again as the *fulcrum* in terms of school direction. Whatever the source: school critics, university researchers, teacher organizations, community's publics, central administration, or the board of education, the principalship continually reappears as the focal point for understanding and improving the quality of the nation's schools. It is the principal who remains on the *firing line* when conflicting issues, ranging from student discipline to problems of personnel administration, or compliance with increasing numbers of state and federal mandates to maintaining a quality educational program that serves a less and less homogeneous school community with its varying students' abilities and parent aspirations. It is the principal who, if effective, will provide responses to such issues as: drug and alcohol abuse, student pregnancies, students' rights and responsibilities, dropouts, students at risk, etc.

School effectiveness and productivity need to be operationally defined. Upon review of the extant literature, it is clear that effectiveness is bound to the defining criteria chosen. For example, select literature characterizes effectiveness as residual gain on standardized test scores, while others favor schools known for their positive socializing effect on children (Glickman 1987 and Cuban 1983). Effectiveness is not unidimensional, but rather a complex construct that is dependent on the criteria used. These may be independent of one another and, indeed may be mutually exclusive. Within a theoretical model or framework, it is difficult to organize the field so as to state unequivicably that one school is more effective than another or that a given set of principals' behaviors and leadership styles are any better than another set of behaviors. To resolve this dilemma, the major models that characterize organizational effectiveness were examined (Parson 1960; Bossert, Dwyer, Rowan, and Lee 1982; Duckworth 1983; Ellet and Wallberg 1979; Pitner 1988; and Hoy and Miskel 1987). In essence, from the perspective of this textbook, school effectiveness can be characterized as the school's ability to control and adjust to the following constructs.

Maintenance — the school's ability to create and maintain its motivational and value structure. For an organization to effectively function over an extended time period there must be a certain sense of client and employee loyalty to the organization, its goals, and culture. Often these values are defined as central life interests, job satisfaction, staff motivation, job commitment, and sometimes included under the generic label, *climate*. They are typically examined through expectancy theory comparing reward value, reward probability, and level of effort (Vroom 1964); job character-istics models comparing skill variety, task identity and task significance (Hackman and Oldham 1980); discrepancy hypotheses comparing indi-vidual motivation with organization incentives (Smith, Kendall and Hulin 1969); inducements contributions theory which examines what is offered vs. contributed (March and Simon 1958); and, dissonance theory compar-ing employees' expectations with actual experience (Festinger 1957). Schools characterized as high on this dimension are described as having committed, dedicated staff who are interested in their work as defined by the school's value system, are protective of their school, and identify with its norms. Employees are seen as investing a large share of time, commitment and energy toward the school in relation to competing life activities.

Adaptation — the school's ability to successfully understand and accom-modate its external environment. The extent to which the school does or does not offer programs consistent with community norms and expecta-tions is often related to difficulty or success in sustaining interest in and support for the school. Schools and school systems can lose the support and respect of their communities if they are not aware of the expectations and desires of their clients. To successfully adapt to changing environ-ments and compete with others for community interest, resources and support, effective schools must fuse bureaucratic expectations, sublimate wishes and individual needs in a way that produces a more powerful influence than the simple additive power of each entity. Schools must maintain a certain degree of harmony to effectively deal with their envi-ronmental pressures and possess sensitive monitoring mechanisms that provide reliable and timely information concerning the external environ-ment. Adaptation is also defined in terms of the ability of schools to keep abreast of the new technologies in the field. This means that the staff is actively experimenting with new instructional methods and constantly surveying available resources for new curricular materials. Planned and meaningful staff development activities that focus on keeping the staff current provide further indications of a school poised to take advantage of many potential opportunities.

Goal Attainment — the ability of the school to define objectives, mobi-lize resources, and achieve desired ends. Unlike the adaptation dimension, goal attainment, the third criteria of effectiveness, is widely recognized as an important measure of effectiveness. Indeed, measures of the *effective school* correlate (goal consensus, strong instructional leadership, close monitoring of the instructional program, and high expectations of stu-dent achievement) are subcomponents of the goal attainment dimension.

Generally, goal attainment is defined through productivity, resource acquisition, efficiency, quantity, and quality standards. (Hallinger and Murphy 1985) offer an instrument which is designed to measure principal instructional management in such areas as: frame the school's goals, coordinate the curriculum, monitor student progress, protect instructional time, maintain high visibility, provide incentives for teachers, promote professional development, and provide incentives for learning. This is another measurement device typical of those designed to assess the goal attainment dimension. In addition to process which might lead to goal attainment such as the establishment of quality control or resource allocation systems, actual outcomes typically defined in student terms are also important dimensions of school effectiveness as operationalized through goal attainment. The most common is academic achievement; however, student affective outcomes such as student self-concept also play critical roles. Other studies have found that student measures such as academic norms, academic futility, future expectations, present expectations, and teacher expectations to be linked with overall school climate and to account for a significant amount of variance in student academic achievement.

Integration — the ability of the school to organize, coordinate, and unify the various school tasks necessary for achievement. The last attribute of effective schools is the extent to which the component subsystems and/or people trust the competence of each other and work together in a coordinated fashion. From a larger perspective, this includes both an integration within and between the various school component groups. In many ways the integration component is related to the conception of coupling that has gained considerable attention within the study; of informal organizations. In this sense, the integration (coupling) construct as it applies to schools typically refers to a pattern of organizational and interpersonal mechanisms that serve to link the various human subcomponents of the school. When coupling is loose and/or trust and respect is absent, the resultant effect is often that the staff and students are exposed to repetition, significant gaps or overlaps in the curriculum, and a general absence of a developmental sequence that capitalizes on prior learning. Other direct measures of integration are the extent of cohesion-conflict among and between different school groups. As conflict arises, coordination of the educational program and social development is curtailed and inefficiency is promulgated.

Integration is also a measure of the degree to which the school has a common sense of purpose or vision and the degree to which the students, staff and community share that vision of themselves; can describe their individual roles in the larger plan; and feel that they play an important role in the organization. Conversely, schools that evidence and exhibit excessive repetition and duplication, conflict, and lack of inter-organizational communication would be considered to be low in integration.

THE PRINCIPAL: THEN AND NOW

The present development of the principal may be traced to the middle of the nineteenth century. The essential features of the principalship became apparent by the close of the twentieth century and have not undergone substantial change since that time. Certainly the duties and responsibilities have grown and increased in complexity, however principals continue to serve the twin functions of providing instructional leadership and managing school affairs today, just as they were called upon to do some one hundred years ago.

We can identify several factors which contributed to the early development of the principalship:

1. the rapid growth of the cities during the 1850–1900 period and subsequent problems accompanying the schooling of an ever expanding school age population,
2. the grading of schools and the introduction of new sets of management problems related to the coordination of pupils and curriculum,
3. the reorganization of schools and the consolidation of departments under a single administrative head, and
4. the establishment of the position of a head assistant to free the principal from teaching responsibilities (Pierce, 1934).

Many of the duties prescribed by lay boards of education for the principal were for the most part clerical in nature prior to 1850. By the late 1800s the emphasis in responsibilities shifted from the maintenance of records and reports to matters of school organization and general management. By 1900, the principal had become the directing manager, rather than the presiding teacher of the school (Pierce, 1934, p. 211). Principals were required to assume increased responsibility for the daily management of schools and had by this time acquired some elements of power and their position carried with it increased prestige.

The right to graduate pupils on the basis of the principal's standards, the right to have orders or suggestions to teachers given only through the medium of principals, and the right to a voice in transfers and assignments of teachers connected with their schools, the right to direct teachers, enforce safeguards to protect the health and morals of pupils, supervise and rate janitors, require the cooperation of parents, and requisition educational supplies

(Pierce, 1934, p. 211).

The role of the principal was extended to include the dimension of instructional supervision when school boards and superintendents were beginning to find that they were ill-equipped, because of training and time, to oversee instructional matters in the schools.

The principal's supervisory role continued to develop by the middle of the nineteenth century, Principals became involved with class visitations, pupil adjustments, measurement of pupil progress, rating of teachers, and instruction in methods, virtually all of the phases of modern supervision (Pierce, 1934, p. 213). By the early 1900s, three critical and enduring functions of the principalship had gained a secure footing:

1. the organization and general management of the school,
2. the supervision of instruction and staff development, and
3. the interpretation of the work of the school to the immediate school community.

The role had evolved from that of a *principal teacher* performing numerous clerical tasks to the prototype of the modern day principal.

The principalship developed in concert with changes in the school's external environments and reflected changes in the superintendent's function. It was (Button 1966) who offered evidence of this in his historical overview of the changing doctrines of educational administration during the one hundred years preceding, in his *Doctrines of Administration: A Brief History.*

The administrative duties of the principal were in place before the supervisory function was fully realized; as a result, the former has often tended to occupy the major portion of the principal's energies and efforts. Further, in many school systems, it was the superintendent who assumed the supervisory role and the improvement of instruction. This was his or her responsibility, if it was to be done at all.

The rapid growth of the schools, the necessity for classification of pupils, installation of grades and courses of study, and the introduction of new or special subjects demanded more time than the superintendent could give. Because of this, the principal was called upon to do this extremely important work. Principals were now conducting teachers' meetings, visiting classrooms, measuring the efficiency of instruction, adjusting pupils' difficulties, rating teachers, and giving teachers instruction in teaching methods.

The early supervisory roles of the principal were centered in the development of a well-grounded system of schools, the ideal for which most superintendents sought. This supervisory function of the principal could generally be characterized, before 1900, as inspection. Unfortunately, this concept of supervision still appears in too many of today's public schools.

The current educational scene is seen as retaining many of the remnants of these earlier doctrines reflected in the principalship. Some of today's principals view themselves as *teachers of teachers,* others as *applied philosophers, managers,* or *professionals* imbued with some special knowledge and understanding of the behavioral sciences as they relate to school administration. Many of today's principals do not envision themselves as change agents in the schools they administer. They prefer to either not respond to or to conceal themselves from the new environments that are bound to appear in today's *non-rational world.*

> The author, in an earlier experience, could have easily assumed the above noted posture. This occurred during the infancy of the formal collective bargaining movement. Early in the 1950s, while serving as a teacher, I was elected to the House of Delegates of the New York State Teachers Association.
>
> During my final year as a delegate, I was appointed to the post of principal of the elementary school in which I had been teaching. Upon returning from that year's teachers' association delegate convention, I was made fully aware that I was no longer viewed by the teachers of the school, or school district, as their representative. The local teacher organization simply avoided calling upon me, this new principal, to report upon the events of the convention.
>
> I recognized the need to fashion new and constructive relationships and to be responsive and understanding of this new internal environment in which the teachers and I now found ourselves. Relationships between teachers and administrators had undergone change with the advent of collective teacher activities, and the ability and preparedness for those affected by what at times was an adversary process posed conditions that required new understandings, sensitivities and sophistication.

The effective and productive principal is able to maintain a balance while performing as an instructional leader and effective school manager. There are a multitude of factors and environmental issues which might suggest that this balance is an impossible goal, however, the author's approach to the principalship would suggest that unless these two, productive instructional leadership and effective school management, are occurring there is little reason to argue for the continuation of the principalship as we know it.

FUNCTIONS OF THE PRINCIPAL

A goodly portion of the schools' publics have a limited understanding of the responsibilities of the principal and the principalship.

> Every school administrator, according to some jokesters, now needs three assistants: one to write proposals and explain to state and federal bureaucrats what changes are about to be made; another to tell the board of education, the community, and the teachers that the changes won't make any difference; and a third to attend meetings called by the first two.
>
> (H. Thomas James, *Education Digest,* Quote)

> And then there was that principal who during a school walk-through proudly announced to this author, *I made it.* When questioned regarding what he had made, he declared proudly, *I made it through the lunch period today.*

Knezevich (1975, pp. 393–395) suggests that more and more the principal is recognized as an executive or administrator and the principalship is viewed as a constellation of positions. He refers to Dean (1960), who conceptualized the office of the principal as one that provides the following school services:

1. A communication center of the school
2. A clearinghouse for the transaction of school business
3. A counseling center for teachers and students
4. A counseling center for school patrons
5. A research division of the school, for the collection, analysis, and evaluation of information regarding activities and results
6. A repository of school records
7. The planning center for solving school problems and initiating school improvements
8. A resource center for encouraging creative work
9. A coordinating center and agency designed to cultivate wholesome school and community relations

Knezevich offers select prescriptions while detailing the principal's tasks, and suggests that the principal is unable to adequately fulfill the role of instructional supervisor, competent to counsel all teachers. He suggests that instructional leadership requires that the principal marshall resources, human and material, that classroom teachers require to perform effectively, and that the principal, due to other administrative functions may not be effective in this function. He presents these observations:

> *The principal in a public school, whether at the elementary or secondary level, is a counselor of students, the school disciplinarian, the organizer of the schedule, the supervisor of the instructional program, the pupil-relations representative for the attendance area, the liason between teachers and the superintendent, the director and evaluator of teaching efforts, the manager of school facilities, the supervisor of custodial and food service employees within the building, and a professional leader.*

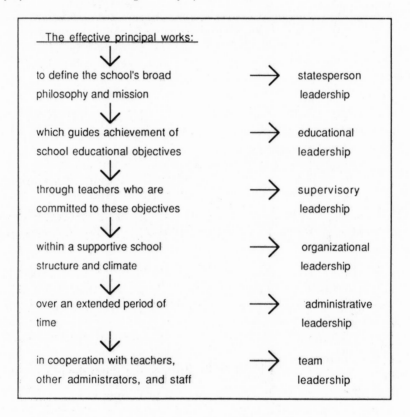

Figure 1: Major functions of principal

Those who are familiar with the principal's position see it as a demanding one. However, few of the earlier studies and writings sought to add a further dimension to this demanding role, that of envisioning, of recognizing the principal as one that views this role in terms of the future direction of public education. It would appear that this dimension is vital if we are to respond with some legitimacy to the current concerns enveloping public education.

Rose and Drake (1974, pp. 13–14) view the principal's function as one that emphasizes a combination of administrative-managerial and educational leadership. They have prescribed this dual emphasis as:

1. *Administrative-Managerial Emphasis*
   a. Maintaining adequate school records of all types
   b. Preparing reports for the central office and other agencies
   c. Budget development and budget control
   d. Personnel administration
   e. Student discipline
   f. Scheduling and maintaining a schedule
   g. Building administration
   h. Administering supplies and equipment
   i. Pupil accounting
   j. Monitoring programs and instructional processes prescribed by the central office
2. *Educational Leadership Emphasis*
   a. Stimulate and motivate maximum staff performance
   b. Develop with staff realistic and objective systems of accountability for learning
   c. Develop cooperatively operable assessment procedures with staff
   d. Work with staff in developing and implementing the evaluation of staff
   e. Work with staff in formulating plans for evaluating and reporting student progress
   f. Provide channels for the involvement of the community in the operation of the school
   g. Encourage continuous study of curricular and instructional innovations
   h. Provide leadership to students in helping them develop meaningful and responsible student government
   i. Establish a professional learning resources center and expedite its use.

Unfortunately, Roe and Drake, suggest in their observations, that it is virtually impossible to assume that the principal can be a real instructional leader and at the same time be held strictly accountable for the general operational and management detail required by the central office. These authors further this position when they maintain that the professional leadership is the one that most principals profess they dream about but can't achieve. They would argue that it is the exceptional principal who tends to emphasize instructional leadership, and that most principal's jobs are dominated by the administrative-managerial emphasis.

In this text, however, the author seeks to promote the instructional leadership role of the principal as his or her primary responsibility. Although it is fully recognized that the principal must successfully deal with a multitude of administrative-managerial functions, the primary purpose of the schools, that of providing effective and productive learning experiences for their students, must be the principal's primary emphasis. Unless this primary role of the principal is dealt with responsibly, all other roles have little or no meaning or purpose.

Further, there is reason to firmly believe that many of the traditional administrative-managerial tasks should no longer occupy nor consume the principal as in the past. What with the addition of various services and personnel and new technologies, many of the traditional tasks that fell solely within the principal's domain do not exist. This author has personally experienced a watering down of central office clerical and other managerial requirements imposed upon the principal. While serving as an elementary school principal during the 1950s, the author was then consumed with the clerical responsibility of assuring the exactness and reporting of each teacher's attendance register, and the additional assignment of overseeing the student transportation program of the school system. Yet his priorities lay with instructional leadership, so classroom visitations and observations, staff development programs, and the creation of classroom libraries, were but some of the instructional leadership functions within the sphere of this principal's role.

What with the introduction of new technologies and procedures, secretarial and clerical personnel, and various support services, such as: guidance counselors, psychologists, assistant principals, department subject/grade level heads and coordinators, central office staff personnel, the empowerment movement, and more, there is good reason to expect that the education leadership role of the principal occupy the primary functions of the principal of today, should he or she wish this to be so.

CONCEPTION OF THE PRINCIPALSHIP

Theorists have identified key administrative task areas and processes for the principalship as: *planning, organizing, leading, and controlling.*

The *planning* function implies the setting of the school's goals and objectives, and developing those strategies necessary to implement them. The *organizing* function is the means by which the principal pulls together those human, financial, and physical resources required to effectively satisfy these goals and objectives. A *leading* function calls for the guiding, coaching, mentoring, and supervising of fellow staff and associates. And finally, the *controlling* function includes the principal's evaluation and review responsibilities of providing feedback and assuring the attainment of the school's goals and objectives.

POSDCoRB is an acronym for another example of administrative processes. This proposal by Gulick (1937) meant: *planning, organizing, staffing, directing, coordinating, reporting, and budgeting.* The American Association of School Administrators (1955) added: stimulating staff and evaluating staff as additional and significant processes.

In 1975, Miklos summarized principalship tasks and functions by encompassing common themes from a variety of study and research resources, including the works of such noted educational administration theorists as Russell Gregg (1975) and Roald Campbell (1971).

RESEARCH ON SCHOOL PRINCIPALS

In educational research literature, the role of the principal, that generally dominates, is that of: leader, instructional supervisor, administrative decision maker, organizational change agent, and conflict manager. The most prevalent image of the principal, as reflected in research, is that of principal-as-leader.

An often repeated concern affecting and impacting upon the principalship is a continuing conflict regarding emphasis, the instructional versus the managerial functions of the assignment. It is obvious that a balance needs to be maintained between the two, and the effective principal is one who responds with appropriate emphasis to these two specific demands.

Some research studies propose that the principal direct his or her attention toward organizational maintenance tasks, commonly observed in many schools, are related to one or more of the following: the expectations of central office administrators, the norms of teachers, the dispositions and abilities of principals, the size of the organization, the in-school administrative resources, characteristics of the student population, and aspects of the larger environment within which the school operates (Greenfield, 1982, p. 14). While leadership is what is sought of school principals, research which emphasizes only this dimension of the principal's role obscures much of what the principal actually does. Most studies, such as these, fail to note the wide range of personal, organization, group, managerial, personnel, and environmental factors that influence the principal.

Four early studies provide the basis for current research. Hemphill, Griffiths, and Frederikson (1962) examined the personal characteristics of principals and the consequences of such differences among principals while executing their tasks as they interact with other critical factors within the schools' environments. Gross and Herriot (1965) identified the principals' roles in the improvement of teacher performance and challenged the argument that principals should provide only routine administrative services. Foskett (1967) anticipated the divergent and often conflicting values and perception characterizing teachers, students, and parent and non-parent community groups. Lipham and Francke (1966) studied the actual work situations of principals and determined a range of interpersonal, and contextual factors related to principals and their promotion.

More recent research on the principalship is not problem-centered, nor does it focus in any meaningful manner on policy issues. Byrne, Hines, and McCleary (1978) propose that the most serious problem faced by secondary principals are: time consuming administrative detail, inadequate time, and variations in the abilities of teachers. Valentine et. al. (1981) suggest that administrative detail, apathetic or irresponsible parents, and problem students prevent middle level principals from performing their assignments. Pharis and Zachariya (1979) noted staff dismissal, student behavior, and declining enrollments as the most serious problems facing elementary school principals. These studies revealed little about the personal characteristics of principals and appeared out of step with the constantly changing demographics, although Gorton and McIntyre (1978) noted several individual qualities that may distinguish effective principals from others.

Some studies view the behaviors of principals. Wolcott's (1973) research portrayed the principalship as characterized by face-to-face interpersonal encounters, and the role of the principal as one that is highly personal and problem centered. In the Salley, McPherson and Baehr (1979) study a job function inventory for school principals was developed. These researchers have found that the single largest category involved the principal's relations with people and groups. They note that principals are captives of their environments. Unless environmental characteristics, particularly those related to the organization of the school and school system, are changed, the principal rarely will be a change agent and his or her work will be routinely predictable. This research revealed basic patterns used by principals in response to their work:

1. emphasizing the involvement and support of groups,
2. focusing on the evaluation and improvement of academic performance,

3. developing qualified staff through personal effort, and
4. emphasizing fiscal control and close relationships with the central office.

They conclude by noting that principals define their positions in terms of administrative rather than instructional functions, and that traditional conceptions of the principal as an instructional leader increasingly conflict with the pressures that accompany the production manager.

Blumberg and Greenfield (1980) found that principals identified by others as effective were strongly committed to certain personal values about schools and children, tended to be active and to take initiatives, and did not permit themselves to become consumed by routine organizational requirements. These principals successfully used a variety of approaches in dealing with these problems thereby suggesting that there is more than one path to the principalship.

Crowson and Porter-Gehrie (1980) identified specific coping strategies used by principals when dealing with inadequate time, enrollment decline, challenges of authority, diverse community and parent expectations, and conflicting role expectations. Although these results were not definitive, they did describe the coping behavior of principals.

Morris et. al (1981) found principals exercising discretion in:

1. monitoring what was happening throughout the school,
2. protecting the school system from the uncertainties of an unpredictable clientele,
3. adapting organizational policies to school needs,
4. realizing their personal goals,
5. acquiring power relative to the larger system,
6. adapting to the reward system of the district, and
7. protecting their school from interference in its instuctional endeavors.

Other recent studies focused more specifically on the principal's nature of work. Peterson (1981) focused directly on the managerial aspects of the principalship. Martin and Willower (1981) studied the managerial behavior of secondary school principals, while Willower and Kmetz (1982) studied the managerial behavior of elementary school principals, and Berman (1982) studied the managerial behavior of female secondary principals.

These studies flagged the relative distribution of effort over a variety of activities, but they do not provide data regarding how well those activities were performed or the consequences of the time given to each activity. Unfortunately, the results of research on the principalship offer limited guidelines for those interested in improving the effectiveness of school site administrators. The complexity of the role itself and inherent methodological and theoretical limitations in studying principals will continue to plague those in search of an applied understanding resulting in improved practices (Bossert et. al. 1981).

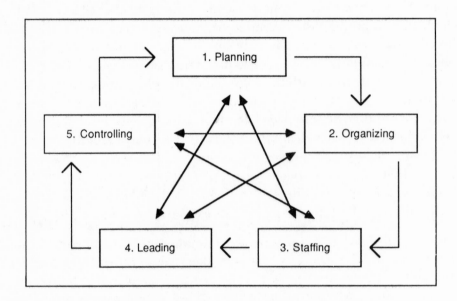

Figure 2 : How principal's functions are related

Nevertheless, there are certain characteristics of the principal's role which research offers as critical to effective performance:

1. the ability to work closely with others on a face-to-face basis,
2. the ability to manage conflict and ambiguity,
3. the ability to integrate a cluster of demands competing for the time and attention of principals,
4. the ability to anticipate and adapt to rapidly changing human social, and environmental conditions,
5. the ability to think and to exercise discretion in formulating action plans and decisions when responding to the contingencies of a system in constant motion, and,
6. the ability to assess and evaluate the consequences of the schooling for

children in light of knowledge regarding effective educational and managerial practices.

Another question that is difficult to study and research is the consequences of the activities and social interactions of principals. There are both design and criterion problems in studying phenomena related to this question.

Researchers are currently systematically observing and recording the day-to-day behavior of principals. Such studies yield substantive data about the kinds of problems principals face and the various ways in which they respond to these problems. Such research provides valued direction to efforts to identify personality and situational variables and relationships regarding principal behavior. This form of descriptive research is a valued strategy in studying school principals and their behaviors. Action research promises to build a desperately needed foundation for both effective practice as well as for a more general understanding of the work of the principal and this is to be encouraged.

REFORM OF PRINCIPAL PREPARATION

The reform movement in education of the 1980s and early 1990s has flagged a further need, that of providing highly competent school administrators, in particular school principals. Accordingly, many of the universities that offer programs leading to school administrator preparation and certification are now designed to provide prospective principals with a more complete knowledge base. In addition to guidelines requiring some teaching experience, an advanced degree, and numbers of courses and credits or semester hours in select major areas, candidates for the principalship are expected to complete an internship or employment as a practicing principal. During this internship or employment the candidate is monitored by the local school district and university, and if successful, awarded temporary certification. Beyond this, the candidate is required to continue his or her inservicing through supplemental course work, which eventually leads to permanent satisfaction of principal certification standards. The primary focus of the internship program provides for supervised practice and the framework for demonstrating on-the-job competence. Another positive element of the program is one that prospective principals are provided with employment opportunities. It provides for closer coordination between school districts and universities, and establishes an appropriate and valued linkage.

INDUCTING PRINCIPALS

Principal induction is the process by which new school principals make the transition from theoretical to operational leadership. There are in in existence several approaches to principal induction, ranging simply from handing over the keys to the building to comprehensive career development programs. Five studies appear in the November 1989 report of the National Association of Elementary School Principals regarding *Inducting Principals* that exemplify the ongoing research and development in educational administration which seeks to fill the gap between the idealized abstraction characteristic of principals' academic preparation and the demanding reality they confront during their first years on the job.

One of the studies recommends, based on the data that had been compiled, that induction programs provide additional orientation in time management, communication with staff, working with parents, budgeting, and curricular instruction. Further, an effort was made to delineate the major problems confronting new principals, offer promising recommendations, and provide a comprehensive guide for the formation of strategies for successful principal induction, including from personal experiences, a practical guide of the *do's and don'ts* for new principals.

PREPARATION FOR PLURALISM

The preparation of principals must be responsive to the *now* environments of their school-communities. Attention must be directed toward issues of race, ethnicity, gender, and social class.

The National Policy Board for Education Administration has responded to this need in its report entitled, *The Importance of Being Pluralistic: Improving the Preparation of School Administrators.* Notes on Reform, No. 6. Part of this report contains the perspectives of graduate students regarding their own experiences during their educational administration preparation programs. These students, of different racial, social, and gender backgrounds, share their reflections and perspectives on the diversity which affected their own education and the conditions of their employment. Another study contained in this report entitled, *Race, Ethnicity,*

Culture, and Values: An Emphasis Needed in Administrator Preparation Programs, describes the urgency of revising preparation programs to include study and reflection about our pluralistic society and schools. This study offers a variety of instructional techniques that are worthy of consideration in the development of school administrator preparation programs.

ASSERTIONS ABOUT SCHOOL ADMINISTRATORS

The vigorous debate about educational reform has pointed to many perceived flaws in American education. In the heat of the debate, many critics of today's public schools have made charges and counter charges about the causes of educational deficiencies. Some charge soft curricula, others blame poor teaching, some blame irresponsible parents, and still others point to a lack of financial support as the root cause.

Efforts to find reasons have included some severe criticisms of educational administration. Some of these criticisms are deserved, and corrections should be made. However, some of the criticisms have been vague, harsh and inflamatory.

Six different assertions about school administration have appeared in the press or other media. These have appeared as: there are too many administrators, the number of administrators is increasing rapidly, administrators are paid too much, increasing amounts of school budgets are going to administration, much of this money for administration could be spent for other purposes, and administration is an unnecessary burden that should be curtailed.

According to the U.S. Bureau of Labor Statistics there are more than 14 staff members per administrator. When this is compared with major industries and services, we find that school administration is not overstaffed when judged alongside of similar management-staffing practices in business. The question does arise: should public school administrators be compared to management of big business and service industries? The answer to this should be a resounding yes, judging the size, range, and importance of their comparative responsibilities.

It is also important to note that the overall administrative staff, including principals, assistant principals, and supervisors, make up only 4.6% of the total staff of most school systems. Also, contrary to a reported quote in *U.S. News and Report* by former Secretary of Education William Bennett (1988) that educational administration was a *blob* that continues to grow, no matter what, statistics show the opposite to be true. Although the number of pupils increased by 11% during 1960 thru 1985, the number of the nation's public elementary and secondary school principals dropped by 15%, from 97,000 to 82,000 during the same period. Pupil-teacher ratios during the same period decreased: one teacher for every 27 pupils enrolled in the public schools to one teacher for every 18 pupils, a change of 33%. Although the number of classroom teachers decreased, numbers of classroom teachers entered other instuctional areas and services. Such shifting has increased the ratio of non-supervisory instructional personnel threefold while the ratio of principals, assistant principals, and supervisors has remained almost constant.

Schools have assumed additional responsibilities in recent years, particularly in response to various newly approved mandates and laws and beginning with 1983, the school reform movement. Some of these additional responsibilities assigned to schools appear as follows:

1. improve staff evaluation
2. institute career ladders and incentive pay for teachers
3. remove asbestos
4. increase basic skills
5. decentralize decision making
6. improve staff development and retraining programs
7. implement objective-reference testing
8. improve standardized test scores
9. increase students' critical thinking skills
10. stiffen homework requirements
11. reduce class size
12. expand the school day and year
13. reorganize middle grades
14. offer tutoring programs
15. develop drug and alcohol abuse prevention programs
16. strengthen career education
17. increase parent involvement
18. focus on computer literacy needs
19. provide sex education
20. increase counseling and crisis intervention services
21. identify at-risk students
22. provide AIDS education

Additional requirements during this time focused on instructional needs for special groups, such as: handicapped, gifted, minorities, students with English as a second language, disadvantaged, pre-kindergarten, potential dropouts, latchkey children, at-risk students, teenage mothers, and the list goes on.

Accordingly, there is support for a contrary contention, that the number of school administrators has not experienced a rapid growth, in spite of the obvious addition of substantial responsibilities assumed by school systems in recent years.

Concerning the question of administrators' salaries, internal data suggest that the gap between teacher salaries and administrator salaries has been closing, and that salaries of administrators have not been growing at the expense of teacher salaries. Unfortunately, external factors to be considered in salary determinations offer little comparative data when viewing salaries paid executives out of education, and this is further complicated when the placement of the principal is considered in this comparison.

With regard to the question concerning administration taking more of the school budget, it can be adequately shown that this too is a misconception. Between 1960 and 1985 that portion of school budgets going to administration has continued to remain at approximately 4.5%. Since such fixed charges as retirement and health care costs have more than doubled for all school personnel during the above noted period, it is suggested that interpreting trends in school finance requires particularly careful analysis.

There is extensive research to show that good management is essential to effective schools, just as it is to profitable businesses and industries. Also, the school principal's job is complex, requiring more than just general management skills. Assertive leadership by public school principals is the key to a school's effectiveness in promoting student learning. The principal sets the tone of the school and is important in conveying high expectations to both students and staff. Research also clearly shows the correlation between enhanced student learning and effective district-level leadership. Common characteristics for good school principals are:

1. assertive instructional role
2. goal and task oriented
3. well-organized
4. conveys high expectations for students and staff
5. frequent classroom visits
6. high visibility and availability to students and staff
7. strong support to teaching staff
8. adept at parent and community relations.

It can be concluded, with valid data in support of this position, that quality management is necessary for the good development and operation of effective schools, and to coordinate effective and efficient school programs. Also, that assertive instructional leadership by the school principal is a key element common to all effective schools. If we are to make substantial improvements in the nation's schools and in student learning, the separation of meaningful facts from harmful fiction is fundamental. Careful examination of available evidence would indicate that, as broad generalizations descriptive of school administration, the assertions presented by select school critics are often myths, not realities (ERS 1988).

Meaningful improvement of the nation's schools depends upon an accurate assessment of the real and important problems affecting student learning and the proper application of known knowledge and resources in addressing these problems. Skillful leadership and effective management are crucial to this endeavor.*

PRINCIPAL EFFECTIVENESS

From 1982 to 1987, 1500 outstanding schools were recognized by the School Recognition Program. This recognition was based upon an analysis of their leadership, order and discipline, community support, and high standards and expectations for all students.

Assuming that these recognized schools collectively represent some of America's better elementary and secondary schools, the administrative skills of the principals of these schools were studied. These selected skills were contrasted with the administrative skills of randomly selected school principals.

Results of this study indicate clearly that the teachers of the recognized schools perceive their principals as more effective than do the teachers of the random schools. The pattern of differences between perceptions of the teachers surveyed supports the belief that more effective schools are administered by more effective principals.

The data gathered from this and other similar studies provide an avenue to improved perceptions; in the educational setting, improved perceptions translate into personal growth and more positive organizational culture. To provide a valid, reliable, and practical instrument for faculty

*(Excerpted from report entitled: Concerns in education: some popular assertions about school administrators: are they myths or realities? Arlington, Educational Research Service, Inc. 1988).

feedback regarding administrative skill, the *Audit of Principal Effectiveness* was developed in 1982. This instrument was statistically analyzed, used in research studies and in hundreds of schools across the country. The revised instrument provides the principal with teacher insight on 80 items of principal effectiveness. Further, teacher perceptions are provided regarding three domains: organizational development containing the factors of linkage, organizational direction, and procedures; organizational environment containing the factors of teacher and student relations, and interactive and affective processes; and the educational program containing factors of instructional and curricular improvement.

Factors scored within the three domains provide the principal with an understanding of personal administrative skills beyond the scope of each individual instrument item.

GUIDELINES FOR CREATIVITY AND INNOVATION

Innovation should be seen as points of departure or catalysts, rather than as things to be implemented.

Creativity is the process by which novel ideas are generated, and innovation is the process by which novel ideas are transformed into things tangible and useful. Creativity forms something from nothing, and innovation shapes that something into practical products and services. Ideas and implementation go together, while creativity without innovation is aimless and innovation without creativity is sterile.

Peter Drucker suggests that innovation is not mysterious, nor does it require genius. In *Innovation and Entrepreneurship* he urges preparation for the following:

1. The unexpected—success, failures, events of all kinds
2. The incongruous—differences between the way things are and the way they ought to be
3. The need to perform tasks better—processes
4. Unforeseen shifts in market demands or industry (school) structure
5. Changes in population—demographics
6. Changes in collective personality—new perceptions, moods, meanings
7. Novel information and fresh knowledge

General rules can help. Some may appear simple and obvious, yet failure by principals to have them in mind will handicap a school as it seeks to generate useful creativity. Here are some guidelines:

1. If overall operating results over a substantial period are less than expected or desired, try something different.

2. If at first you don't succeed with an idea, do not try it again and again, change it.

3. If things are working out well, don't alter anything unless you have first asked why the success is occurring. Plan to achieve future success through creative effort based upon understanding how present success is achieved.

4. The best way to be confident about anyone's creative strength is to see steady record of proven good ideas generated by that individual. Meaning care must be taken to uncover creative effort that has worked out well, trace its origins to the people responsible for it, and support those employees in their future proposals.

5. Good communication is needed between a management interested in creativity and the originators of creative ideas if there is to be useful assessment and employment of creativity.

6. The development of a concept to full utilization usually will involve multiple joint actions by many. A group of creative people who communicate their rough ideas to one another will bring forth finished and beneficial innovation far more certainly and rapidly than will a collection of lone contributors.

7. Steady mass touting and urging of novel proposals should not be confused with generating true creativity because too many of the submissions will be harebrained.

8. A highly creative individual will make many times as many contributions as one who is only marginal creative.

9. Whether a school is large or small, innovation is more likely to be successful if proposal ideas are discussed with all entities who will be critical to success, from research to school, from inventor to potential consumer.

10. Don't overplan and overformalize in the early stages of the creative process. Nothing can be more discouraging to someone pregnant with an idea than being pressed to prove what the embryo will turn into when fully developed, especially if the seed idea is then no more than a gleam in the inventor's eye.

11. Do not think of creativity as always connoting breakthroughs, radical inventions, or major reorganizations. Ingeniously conceived, well implemented, small deviations from existing practices can yield spectacular results.

12. The right organization to turn small deviations into high payoffs may differ greatly from one geared to seeking the big, super valuable

discontinuity. Most schools will find that some sponsoring of each kind of creative effort is appropriate.

13. Don't generalize about how to encourage and use creative effort. Doing it right depends on the detailed area of endeavor and current circumstances. If the opportunities are understood and a healthy respect exists for the potential of creative efforts in handling them, the best way to employ creativity will virtually suggest itself.

14. Creative people need not be put on special pedestals, and extreme prima donnas need not be tolerated. However, the school must be prepared to act promptly on ideas coming from those individuals with proven creativity. If the new idea should not be carried further, the decision should be made quickly. A truly creative person will usually shift attention to something else.

15. To encourage creativity, it must be rewarded. Bonuses are excellent but constitute one dimension of the remuneration process. The innovative accomplishments of individuals should be well-publicized, both inside and outside of the school.

16. A principal that is reluctant to engage in a special effort to put creativity to work is unlikely to realize productive yields. Proactive investments in, creativity however, will generate substantial school benefits (Kuhn 1988).

SUMMARY

The principal required to effectively and productively orchestrate and lead the restructuring, renewal and reforms that are needed in education today is a new breed of school administrator. His or her preparation and professional development programs must focus on the areas of content knowledge, skills and leadership ability required of those who are to make a difference in the schools.

Earlier preparation and training of principals emphasized the technological problems of school management. The *new movement,* however, delves; into the importance of administrative theory, the application of the behavioral sciences to the problems of educational administration, the social context in which educational administration takes place, the analysis of the school organization as a social system, the analysis of the reciprocal relationships of diverse roles within the organization, the interpretation of educational administration within the broader sphere of public administration of the public schools, and a substantial increase in supervised clinical experiences (Goldhammer, Suttle, Aldridge and Becker, 1967, p. 1).

Beyond this, practicing and aspiring principals who are inclined to effective school leadership will find the emphasis will be on those aspects of professional development about which they should be most aware and concerned, that is the means to affect their mission, the quality of student learnings, and their education.

DISCUSSION QUESTIONS

1. What are the major expectations of students, parents, teachers, and superiors for the role of the principal?
2. Discuss how the following social factors have affected the role of the principal: collective bargaining, student and parent activism, increased involvement of the courts and legislatures in school affairs, societal expectations that the school solve social problems, and increased size and complexity of schools and school systems.
3. Why is it so important for the principal to be competent in the process of problem identification and problem diagnosis?
4. As a principal, what do you think is the proper function of a school: (a) To accept the existing social order but appraise it critically with a view to shaping its future; (b) to accept the social order as it exists and hope it will shape itself; (c) to plan a new social order and encourage children to accept it; (d) forget the social order and concentrate on academics (Drake and Roe, 1986, pp. 14–15).
5. Review the advantages and disadvantages of various entry positions in school administration.
6. More and more schools are being evaluated by many states and school districts on the basis of educational goals or outcomes, i.e., how well are the students achieving rather than how smoothly is the school running administratively? How could this trend make a dramatic change in the time and efforts in the practice of the school principal.
7. Discuss how the social system or community in which the principal works provides a major influence upon his or her role behavior.
8. Some experts have determined the proper preparation of principals on the basis of the (Katz, 1955, pp. 33–42) three-skill approach to administration: technical skills, human skills, and conceptual skills. Discuss this.
10. Can you offer a list of the special competencies that mark the high performing principal?

REFERENCES

American Youth: A Statistical Snapshot, Washington. Commission on Youth and America's Future, June 1987.

Blumberg, Arthur and Greenfield, William: *The Effective Principal: Perspectives on School Leadership.* Boston, Allyn and Bacon, 1980.

Bossert, E. L. et al.: *The Instructional Management Role of the Principal: A Preliminary Review and Conceptualization.* San Francisco, Far West Laboratory for Educational Research and Development, 1982.

Boyan, E. L.: Follow the leader: commentary on research in educational administration. *Educational Research, 10:*2, February 1981, pp. 6–21.

Button, H. W.: Doctrines of administration: a brief history. *Educational Administration Quarterly, 2:*3, Autumn 1966, pp. 216–24.

Byrne, David R. et al.: *The High School Principalship: The National Survey.* Reston, National Association of Secondary Principals, 1978.

Campbell, Roald, et al.: *Introduction to Educational Administration, 4th ed.,* Boston, Harper and Row, 1971.

Cline, H. D. and Richardson, M. D.: The reform of school administrator preparation: the Kentucky principal's internship model. Kalamazoo, *National Council of Professors of Educational Administration,* August 1988.

Crowson, Robert L. and Porter-Gehrie, Cynthia.: The discretionary behavior of principals in large city schools. *Educational Administration Quarterly. 16,* Winter 1980, pp. 45–69.

Cuban, L.: Effective schools: a friendly but cautionary note. *Phi Delta Kappan, 64:* 10, 1983, pp. 695–696.

Drake, Thelbert L. and Rose, William H.: *The Principalship.* New York, Macmillan, 1986, pp. 14–15.

Effective School Principals. Atlanta, Southern Regional Education Board, 1986.

Foskett, J. M.: *The Normative World of the Elementary School Principal.* Eugene, Center for the Advance Study of Educational Administration, 1967.

Glickman, C.: Good and/or effective schools: What do we want? *Phi Delta Kappan. 48,* 8, 1987, pp. 622–24.

Goldhammer, Keith, Suttle, John E., Aldridge, William D. and Becker, Gerald L.: *Issues and Problems in Contemporary Educational Administration.* Eugene, Center for the Advance Study of Educational Administration, 1967, p. 1.

Gorton, Richard A.: *School Administrators and Supervision,* 2nd ed., Dubuque, Brown, 1983,

Gorton, Richard A. and McIntyre, Kenneth E.: *The Senior High School Principalship.* Reston, National Association of Secondary School Principals, vol. 11, 1978.

Greenfield, William D.: *The Effective Principal.* Washington, National Association of Secondary Principals, 1982.

Gregg, Russell T.: *Administrative Behavior in Education.* New York, Harper and Row, 1957.

Griffiths, D. E.: *Educational Administration Reform PDQ or RIP.* Tempe, University Council for Educational Administration Occasional Paper #8312, 1988.

Gross, N. and Herriot, R. E.: *Staff Leadership in Public Schools:* A Sociological Inquiry. New York, Wiley, 1965.

Gulick, Luther and Urwick, L. (Eds.): *Papers on the Science of Administration.* New York, Institute for Public Administration, 1937.

Hallinger, P. and Murphy, J.: Assessing the instructional leadership behavior of principals. *The Elementary School Journal, 86:2,* 1985, pp. 217–248.

Hemphill, J. K. et.al.: *Administrative Performance and Personality.* New York, Teachers College Press, 1962.

Hoy, W. and Miskel, C.: *Education Administration: Theory Research and Practice.* New York, Random House, 1987.

Katz, Robert L.: Skills of an effective administrator. *Harvard Business Review, 33:1,* 1955, pp. 33–42.

Knezevich, S.: *The American School Superintendent.* Washington, American Association of School Administrators, 1971.

Kuhn, Robert L.: *Handbook for Creative and Innovative Managers.* New York, McGraw-Hill, 1988.

Levine, D. and Lezotte, L.: *Unusually Effective Schools.* Madison, National Center for Effective School Research and Development, 1990.

Lipham, J. M. and Francke, D. C.: Non-verbal behavior of administrators. *Educational Administration Quarterly, 2:2,* Spring 1966, pp. 101–09.

Martin, W. J. and Willower, D. J.: The managerial behavior of high school principals. *Educational Administration Quarterly, 17:*1981, pp. 69–70.

McCurdy, J.: *The Role of the Principal in Effective Schools: Problems and Solutions.* Arlington, American Association of School Administrators, 1983.

Miklos, Erwin: *Educational Leadership in Schools.* Geelong, Australia, Deokin University, 1980.

Morris, Van Cleve. et al.: *The Urban Principal: Discretionary Decision-Making in a Large Educational Organization.* Chicago, University of Illinois at Chicago, March 1981.

Morris, V., Crowson, R.L., Hurwitz, E., Jr., and Porter-Gehrie, C.: The urban principal: middle manager in the educational bureaucracy. *Phi Delta Kappan, 63:*1982, pp. 689–692.

Peters, T. J. and Waterman, R.H.: *In Search of Excellence.* New York, Harper and Row, 1982.

Peterson, Kent D.: *Making Sense of Principals' Work.* Los Angeles, American Educational Research Association, April 1981.

Pharis, William L. and Zachariya, Sally Banks: *The Elementary School Principalship in 1978: A Research Study.* Arlington, National Association of Elementary School Principals, 1979.

Pierce, P. R.: *The Origin and Development of the Public School Principalship.* University of Chicago Press, 1935.

Pitner, N.: *Handbook of Research in Educational Administration.* New York, Longmans, 1988, pp. 99–122.

Roe, W. H. and Drake, T. L.: *The Principalship.* New York: Macmillan, 1974.

Salley, C. et al.: What principals do: a preliminary occupational analysis. In Erickson, D.A. and Reller, T.L. (Eds.): *The Principal in Metropolitan Schools,* edited by D. A. Erickson and T. L. Reller. Berkeley, McCutchan, 1979.

Shoemaker, J. and Fraser, H. W.: What principals can do: some implications from studies of effective schooling. *Phi Delta Kappan,* 1981, pp. 178–182.

Staff Relations in School Administration. Washington, American Association of School Administrators, 1955.

The Importance of Being Pluralistic: Improving the Preparation of School Administrators. Charlottesville, National Policy Board for Educational Administration, December 1989.

Valentine, Jerry.: *The Audit of Principal Effectiveness: A Process of Self-Improvement.* Washington, Department of Education, April 1989.

Valentine, Jerry and Bowman, Michael L.: *Principal Effectiveness in National Recognition Schools, A Research Project Summary Report.* Washington, Department of Education, July 1989.

Valentine, Jerry. et al.: *The Middle Level Principalship: A Survey of Middle Level Principals and Programs.* Reston, National Association of Secondary Principals, vol. I, 1982.

Weick, K. E.: Educational organizations as loosely coupled systems. *Administrative Science Quarterly,* 1976.

What Next? More Leverage for Teachers? Denver, Education Commission of the States, July 1986.

Woolcott, H. F.: *The Man in the Principal's Office: An Ethnography.* New York, Holt, Rinehart and Winston, 1973.

Chapter II

THE PRINCIPAL
AND INSTRUCTIONAL LEADERSHIP

INTRODUCTION

Every educational system has a moral goal that it tries to attain and that informs its curriculum. It wants to produce a certain kind of human being. This intention is; more or less explicit, more or less a result of reflection; but even the neutral subjects, like reading and writing and arithmetic, take their place in a vision of the educated person. In some nations the goal was the pious person, in others the warlike, in others the industrious. Always important is the political regime, which needs citizens who are in accord with its fundamental principles. Aristocracies want gentlemen, oligarchies, men who respect and pursue money, and democracies lovers of equality. Democratic education, whether it admits it or not, wants and needs to produce men and women who have the tastes, knowledge, and character; supportive of a democratic regime. This education has evolved in the last half-century from the education of democratic man and woman to the education of the democratic personality.

Allan Bloom

Various materials, reports and research on the principal identify three major components of the building administrator's role: chief school administrator, operations manager, and instructional leader. Research would show further that principals spend most of their time responding to administrative and managerial tasks, at the expense of instructional leadership. Yet, the effective schools' movement calls for principals to become strong instructional leaders.

We do not know much about the specific processes by which instructional leadership affects teaching and learning. Literature about effective schools and principals suggests that school leadership and teaching and learning are connected, but they do not reveal the specific links between them. This need for studies that can trace the links between the various dimensions of the principal's instructional leadership and teaching and learning is recognized by the U.S. Department of Education, which has in motion a five-year research and development project to consider this very issue. Although the planners of this research project maintain certain differences with regard to the role of the department in the area of research and development on educational leadership they do highlight:

1. *The center should focus on leadership at the school or building level.* It should not ignore leadership at the classroom, district or state levels, but should consider these in terms of how they are mediated by building level leadership.

For example, how does building-level leadership filter or translate central office decisions to the classroom and what effect does this have on teaching and learning? To what extent does building-level leadership buffer teachers from community pressures or link them to parents, and to what effect on teaching and learning? How does school district leadership help or hinder leadership at the school level? How are they interdependent?

2. *The research should be interdisciplinary and collaborative* in the sense that it should not be limited to a single institutional, discipline, perspective, methodology, or model. Moreover, the research should not bias respondents toward a strictly quantitative or qualitative methodology, but should encourage an appropriate mix of the two.

3. *The project should quickly result in some type of practical outcome* and this development phase should be explicitly linked to the research.

The center is to establish, as its main mission, an institute for school leadership to be developed and to teach a curriculum designed specifically for those who would teach and train education policy makers and school leaders.

To be fully effective, principals must be more than managers; they must be instructional leaders. This position of the author is supported by considerable literature, research and his personal and professional experiences as a principal and school administrator during a period of more than three decades. Although John Gardner wasn't thinking specifically of principals when he wrote about leadership; it is noteworthy to examine his *tasks performed by leaders.* These nine tasks seem to be the most significant functions of leadership, they get to the heart of some of the important questions frequently appearing concerning leadership.

1. *Envisioning goals.* Leaders perform the function of goal setting in diverse ways. Some assert a vision of what the group can be at its best. Other leaders point us toward solutions to our problems. Still others, presiding over internally divided groups, are able to define overarching goals that unify constituencies and focus energies.

2. *Affirming values.* Not only leaders of the society at large but leaders of organizations and groups must concern themselves with the affirma-

tion of values. They do so not only in verbal pronouncements but in the policy decisions they make, the kinds of people they surround themselves with and the way they conduct themselves.

3. Motivating. Leaders do not normally create motivation out of thin air. They unlock or channel existing motives. They create a climate in which there is pride in making significant contributions to shared goals.

4. Managing. Those aspects of leadership that one might describe as managing are: planning and priority setting, organizing and institution building, keeping the system functioning, agenda setting and decision making, and exercising political judgment.

5. Achieving workable unity. Leaders must deal with both external and internal conflict. Today they live in a world of interacting, colliding systems. Under the circumstances, all of our leaders must spend part of their time building community, dealing with polarization, creating loyalty to the larger venture.

6. Explaining. Leaders teach. Teaching and leading are distinguishable occupations, but every great leader is clearly teaching, and every good teacher is leading.

7. Serving as a symbol. The leader is inevitably a symbol of management.

8. Representing the group. A distinctive characteristic of the ablest leaders is that they do not shrink from external representation. They see the long term needs and goals of their constituencies in the broadest context, and they act accordingly.

9. Renewing. We are buffeted by events over which we have no control, and change will occur. The question is, will it be the kind of change that will preserve our deepest values, enhance the vitality of the system and ensure its future.

John W. Gardner, U.S. Secretary of Health, Education, and Welfare from 1965 to 1968, has written extensively about leadership. This passage is excerpted with the author's permission from The Tasks of Leadership, one of twelve papers published by the Independent Sector.

There are certain authors of writings on the principal and some practitioners who consider it impractical to expect most principals to perform two roles, that of management and instructional leadership. They would suggest that school management and instructional leadership are two separate tasks that cannot be performed by a single individual.

We question whether it is practical to expect most principals to perform two roles that are so different and require such diverse skills. We suspect that only someone with a split

personality and the time of two people can perform both functions well. We suggest that
the first realistic step in school improvement is to recognize that school management and
instructional leadership are two separate tasks that cannot be performed by a single
individual.

(Rallis and Highsmith 1986)

It is they who suggest that we have two problems: 1) schools need instructional leadership, but the principal's time is consumed by management tasks; and 2) teachers wish to improve their profession, but they want the leadership and control to come from within their own ranks.

This author would propose, to the contrary, that numerous examples exist in which principals have redefined their priorities. These principals are in fact the instructional leaders of the schools in which they find themselves and they also tend to the management requirements of those schools. Secondly, instructional leadership must come from both the principal and the school's staff. All teachers are neither prepared for positions of instructional leadership, or want to assume the leadership and control to come from within their own ranks. Reference is made to an article entitled *Teachers discover plan's drawbacks: flaws seen in schools' decision-making program* which appeared in the December 25, 1990 issue of Florida's *Sun-Sentinel.* Select statements in this article, included here, provide further support for the author's view.

They got the word at the end of last school year: Teachers, we're putting you in charge. You've told us things could be better if you ran the show. Well, here's your chance. Go for it.

. . . some teachers have begun to resent the pressure inherent in those words. The idea is great but they don't give us any money, they don't give us any time, and they want results.

Some teachers are enthusiastic and they have made decisions affecting their jobs, but at other schools problems abound. Teachers complain about power-hungry colleagues, lack of time and money, and dwindling attendance at meetings. The bottom line: It's not easy getting dozens of teachers to agree. When it gets down to the mundane meetings to try to modify things, you get kind of discouraged. Progress seems to be hindered by personality conflicts. Some teachers worry that others will sabotage ideas they do not like.

In light of the many and varied criticisms being levied upon the schools, particularly regarding the status of their effectiveness, or lack of same, principals must redefine their priorities, and professional instructional leadership should appear as their number one role. Obstacles to exercising instructional leadership must be overcome. Unless principals do indeed offer leadership in this vital area there is truly little to support the argument that the current certificated or licensed principals do offer something special or unique to school administration, something that may not be equally offered by others trained in *other* management areas.

Thanks to research on effective schools and business organizations, today's knowledge base is substantial and the skills necessary for successfully providing instructional leadership are known and attainable. It is generally known that instructional leadership skills include: envisioning, communicating, developing trust, motivating others, decision making, risk taking, modeling, planning, and promoting collegiality. Equally important are the leader's belief systems, especially his or her self-concept and treatment of others. The effective principal blends knowledge, skills, and beliefs, when working with teachers, pupils and parents, to develop an educational philosophy (mission) that shapes the school's goals and objectives. The principal furthers this effort by fostering and ensuring purposeful and quality programs of staff development, a positive and productive school climate, and active and meaningful school-community involvement. This restructured teaching force increases local school autonomy (site based management-decentralization), and offers the principal the greatest instructional leadership challenge he or she has yet to face.

In this chapter the author concentrates upon the instructional leadership role of the principal and portrays it as a major contributor to educational excellence and school productivity.

IMPROVEMENT OF CURRICULUM LEADERSHIP

A school has standards when it has high and consistent expectations of *all* learners in *all* courses.

There are a number of tenets that are useful as guides for principals who seek to become effective curriculum leaders. They are not necessarily formulas for success, but they do represent different ways of looking at curriculum leadership (Bailey, 1990).

1. curriculum leaders' actions are guided by a curriculum model
2. leaders use curriculum governance documents to identify and clarify the directions, roles and responsibilities of all stakeholders in the curriculum monitoring process.
3. leaders create and use curriculum materials that are tied to school district guiding documents
4. curriculum leaders know the difference between curriculum con-

struction and curriculum monitoring, and employ leadership skills accordingly

5. curriculum leaders see curriculum development as a continuous process

6. curriculum leaders empower others in curriculum construction and monitoring

7. curriculum leaders see the interconnectedness of curriculum supervision and staff development

8. curriculum leaders are trained, not born

9. curriculum leaders are guided by research in the decision-making process

10. curriculum leadership emerges from the ranks of all the stakeholders in the school district and school building

11. curriculum leaders believe in self-improvement, staff-development and supervision as tools of improvement, and

12. curriculum leaders operate as facilitators and seek consensus rather than compromise.

THE ASSESSMENT OF INSTRUCTIONAL LEADERSHIP

... the principal's role comprises three dimensions of leadership activity: defining the school mission, managing the instructional program, and promoting the school learning climate.

Philip Hallinger

There is general agreement that principals should be strong and effective instructional leaders. However, research (Hallinger and Murphy 1982, 1985) and experience suggests that principals do not provide this leadership unless certain conditions are satisfied.

1. School system decision makers have reduced those obstacles that keep principals from fulfilling their instructional leadership role

2. Instructional leadership is understood and observable, and therefore able to be implemented.

3. The assessment of instructional leadership behaviors results in reliable and valid information, and provides the principal with useful development data.

Those obstacles that seriously limit the principal's ability to apply strong instructional leadership in the school include: a limited knowledge of curriculum and instruction, professional standards, district office requirements and expectations, and function diversity.

Limited knowledge of curriculum and instruction. Although principals were once teachers there is little reason to believe that this has prepared them with the tools to provide instructional leadership. Surely, teacher preparation programs do not ensure the necessary skills for evaluating other teachers, their teaching, helping teachers improve classroom instruction, or developing, coordinating, constructing, implementing, and evaluating curriculum. Principal certification and licensure programs now in place at most universities offer very little in terms of curriculum and instruction, and even less in the area of skill-oriented staff development programs. In other words, currently, principals generally enter their initial administrative posts with limited knowledge, understanding and experience in instructional and curriculum development and shallow background for instructional leadership.

Professional standards. Principals, sometimes referred to as middle management, are known to exchange their responsibilities and function in the areas of curriculum and instruction for what may appear as contract limitations resulting from collective bargaining agreements negotiated by the school district and its teachers. Generally, such matters as teacher assessment purposes, procedures and policies do not appear within the language of the agreement, accordingly, they lend themselves to extended understandings and interpretations.

School district requirements and expectations. Unfortunately, many school systems consider the principal's managerial efficiency and political stability as being of greater importance than his or her instructional leadership. In fact, little encouragement is offered the principal, in those school systems, to actively involve himself or herself in curriculum and instruction. In those systems, the principal's immediate and solid responses to community or management related problems is about all that administrators at the central office level seek from the building level administrator.

Differences in role characteristics. The principal's work is influenced by numerous interactions with a variety of participants and situations, and his or her schedule often provides limited opportunities for uninterrupted blocks of time needed for planning and assessing curriculum, teacher observations and conferences. Further, all members of the school-community: teachers, parents, students, central office administrators, and board of education hold substantively different expectations of the principal. This multiplicity of roles and expectations often lead to a fragmentation of the principal's vision of the school.

These obstacles to instructional leadership are further complicated because of the failure to provide clear definitions of the principal's role.

However, there has been considerable movement toward providing clearer understandings of the principal's function as the school's instructional leader (Bossert et al. 1982, Hallinger and Murphy 1985, Hallinger et al. 1983).

There is a general consensus held by those doing research and practitioners alike that the principal's role, while performing as an instructional leader, appears as: defining the mission of the school, managing the instructional program, and promoting the learning climate within the school.

Defining the mission of the school. The principal who is an effective instructional leader clearly envisions the school's purpose and what it seeks to accomplish. This defining of the school's mission includes leading the entire staff during the development of school-wide goals and objectives and communicating them to the total school community. In turn, this encourages the staff, students, parents, and community to arrive at a sense of common and shared purpose and unites all the school's activities. This articulation of the school's mission promotes accountability, a sense of personal ownership, and instructional improvement.

Managing the instructional program. Traditionally, the principal's role as instructional manager was limited to the supervision and evaluation of instruction. Within this proposed environment, the principal is found working with the staff in the evaluation, development, and implementation of the school's curriculum and instructional programs. Further, research on effective schools and school improvement urges principals to apply themselves to such functions as: coordinating the curriculum and monitoring student progress. Through curriculum coordination, students are assured of appropriate instruction in all areas identified by the school system as its offerings. Also, the principal, as the school's instructional leader, monitors student progress within the classrooms and across the grades, a vitally important role that justifies the school's mission.

Promoting a positive climate. The norms and attitudes of the staff and students that influence learning in the school is the school learning climate, and principals are seen as shaping this learning climate by:

1. maintaining high visibility, thereby communicating priorities and model expectations;
2. creating a system of rewards that reinforces academic achievement and productive effort;
3. establishing clear, explicit standards that embody the school's expectations;

4. protecting instructional time;
5. selecting and participating in effective and purposeful staff development programs that are consistent with the school's mission.

In order that assurances are provided that strong and effective instructional leadership is provided by the principal, reliable and valid methods of assessing the principal's leadership behaviors must be in place. In select instances, assessments serve as a means of evaluating personnel and satisfying accountability-oriented purposes. In these instances, the data must meet legal and professional standards of reliability, objectivity and validity (Latham and Wexley 1981). There is substantially greater flexibility where assessments are utilized primarily for professional improvement.

Methods of assessing instructional leadership. Principals' skills can be assessed through direct observation, interviews, document analysis, and questionnaires.

Direct observation has been pioneered in such professional development programs as Peer-Assisted Leadership (PAL) piloted at the Far West Lab in San Francisco (Barnett and Long 1986). Here principals utilize the results to aid one another in the creation of individualized professional development programs. Although direct observation is a highly useful method of assessing instructional leadership, it requires multiple observations and is somewhat time consuming.

Interviews with the principal, staff, and students can aid in this assessment of the principal's instructional leadership. This too, although useful in helping to clarify the principal's instructional leadership image, is limited in its validity and often time consuming.

An analysis of school documents does provide data on the principal's instructional leadership. This analysis of goal statements, newsletters, memos, bulletins, minutes of meetings, and other school documents does provide a revealing picture of the principal's concerns, priorities, and communicating personality.

Questionnaires offer a quick and convenient way of gathering assessment data. Although they rely on staff, student and parent perceptions, rather than upon concrete observed behavior, they are found to provide reliable information on the principal's instructional leadership behavior (Latham and Wexley 1981).

A combination of these methods of assessing the principal's instructional leadership within the school is recommended.

PRINCIPALS IMPROVE THE CURRICULUM

The principal who is committed to substantive educational principles will establish practice-based guidelines and review current literature and research for the improvement of the school's curriculum. This principal recognizes that for the most part the curriculum of many schools is treated as isolated and disjointed subjects to be accumulated as units towards the satisfaction of grades level or diploma requirements. This isolation and disjointedness or departmentalization of the curriculum is a major challenge, for it is recognized that this has historically left students with the inability to make connections in situations that call for the uses of knowledge that provides for a needed linkage or crosses subject matter boundaries.

It is Whitehead (1929) who commented that the curriculum which is seen and treated as a list of disconnected subjects can have limited vitality. The best that can be said of it is, that it is a rapid table of contents which a deity might run over in his mind while he is thinking of creating a world and had not yet determined how to put it together.

Legislators throughout this nation have, since the issuance of *A Nation at Risk* (1983), legislated increases in the numbers of academic credits required of students. This increase in the mandated curriculum may have somehow given credence to an erroneous thinking that the curriculum is a matter of policy determination—set at a level beyond the school. Such state mandated lists of subjects and units required toward high school completion do not define the manner in which these subjects are to be offered or coordinated as a curriculum. Also, there is no direction offered within these mandates for the improvement of the curriculum.

Professional literature abounds with research and successful practice and offers principles for curriculum improvement. An extensive list of criteria for judging a school appears in *Supervision in Education: Problems and Practices* (Tanner and Tanner, 1987). The following principles are derived largely from this list.

1. The responsibility for putting the curriculum together and improving the curriculum resides with the professional staff of the school and school district.

Effective schools engage in schoolwide curriculum organization and articulation (Kyle, 1985). Curriculum development is not a fragmented matter. It is a shared responsibility of the principal, the faculty and the central office, and state curricular mandates are not viewed as an excuse for the avoidance of this responsibility.

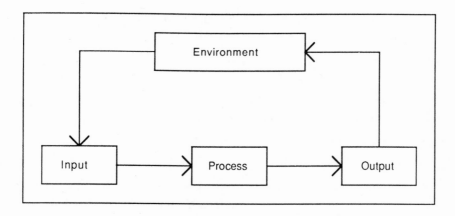

Figure 3 : General Systems Model

2. The principal is responsible for marshalling the professional staff and resources of the school for curriculum improvement.

Effective schools research reveals that the principal is more than a school manager. As the school's educational leader, the principal offers an understanding of a vision of the total, all encompassing, curriculum and he or she shares this vision with the school's professional staff (Kyle, 1985; Rutter et al., 1979).

3. The curriculum is more than the sum of its parts.

A curriculum is determined by how the parts are connected and articulated to each other and the whole. As stated by Tanner and Tanner (1980), the concept and function of general education emerged from the need in a free and polyglot society to develop a common universe of discourse, understanding, and competence in the face of increased specialism.

Although legislatively-mandated courses are generally listed as separate subject fields, these listings do not preclude a correlation or linkage of mathematics with science, for example, or this fusion of science with social studies. The manner in which the curriculum is organized and implemented remains a responsibility of the school's professional staff.

4. In addition to a coherent core of studies to meet the common needs of students, the curriculum encompasses diversified studies to meet the exploratory, enrichment, and specialized needs of a student body coming from a pluralistic society.

Students pursue their diversified studies without being tracked or segregated (Goodlad, 1984).

5. *The balance and coherence of the curriculum is maintained in the face of any special priorities that may be established.*

Care is taken to assure that priorities given to specific disciplines are not at the expense of other disciplines within the school.

6. *The curriculum is articulated horizontally (interrelating the various subject fields) and vertically (from grade level to grade level within the subject fields).*

The principal, departments and staff do not work in isolation according to subject specializations (Tanner and Tanner, 1987).

7. *The value of any subject is determined in large measure by what it contributes to the student's understanding of other subjects in the curriculum and to the life of the student in the real world* (Weinberg, 1967).

Students are able to apply their learnings in one discipline to the other disciplines. A curriculum which narrowly concentrates on facts and mechanical skills fails to enable students to use these skills and information in new and varied situations. Learnings become the student's intelligence for it is generalized and made useable in a wide variety of new and differing situations within his or her internal and external environments.

7. *Curriculum improvement is treated as a problem-solving process.*

Problems are seen as opportunities for improvement, not merely obstructions and improvements occur as problems are identified and resolved.

8. *Curriculum improvement and instructional improvement are inescapably interconnected; curriculum improvement and staff development are linked.*

To work on instructional improvement apart from curriculum improvement is like separating the act of eating from the food that is being eaten (Dewey, 1916). Such activity is sterile and mechanical, and as stated earlier, the relegation of curriculum to educational policy above and beyond the school unit, serves to diminish the roles of the principal and teachers as professionals.

9. *Teacher effectiveness is determined by the readiness and capacity of the teacher to identify significant problems, and to seek help in solving these problems.*

Teachers reveal rather than conceal problems, and in turn, fewer problems appear and are at issue. It is through effective staff development programs that teachers learn to identify and resolve curricular and instruction problems.

10. Curriculum and instruction are idea-oriented rather than error oriented.

An undue emphasis on facts and mechanical skills offers a narrow focus. It places to much importance upon error-oriented teaching at the expense of idea-oriented teaching. Student errors offer fertile opportunities for clarification and improvement, while the avoidance of student errors is generally accompanied with limited risk taking and minimal production and effort. Idea-oriented teaching stimulates student skill development, it stimulates improvements of the skills for making knowledge applications, and for higher order thinking in school and life situations, while increasing and motivating student interests.

11. Teachers and students have complete access to rich and varied curricular resources.

School budget provisions for curricular materials, including textbooks, are known to represent too small a percentage of the total operating budget, and movement should be made to assure that minimal standards, such as those established by the American Association of School Librarians, are exceeded.

12. The responsibility for the curriculum, including the selection and use of curricular materials, resides with the professional staff.

The expertise of the professional staff in determining the appropriateness of curricular materials is clearly and fully recognized and supported by the board of and the school system's publics. When individuals or special interest groups within the internal and/or external school environments offer objections to curricular materials, appropriate guidelines are in place. (See Appendix A and Appendix B)

13. Teacher prepared tests are designed to develop higher order thinking abilities, rather than being geared primarily to rote learning and mechanical exercises.

The emphasis is placed on interpretation and application of knowledge, rather than on the mere recall of information or the mechanical use of narrow and limited skills. Such tests offer valued instruments to teachers in their efforts to evaluate their own efforts in effecting student growth and achievement (Goodlad, 1984).

14. Multiple, comprehensive criteria are used in evaluating student achievement rather than relying primarily on test results.

The curriculum should not be determined by standardized or other external tests. Teachers should regard teaching-to-the-test as counterproductive (Boyer, 1983; Goodlad, 1984).

15. The school schedule functions to facilitate the curriculum, rather than to constrain it.

The schedule is designed to permit students to participate fully in the school's program of studies and student activities. Scheduling considerations do not result in student tracking or isolation (Boyer, 1983; Goodlad, 1984).

16. Classroom work and extraclass activities provide all students with opportunities to develop initiative, responsible self-direction, and cooperation through student-initiated individual and group projects.

Classroom work and extraclass activities are seen to involve teachers and students in cooperative planning and evaluation, thereby creating a sense of community within the school (Kyle, 1985) and those competencies required for success in school, college, and society (Goodlad, 1984; Raven, 1984).

17. Students are periodically asked for suggestions on curriculum and school improvement.

Follow-up studies are made of graduates, transferees, and dropouts, and a school-community dropout prevention program is in place. These activities are integrated with the curriculum (Boyer, 1983).

18. The summer session includes not only make-up, remedial, and accelerated course offerings, but enrichment studies, purposeful recreational activities, and community service projects.

The summer session responds to diversified interests, talents, and needs of the school's students.

19. The test of the school's philosophy is its curriculum in action.

Schools offer statements of philosophy and it is the curriculum which give these meaning, purpose and validity.

This commitment of the school's principal and professional staff to sound educational principles, such as those noted here, offer direction and purpose to the total school-community. They minimize the advancement of ill-conceived and misdirected educational reforms, and maximize effective measures designed to provide for instructional improvement.

MODELING FOR CURRICULAR UNITY

One of the most powerful tools a principal possesses is the knowledge of how to improve the effectiveness of the school *as a school.* This means that the principal visualizes what is happening at the school, not as a matter of simply coordinating independent responses, but as a matter of *integrating* the total responses of a school (English, 1987, p. 35).

The effective principal recognizes that the actions of individual teachers, unless in harmony with one another, do not advance consensus or the satisfaction of the school's mission. That principal's goal must be *synergy*, a combining and adapting of the school's staff, which in turn produces teachers who teach toward common goals. The principal who affects a curricular harmony within the school, is the creator for that synergy. This curricular harmony is seen as a: singleness, unity and an identity or coincidences of interests, purposes, or sympathies among the members of the school's professional staff. It is seen to include three separate but necessarily interactive parts: the written curriculum (work design), the taught curriculum (the work), and the tested curriculum (work measurement) (English and Steffy, 1983).

The written curriculum is viewed as those materials that direct teaching. This includes, but is not limited to, textbooks, scope and sequence charts, course syllabi and catalogs, policies and guidelines, subject content specifications. The taught curriculum includes the content and method, while the testing of students and evaluation of teachers and teaching are integral parts of the tested curriculum.

These three curricular components, although they exist in all schools, often operate in isolation and independently. Accordingly, what appears as the school's written curriculum is not necessarily in accord with what teachers teach or the knowledge expectations of the students. What teachers teach and student learn may be free of the influences, guidance, or controls of one another. Because teaching deviates, or is idiosyncratic in any functional relationship, from the other curricular components, it fails to contribute to the school's synergy. Under these circumstances teaching can only be improved idiosyncratically and the school fails to function as a system. It is neither more efficient nor effective as an independent organization.

The concept of curricular unity, the optimization of work in the schools, tends to focus the energies and efforts of the principal on those unifying activities that encourage oneness.

In order that curricular unity is achieved, the principal needs to anticipate select problems and issues which require solution. He or she needs to recognize that school scheduling may serve as either a means or a barrier to the attainment of curricular unity. Also, the process of curriculum alignment is one tool for introducing a workable linkage between tests (work measurement) and teaching content, for tests, particularly standardized tests, are not necessarily measures of the school's curriculum (English, 1985).

Another problem which the principal faces is that of teacher autonomy and isolation. The cellular structure of the school works against creating curricular articulation, horizontally and vertically within the school and school system (Lortie, 1975). This form of school structuring does encourage greater specialization, however this approach does tend to limit creativity.

> *Everything we know indicates that creativity can become effective only if the basic tools are given. Everything we know also indicates that the proper structure of work, of any work, is not intuitively obvious.*
>
> Rousseau

Nothing suggests that curricular unity will occur without the leadership of principals, or the *principal-less school,* who work to articulate and integrate the total school curriculum. Also, confusion continues to exist within often held understandings of instruction and curriculum. Instruction is teaching directed by the curriculum, therefore lead. The function of the curriculum is to lead and form teaching and the cumulative strength of teaching is created by the curriculum.

We do know that unrelated teaching does occur within the school. In these instances schools are little more than collections of teachers, each doing his or her own thing. Some schools have attempted to respond to this condition by introducing various accountability measures, including teaching models (Hunter, 1982). However, these approaches do little unless they are directed toward a valid and coherent curriculum. These teaching models can aid in the development of a school-based synergy when the curriculum provides the framework and teaching becomes instruction. In other words, teaching must be linked to the curriculum and in turn be firmly based in the tools of work measurement for curriculum unity to occur.

There are steps that principals can take which lead towards the implementation of curricular unity in their schools.

1. Develop concise and valid statements of desired work content.

These are stated goals that teachers are to accomplish. Care should be taken to assure that curriculum statements are neither ambiguous nor nonfunctional and their use encouraged. Also, the usual behavioral objectives are nonfunctional because they are statements of work measurement, not work content. These behavioral objectives indicate what students should be able to do and not what teachers are to accomplish. These objectives are not statements of work content.

2. Develop valid and reliable work measurement instruments.

The development of valid and reliable work measurement instruments follows the creation of work content prescriptions. Whatever form these instruments take, they should be preceded by appropriate alignment data. This alignment provides assurances that the measurement instruments are part of the curriculum.

3. Ensure that the textbooks selected agree with the curriculum and related measurement instruments.

The content decisions made by teachers in the classrooms are greatly influenced by the textbook. In fact the textbook has been called the curriculum surrogate (English, 1986), therefore, textbooks need to be aligned with the curriculum and evaluative materials.

4. Monitor the delivery of the curriculum.

An essential responsibility of the principal is the maintenance of the school's curriculum unity, and this is accomplished through monitoring. This ensuring of curriculum unity occurs when the principal insists upon linkage occurring during teacher observations and the review of plan books. With this insistence, instruction is not neglected and the result is effectiveness and synergy.

5. Common use is made of feedback.

Work measurement data is used as the data base for creating improved curricular unity, and this is contingent upon the extent to which this data accurately and fully considers the curriculum.

Principals who use curricular unity, and use it effectively, will find it to be a strong concept, one that does provide better results, however, it does not relieve them of the task of selecting the right content for classroom delivery before linking it the evaluative materials.

ACTUALIZING INSTRUCTIONAL LEADERSHIP

There is a growing body of evidence on effective instruction, school productivity, school learning climate, and learning styles that emphasizes that leadership is critical to initiate and sustain any process of school improvement. Much of this knowledge converges on the principal, arguing that certain behaviors set into motion effective leadership. Instructional leadership competence is generally seen in three forms:

1. **Content competence** implies a knowledge of subject matter practices and trends; the ability to assist teachers in organizing and presenting academic content, skills, and resources of instruction.

2. **Methodological competence** presumes a knowledge of instructional strategies and modalities; the ability to assist teachers in improving instructional delivery, from establishing set and stated objectives to choosing competing methodologies.

3. **Supervisor competence** involves a knowledge of the administrative and interpersonal skills of instructional supervision; the ability to assist teachers in implementing effective instructional practices; the skills of clinical supervision and/or performance appraisal (Keefe, 1987, p. 50).

Although instructional leadership embraces all of these competencies it may be somewhat unrealistic to expect the principal to achieve an equal facility or competence in each of them. If this is so, what then is instructional leadership for the principal? *It is the principal's role in providing direction, resources, and support to teachers and students for the improvement of teaching and learning in the school.*

Instructional leadership may appear within these four broad domains:

1. **Formative.** The effective instructional leader is aware of significant trends in school curriculum, new school organizational approaches, and the status of present instructional media and technology.

2. **Planning.** The principal who is aware of educational trends has available the necessary knowledge base for the planning domain of instructional leadership.

3. **Implementation.** Effective schools emphasize academics, quality teacher pupil interactions, and incentives that encourage student outcomes.

This school climate, which encourages learning, is the collective yield of the efforts of the principal, teachers, parents and students and students. The successful principal brings into harmony the skills and abilities of these groups to cause conditions of excellence.

The principal should use techniques that stimulate teachers to renewed group activity by reducing the barriers between them. An important aspect of this stimulation is the extent to which the leader is able to interpret to his or her colleagues the results of their group work. This role stems from a genuine respect for the contributions of each individual.

The leader must understand the need for involvement of the staff, he or she must be able to help groups state achievable objectives and develop a plan for implementation and evaluation (Bookbinder, 1972, p. 57).

4. Evaluation. The school that aids students in their growth and learning has the resources to offer sufficient evidence that this has occurred. This may appear in such vital signs as: achievement test scores, average daily attendance, library and media usage, and success of the school's graduates. By responding with this evidence, the effective principal can provide the basis for program improvement and community understanding and support.

Instructional leadership assumes that the principal has knowledge of effective instructional practices and the characteristics of learners. His or her effectiveness does ultimately depend upon understandings between the nature of the program and learner success. If limitations do appear with instructional leadership, these do arise primarily because of insufficient understandings of the complexities involved, and the fact that students learn in defineably different ways.

THE INSTRUCTIONAL IMPROVEMENT PLAN

When the principal does perform as an instructional leader he or she necessarily is required to respond to the demands for creating a systematic plan for involving a coalition of the school's administration and staff in clarifying the school's mission, setting mutually agreed upon objectives, developing a data base for program change, identifying staff development needs, implementing the desired changes, and evaluating program effectiveness. A number of related questions must be responded to when this instructional improvement plan is formulated.

   1. Agreed upon objectives. Establish what is to be done.
    a. What are the needs of the learners being served by the school?
    b. What are the outcomes being sought?
    c. What are the current student achievement expectations?
    d. What instructional methodologies will achieve desired results?
   2. Develop a data base. Assemble school and effective educational practices data that offer useful intelligence.
    a. What are the school's earlier test results?
    b. Are school program descriptions available and current?
    c. What are the school's student grouping practices?
    d. Has effective schools research effected instructional design?
    e. Are teachers employing effective teaching strategies?
    f. What is the nature of planning being utilized to effect change

3. Staff development requirements. Fix teacher needs for implementing the determined program changes.

    a. What are the current skills of the school's continuing staff?

    b. What new skills must teachers develop?

    c. Is there a need for additional staff?

    d. What other or new resources are required?

    e. Does the school/district have staff development capabilities?

    f. What is the availability of consultation services?

4. The implementation of desired changes. Desired program(s) and methodologies are determined and organized.

    a. Are reasonable student achievement expectations in place?

    b. Will the ongoing school programs achieve desired results?

    c. Has a timeline been set for desired staff development?

    d. What are the desired changes in scheduling and/or grouping?

    e. What approach to instructional supervision will used?

5. The evaluation of program effectiveness. Assess the degree of program implementation and the level of student achievement and program effectiveness.

    a. What are the student test scores?

    b. What are the trends in meaningful data?

    c. Are students achieving?

    d. How are educationally disadvantaged students achieving?

    e. What is the level of participation in program-related actions?

    f. Are student attitudes toward instruction positive?

    g. What are the achievements of program graduates?

This improvement plan, once formulated and implemented, must be carefully monitored. The instructional leadership must provide assurances that a collaboration between the principal and teachers is occurring in order that the liabilities arising from professional isolation and adversarial relationships are offset (Keefe, 1987).

SUMMARY

This chapter focused on the principal's instructional leadership goals and functions. Providing leadership for the instructional program requires understandings of educational techniques and a personal vision of academic excellence that is translatable into effective classroom strategies. This is supported by research which shows that principals can have a profound effect on students' learning experiences.

Although there are many tasks performed by principals, five most clearly influence a school's instructional program:

1. defining the school mission,
2. managing the curriculum and instruction,
3. promoting a positive learning climate,
4. observing and giving feedback to teachers, and
5. assessing the instructional program.

The key to effective instructional leadership lies in the principal's knowledge of his or her environments, current instructional methods and technologies, ability to prioritize his or her emphasis upon school management, organization and supervision, the decentralization of the decision making process, flexibility in sharing duties, and understandings of the critical leadership functions.

> Instructional leadership is the principal's role in providing direction, resources, and support to teachers and students for the improvement of teaching and learning in the school (James Keefe and John Jenkins 1984).
>
> We broadly interpret the concept of instructional leadership to encompass those actions that a principal takes or delegates to others, to promote growth in student learning. Generally such actions focus on setting schoolwide goals, defining the purpose of schooling, providing the resources needed for learning to occur, supervising and evaluating teachers, coordinating staff development programs, and creating collegial relationships with and among teachers (Wynn De Bevoise).
>
> Instructional leadership is leadership that is directly related to the processes of instruction where teachers, learners, and the curriculum interact. To exert leadership over this process, the principal must deal with, in the case of teachers, supervision, evaluation, staff development, and inservice training. In governing the content of instruction, that is, the curriculum, the instructional leader will oversee materials selection and exercise choices in scope and sequence, unit construction, and design of activities.

Principals can meet the demands for instructional leadership by identifying and meeting those needs vital to improving student performances. In addition, sharing leadership means involving the whole faculty in the pursuit of excellence in learning, a pursuit that can be contagious.

DISCUSSION QUESTIONS

1. Effective schools require principals who can perform as both competent managers and instructional leaders. Can these two distinctly different tasks be performed by a single individual?
2. What does it take to be an effective instructional leader?

3. What are the distinguishing characteristics of effective instructional leaders?

4. There are those who believe that many principals have a weak knowledge base in curriculum and instruction, which in turn keeps these principals from carrying out their instructional leadership roles effectively. Do you agree with assessment? What then might you recommend, in terms of principal preparation and development, that would provide for the resolution of this concern?

5. What steps may be taken to strengthen the principal's role and his or her effectiveness as an instructional leader?

6. What are some desirable approaches to the assessment of principal's instructional leadership?

7. Personal characteristics and beliefs affect principals' decision-making processes and their style of instructional leadership. Discuss this.

8. How does the principal, as an instructional leader in the school, influence what occurs in the classroom?

9. What criteria can a principal use to identify the need for curriculum improvement?

10. How can the principal encourage and evaluate curriculum improvement proposals?

REFERENCES

Bailey, Gerald D.: *How to Improve Curriculum Leadership, Twelve Tenets.* Reston, *National Association of Secondary School Principals,* January 1990.

Bookbinder, R. M., et al.: *Critical Issues in Education: A Practical Guide for School Administrators,* Englewood, Prentice-Hall, 1972, p. 57.

Bossert, Steven. et al.: *The Instructional Management Role of the Principal: A Preliminary Review and Conceptualization,* San Francisco, Far West Laboratory for Educational Research and Development, 1982.

Boyer, Ernest L.: *High School,* New York, Harper & Row, 1983.

Dewey, John: *Democracy and Education,* New York, Macmillan, 1916.

Drucker, Peter: *Management,* New York, Harper and Row, 1974.

English, Fenwick: *Getting the Most From the New Jersey HSPT: A Practical Guide to Resolving Design and Delivery Problems in the Schools.* Trenton, State Department of Education, 1985.

English, Fenwick: *Developing Total Curriculum Quality Control: Responding to the Challenge of the HSPT.* Trenton, State Department of Education, 1986.

Goodlad, John I.: *A Place Called School,* New York, McGraw-Hill, 1984.

Hallinger, P. and Murphy, J.: Assessing the instructional leadership behavior of principals. *The Elementary School Journal, 86:*286, 1985, pp. 217–248.

Hallinger, P., Murphy, J., Weil, M., Mesa, R., and Mittman, A.: School effectiveness: identifying the specific practices and behaviors of principals. *The NASSP Bulletin, 67:*463, 1983, pp. 83–91.

Hunter, Madeline: Mastery Teaching, El Segundo, TIP, 1982.

Irwin, C.C.: Model describes how principals can achieve quality instruction. *The NAASP Bulletin,* September 1985.

Kaufman, Roger and English, Fenwick: *Needs Assessment: Concept and Application.* Englewood Cliffs, Educational Technology, 1979.

Keefe, James W.: The critical questions of instructional leadership. *The NAASP Bulletin, 71:498,* 1987, pp. 49–56.

Keefe, J. W. and Jenkins, J. M. (Eds.): *Instructional Leadership Handbook.* Reston, NASSP, 1984.

Kyle, Regina M. J. (Ed.): *Reaching for Excellence.* Washington, National Institute of Education, 1985.

Latham, G. and Wexley, K.: *Increasing Productivity Through Performance Appraisal.* Menl Park, Addison Wesley, 1981.

National Commission on Excellence in Education: *A Nation at Risk.* Washington, U.S. Department of Education, 1983.

Raven, John.: *Competence in Modern Society.* London, H. K. Lewis, 1984.

Russell, J. S., Mazzarella, J. A. White, T. and Maurer, S.: *Linking the Behaviors and Activities of Secondary School Principals to School Effectiveness: A Focus on Effective and Ineffective Behaviors.* Eugene, Center for Educational Policy and Management, 1985.

Rutter, Michael, et al.: *Fifteen Thousand Hours: Secondary Schools and Their Effects on Children.* Cambridge, Harvard University Press, 1979.

Tanner, Daniel, and Tanner, Laurel: *Curriculum Development: Theory Into Practice, 2nd ed.* New York, Macmillan, 1980.

Whitehead, Alfred North: *The Aims of Education and Other Essays.* New York, Macmillan, 1929.

Chapter III

EFFECTIVE SCHOOL MANAGEMENT

INTRODUCTION

Time, unless it is managed, nothing else can be managed.
Peter Drucker

This chapter is about the school management responsibilities of the principal. It describes how principals manage the people, programs, services, facilities, and activities of the schools so that schools' goals, as well as their own personal goals, will be achieved.

The author has attempted in this chapter to convey a positive view of the principal's managerial role, for he believes that this managerial responsibility can be among the more exciting, challenging, and rewarding functions within the principal's total responsibility. Major achievements occur in affectively managed schools because they bring together a wealth of talents and resources that significant accomplishments require.

The societal problems and issues of today, and most likely the problems to be faced in the foreseeable future, require both large and small-scale solutions that the school, as an effectively managed organization can respond to. The skill of the principal, while performing as the school's manager, is a vital factor in the school's ability to respond to its internal and external environmental tasks and challenges. The information in this chapter is designed to help the potential principal and practicing principal develop these managerial skills which offer increased potential for school effectiveness and productivity and also career success.

Management, the process of directing, influencing, and motivating employees, is important whether the leader is a manager of a business, industrial operation or school. Numerous empirical studies have appeared that have dealt with the leadership effectiveness of managers, some of these are quality studies of principal effectiveness.

The field of management has grown and the works of select management writers, theorists and major schools of management thought are described in this chapter. An effort is made to integrate the major

59

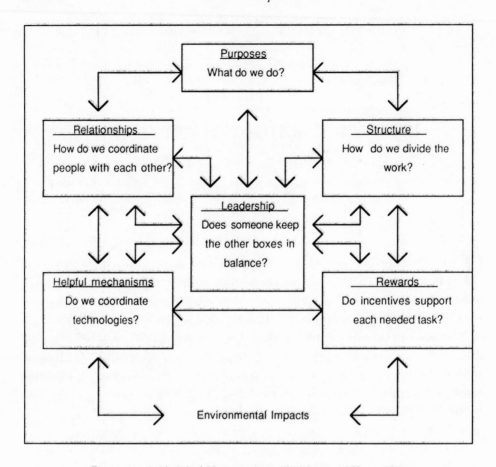

Figure 4 : A Model of Management (Weisbord, 1976, p. 430)

management approaches, the classical, behavioral, and quantitative, and the emerging systems and contingency perspectives. The structure of the chapter is largely based on the classical approach because:

1. principals find it operational;
2. aspiring principals find it to be a good lead-in to the management field; and
3. it provides an excellent organizing framework for all of the management approaches.

The author has made a distinct effort to note some of the important differences in the underlying values, assumptions, and action implications of the various approaches.

THE EVOLUTION OF MANAGEMENT THEORY

There are three major schools of management thought. One of these is scientific management which rests on four basic principles (Taylor 1911):

1. The development of a true science of management, so that, for example, the best method for performing each task could be determined.
2. The scientific selection of the workers so that each worker would be given responsibility for the task for which he or she is best suited.
3. The scientific education and development of the worker.
4. Intimate, friendly cooperation between management and labor.

The second major school of management thought, referred to as classical organization theory, grew out of the need to find guidelines for managing complex organizations. Henri Fayol (1841–1925) is acknowledged as the founder of this classical management school of thought because he was the first to systematize it. Fayol believed that sound managerial practice falls into certain patterns that can be identified and analyzed, and he developed the blueprint for a cohesive doctrine of management, one that retains much of its force to this day. His primary focus was on the managerial activity of his organizational structure and he defined this in terms of these five functions:

1. *planning*—devising a course of action,
2. *organizing*—mobilizing material and human resources,
3. *commanding*—providing direction for employees,
4. *coordinating*—making sure resources and activities are in sink,
5. *controlling*—monitoring the plans.

As the classical school has evolved, it has become known as the *management process* or the *operational approach.*

The behavioral school, the third major school of management thought, emerged because managers found the classical approach to be one that failed to achieve complete production efficiency and workplace harmony. Managers continued to face problems because people do not always follow predicted or rational patterns of behavior. This school, the behavioral school, has made impressive contributions to our understanding of individual motivation, group behavior, interpersonal relationships at work, and the importance of work to human beings. Because of this, managers have become more sensitive and sophisticated in dealing with their personnel and have gained new insights in such important areas as leadership, conflict resolution, the acquisition and use of power, organizational change, and communication.

Various approaches to management have made their appearance as a result of the schools just noted. One of these, the *systems approach* to management, views the organization as a unified, purposeful system composed of interrelated parts. Rather than dealing separately with various parts of the organization, the systems approach gives managers a way of looking at an organization as a whole and as part of the larger external environment. In so doing, systems theory reminds us that the activity of any part of an organization affects the activity of every other part.

Certain key concepts of general system theory have found their way into the language of management, and familiarity with the systems vocabulary is helpful in keeping pace with current developments.

1. *Subsystems* are the parts that make up the whole of a system.
2. *Synergy* means the whole is greater than the sum of its parts.
3. *Open and closed systems* are those that interact with their environments, or they don't.
4. *System boundary* is what separates the system from its environment.
5. *Flows* are the information, materials, and energy (including human), that enter the system from the environment, undergo transformation process within the system, and exit the system as outputs.
6. *Feedback* is the key to systems controls for it insures that information be returned to the appropriate people so that assessments can occur.

The systems approach has permeated current management thinking and has become an integral part of the thought processes and research designs of practitioners and academic theorists of all three major schools.

Another of the approaches to management that has been touted as appropriate and purposeful is the contingency approach. This author experienced this management approach during one period of his World War II service time at Fort Benning's Officer Candidate School. A frequent response to questions regarding military tactics was, *it depends upon the situation and terrain.* This is an appropriate response to current questions for it focuses on the interdependence of the various factors involving managerial situations.

This *contingency* approach was developed by managers, consultants, and researchers in their efforts to apply concepts of the major schools to *under particular circumstances, and at a particular time, best contribute to the attainment of his or her management goals.* real-life situations. They found that methods that were highly effective in one situation would not be so in other situations. They found that results differ because situations differ, or techniques suitable in one situation will not necessarily work in all cases. Accordingly, *the task of managers is to identify which technique will, in each situation, under particular circumstances, and at a particular time, best contribute to the attainment of his or her management goals.* It is then notable that the systems approach emphasizes the interrelationships between parts of the organization. The contingency approach builds upon this perspective by focusing on the kinds of relationships existing between these parts. It would define those factors that are necessary to a specific task or issue and to clarify functional interactions between related factors. It is because of this that advocates of the contingency approach see it as a leading branch of management thought today.

CREATIVE MANAGEMENT MEANS CREATIVE CULTURES

In order to transform schools successfully, educators need to navigate the difficult space between letting go of old patterns and grabbing on to new ones.

To exist is to change. To exist a long time is to change often. So said the English churchman and writer John Henry Cardinal Newman almost emeshed in the process. Concerned persons in public education are certain that two things are sure about change: it must occur, and the uncertainties of its outcomes must be reduced.

In order for change to be beneficial, original thinkers are needed to share and communicate what has been created. The principal will recognize a good idea when it is presented effectively and understandably.

Creativity is heralded as the procedure for transforming problems into opportunities, for energizing the development of unusual ideas and innovation. Innovation is the mechanism for dealing with uncertainty, for assuring control over volatile events. Accordingly, the issue is one of *leveraging* creativity, of maximizing its appearances and implementation. Creative and innovative management is one key to the effective and productive positioning of the school.

New disciplines in management do bring with them considerable excitement and interest. In the 1950s it was management science, the application of quantitative methods to solve administration problems. In the 1960s it was behavioral science, the use of psychological theory for organizational understandings. In the 1970s it was long range planning, the use of formal methods for planning futures and stimulating organization responses. In the 1980s and 1990s it is creative and innovative management, the generation of original solutions for complex problems.

Today's world is a world of change, and schools are struggling to respond and be responsive, and yet the prevailing way of thinking about school organizations comes from several fixed assumptions about the world in which educators work. These assumptions need to be challenged and new and creative presuppositions can be seen as more accurately describing the work of today's educator.

1. Organizational Goals
   a. *Old Assumption:* School systems are guided by a single set of uniform goals.
   b. *New Assumption:* School systems are necessarily guided by multiple and sometimes competing sets of goals.
2. Power
   a. *Old Assumption:* Power in school systems is (and should be) located at the top.
   b. *New Assumption:* Power in school systems is distributed throughout the organization.
3. Decision Making
   a. *Old Assumption:* Decision making in school systems is a logical problem-solving process that arrives at the one best solution.
   b. *New Assumption:* Decision making in school systems is inevitably a bargaining process to arrive at solutions that satisfy a number of constituencies.
4. External Environment
   a. *Old Assumption:* The public is supportive of school systems and influences them in predictable and marginal ways.
   b. *New Assumptions:* The public legitimately influences school systems in major ways that are sometimes unpredictable
5. Teaching Process
   a. *Old Assumption:* There is one, and only one, best way to teach for maximum educational effectiveness.
   b. *New Assumption:* There are a variety of situationally appropriate ways to teach that are optimally effective (Patterson, Purkey and Parker, 1986, p. 8.).

Today's world is so very different. Although we have gained considerably in technology and sophistication, we have lost some of our stability and vigor. Progress has been made in collective power, however we have moved backward in individual control. The modern school cannot assimilate the pyramiding data that is being constantly thrust upon it, and is often overwhelmed by its internal and external environmental challenges. Designs are needed to simplify and reduce, replacing precision for accessibility and accuracy for comprehension.

Today, the management of schools, is the story of theory striving to keep pace with practice. Even strategic planning, which has promised to forecast and guide, often extrapolates the past and misses the future. The past does not forecast the future and today's problems do not arrive in neat component parts, are difficult to factor and offer little in simple solutions. Management of todays' schools requires new forms of thinking.

Creative management is not easily quantified and verified. Originality is not quickly judged, and creative solutions are not easily measured by conventional measuring devices.

WHAT PRINCIPALS DO AS SCHOOL MANAGERS

School managers are described as organizational planners, organizers, leaders, and controllers. In actuality every school manager assumes a much wider range of roles in his or her efforts to move the school toward its stated objectives. School managers, more specifically, do the following.

The principal works with and through other people. The term *people* includes, not only, teachers, students and other school level personnel, and central office administrators, but also other principals in the school system. People also includes individuals outside the school, parents, taxpayers, union representatives, special interest groups, and so on. The principal, then works with anyone at any level within or without the school who, in one way or another, impacts upon the school or its goals.

In addition, principals work with each other to establish, plan, and achieve the schools' and school systems' horizontal and vertical long range goals. They also work with one another to provide accurate information, thus *principals act as channels of communication within the school and school system.*

Principals, as managers, are responsible and accountable. Principals are responsible and in charge of seeing that specific tasks are completed successfully. Not only are they usually evaluated on how well they arrange for these tasks to be accomplished, they are also responsible for the actions of the personnel with their assigned schools. This success or failure of the school's personnel reflects directly upon the principal's success or failure. Although all school personnel are responsible for their particular tasks, the principal is held responsible, or accountable, not only for his or her own work but also the work of others. This brings with it increased elements of risk and anxieties because the principal's responsibility for achieving things, will, at times, reach beyond his or her immediate control.

Principals balance competing goals and set priorities. At any given time, every principal faces a number of organizational goals, problems, and needs, all of which compete for the principal's time and resources (both human and material). Because such resources are always limited, each principal must strike a balance between the various goals and needs. Many principals, for example, prioritize each day's tasks, the most important are addressed immediately, while those of lesser importance are responded to later.

Principals also determine who are to perform particular tasks and make assignments appropriate to the personnel involved. Often limited human or other resources dictate that the principal deviate from the desired practices and these deviations cause the principal to be caught between conflicting human and organizational needs and the identification of priorities.

Principals must think analytically and conceptually. The principal, who is an analytical thinker, breaks each problem down into its components, analyzes these components, and then arrives at a feasible solution. Even more important is the principal who is a conceptual thinker for he or she is able to view the entire task in the abstract and relate it to other tasks. Although considering a particular task in relation to its larger implications is no simple matter, it is essential that the principal work toward the whole school's goals.

Principals are mediators. Schools are composed of people, and people do differ and disagree. Disputes within the school lower morale and productivity, and are at times so extremely disruptive that highly effective personnel may even seek to leave the particular school unit. Such occurrences hinder work toward the school's goals; therefore, principals must at times serve as mediators and resolve the disputes at hand. Resolving personnel differences requires skill and tact.

Principals are politicians. This does not mean that the school expects its principal to campaign for this office. It means that the principals must build relationships, and use persuasion and compromise to promote organizational (school) goals, just as politicians do when they move their programs forward. Principals should also develop other political skills, such as: building alliances and coalitions, and drawing upon these relationships to win support for proposals or decisions or to gain cooperation in carrying out various activities (Kanter, 1979).

Principals are diplomats. Principals serve as the official representatives of their schools at school and school system organizational meetings. They represent the entire school as well as its sub-units in dealing with personnel within their school's internal and external environments.

Principals as symbols. The principal personifies for the school's members and outside observers a school's successes and failures.

Principals make difficult decisions. Schools do not run smoothly at all times and there are no limits to the number and types of problems that may arise: resource limitations, pupil personnel issues, problems with personnel, or differences of opinion concerning school policy, to name just a few. Principals are expected to provide solutions to difficult problems, even though their decisions are at times unpopular.

Briefly, these managerial roles require that the principal be many things to many people, and that he or she must be alert to the particular role needed at any given time. The effective principal is able to recognize the appropriate role to be played and to change roles as needed.

MANAGEMENT TECHNIQUES THAT IMPROVE EFFECTIVENESS

The principal who understands and practices those principles and techniques of management that are most critical to his or her success is more apt to experience *consistently* good results and to be appraised as the *effective one.* The following appeared in the *Front Line Management Program,* a publication of The Economics Press, Inc., as key management techniques and are worthy of note at this juncture in this text.

1. maximizing productivity through delegation
2. make more effective decisions
3. challenging people to improve output
4. improving work through successful criticism
5. building teamwork to increase results
6. reduce lateness and absenteeism
7. communicating with employees to improve morale
8. keeping working conditions safe and pleasant
9. using appreciation and praise
10. evaluating employees to upgrade performance

11. handling employee complaints and grievances
12. developing practical, useful suggestions
13. giving instructions and orders effectively
14. scheduling to achieve greater productivity
15. establishing and meeting deadlines
16. giving orders that get followed completely
17. communicating a sense of urgency for extra effort
18. setting an example that brings out the best in employees
19. correcting errors so that they don't reoccur
20. avoiding resentment while implementing needed change
21. handling disputes to maintain employee teamwork
22. orienting employees so they get started right
23. motivating employees to get all they are capable of giving
24. supervising fairly to avoid the pitfalls of favoritism

THE SCHOOL'S CULTURE

Researchers have looked to anthropological works on groups when attempting to understand school-specific characteristics. They have borrowed the concept of culture to explain school behaviors as a specific type of clan. Schools, like other definable groups, are units whose decisions and behaviors are guided by many tacitly held beliefs and values developed over time. Culture is collective programming of the mind that is relatively stable over time and leads to nearly the same behavioral pattern in similar situations (Hofstede, 1980). The concept draws attention to the importance of values and beliefs for organizational structures, procedures, and behaviors. Viewers see shared values (what is important) and beliefs (how things work) interact with a school's people, organizational structures, and control systems to produce behavioral norms (the way we do things here) (Uttal, 1983).

The concept of school culture has attracted considerable attention, but continues to be difficult to define, and hard to operationalize. Its attractiveness has resulted in a number of popular writings that have sought to indicate that cultures can be defined as *excellent* or *strong* and that schools having such excellent cultures also excel in performance (Peters and Waterman, 1982). This is a rather simplistic viewing of subjective *vibes* often experienced by those who attempt to interpret a school's climate, and has serious drawbacks. It implies that cultures can be manipulated at will to integrate selected characteristics of excellence in order to ensure school effectiveness and productivity, a suggestion that is untenable and impossible to implement. The usefulness of school culture as a concept lies more in the differentiation of a school's decision-making and implementation style, its very recognition of individuality.

The important question for the principal and school management is: How does organizational culture influence a school's ability to deal with change? Culture is a filter with inherent strengths and weaknesses affecting the school's ability to respond to the entire range of environmental challenges. Understanding school culture can help explain why a school might be sensitive or insensitive to certain types of issues and effective or ineffective in dealing with them. How can creative management shore up weaknesses and build on strengths? This task requires assessing school responsiveness and identifying the influence of school culture, and improving performance in all areas, assuring comprehensiveness and well-balanced, environmentally sensitive, school management.

The recognition of the role of a school's culture in school management takes into account the inner school environment. Creative principals must therefore search for innovative tools that are designed to satisfy these requirements. In addition to the demands of an increasingly complex environment and the requirements for new roles and responsibilities of public education, principals find that they must also respond to the schools' cultures. To meet these needs, effective schools need an *integrated management* that combines a sociological planning function; an internal and external reporting function on school performance of the individual principal and the school as a whole.

FOSTERING A CULTURE THAT INSPIRES CHANGE

Good planning and collaborative decision-making pay off in a revitalized school. This is furthered by fostering conditions that encourage teacher initiatives and morale and galvanize community support for school improvement. When this occurs the school is seen as providing meaningful parent and community participation in the school's programs and services, and substantially more purposeful and increased teacher involvement. In turn, the community is convinced that it wants and deserves a better school. Teachers are noted as offering leadership in staff development activities on a regular and continuing basis and committed to grade level, subject matter, school building and district-wide curriculum development and improvement. The principal and teachers work collaboratively, in a non-threatening environment, on alternative approaches to assessment, including faculty advisor-advisee programs developed in cooperation with universities and colleges. The school-community learns that it can work together toward a common cause, maintain positive hopes for the future, and recognize that true change occurs over the long term.

Input is sought for goal-setting from all groups that make up the school: teachers, principals, central office staff, support service personnel, students, parents, and other community members. This collaborative or decentralized approach to decision making may be a new experience for many schools and in order that it to become a part of a school's culture, its effectiveness, that the school is doing things better, must be communicated to all of the school's clients.

Examples of such efforts that impact upon the school's culture include:

1. Consistent with the school's interest in developing collaborative structures, evaluation approaches that embrace goal-setting are selected.
2. A broad base of support, including school board members, teachers, principals, central office administrators, parents, students, teachers' organization representatives, and community business organizations, is sought.
3. Demonstrations that provide assurances that this collaborative process is workable and that it does produce satisfying results for all applicable constituents and clients.
4. Assure substantial staff involvement, while clearly defining school problems and concerns before arriving at carefully projected and discussed first apparent solutions to these issues.
5. Accept and understand that the pace or time spent in determining the real issues is often cause for wonder, however collaborative and decentralized decision making is time consuming.

Good planning and collaborative decision making are excellent strategies for making the best possible use of scarce resources and the resulting school goals become part of the school's culture. This is accompanied with the opening, creating, and extending of available lines of communication because the ability to explain to others what the school wishes to accomplish and what it takes to accomplish this is understood and supported by a broad cross-section of the total school-community.

All members of the school-community, particularly teachers, need to be motivated to utilize innovative ideas. They need to be encouraged to become risk takers. We suspect that, if teachers are able to perceive their school as improving, their ideas being incorporated into concrete changes, they in turn will direct their energies to the examination of their own classroom practices.

Building and district-wide staff development teams are seen as encouraging the move toward examining teaching practices, and forming school-university partnerships. Teachers are able to review their teaching practices with colleagues from their own system and other systems and university experts associated with the partnership. These associations emphasize the key questions of reflective practice, What am I doing and why am I doing it? All this brings with it a clear message to teachers, they are professionals working with children and young adults in a learning setting. They now see how children make sense of their internal and external environments and more fully understand the content material they are working with.

Schools in which principals assume the greatest interest in promoting and encouraging these collaborative efforts push the reflective practices within their schools farthest. Also, teachers in schools involved in various teacher-led staff development activities that flow from common assumptions know much about children's learning and are capable of learning much more.

Developing a school-wide culture for change takes courage, patience, conviction, and vision. Robert Schaefer, in his 1967 book *School as a Center of Inquiry,* suggests some guiding concepts. He proposed that we are all learners in the school setting and that teachers can be genuine partners in helping to engage children in their own learning. Teachers are also able to broaden their scholarship and knowledge base through university partnerships, and must assume a leadership in curriculum and develop their confidence as scholars if they are to be real partners in education.

Defining teachers' roles as major partners in decision making raises issues of trust and accountability, often making teachers and principals uncomfortable. This concept makes teachers responsible for more than ordering textbooks and curriculum guides, they are the ones who outline the curriculum. We do know that many teachers are not ready to assume this decision-making role. Furthermore, openly raised questions of practice means living through periods of considerable ambiguity, and efforts must be made to address such problems by acknowledging their existence and by extending a genuine respect toward diverse viewpoints.

As the school moves towards an understanding of the implications of operating in a center of inquiry it must recognize that teachers need practice digging into their intuitive experience to try to articulate what they think. Learning how to build such discussion into the organizational structure of the school which has not valued this type of expression in the past is a real challenge, and change of this sort must occur slowly and carefully.

Principals must now be leaders of leaders. It is no longer satisfying to tell others what to do. Their roles require people skills and the ability to find consensus in a wide range of differing interests. They must understand and accept controversy and consider it healthy when it occurs openly and in the spirit of seeking to define problems and arriving at genuine solutions. Principals who are leaders serve as models for teachers by respecting their staff's opinions and explaining the reasons for their own personal actions. These principals bring the staff together with clearly expressed sets of common values. Once consensus is reached, principals become the agents for confronting problems of practice and they must be aware that situational perceptions differ substantially. Confrontation, then, provides opportunities for teachers and principals to verbalize their perceptions. Further, the principal cannot simply be the *fixer*. He or she is the catalyst for reflective practice helping teachers think through their practices and how this affects student learning.

When the decision making processes are effective, teachers and principals are better equipped and prepared to respond intelligently to the numerous questions that arise throughout the school-community. However, not all decisions need be made by committee, and not all complaints indicate a problem. Also, the willingness of the board of education and central office to support the risk-taking inherent in this change process is vitally important.

Although what is suggested here is fairly basic and appears to be traced to organizational common sense, it is at best difficult in the educational environment to forego past practices. If a culture change is to occur, the school must focus upon the possible, now that we know we can do something, why not try something *really* difficult, like making a real difference in the learning achievements of all children and youth?

THE PRINCIPAL AS AN EFFECTIVE PLANNER

A major task for principals, while performing their managerial roles, is to plan the efforts of the school and its members and the use of those available resources necessary to achieve state organizational goals. The effective manager (principal) is alert to the central importance of planning. It is Peter Drucker's distinction between *effectiveness,* doing the right things, and *efficiency,* doing things right, that parallels the steps included in choosing goals and then determining how these are to be achieved.

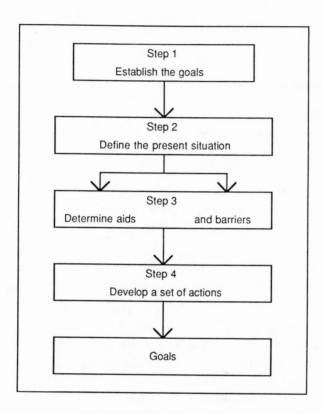

Figure 5 : Basic steps in planning

The specific elements of the planning process are closely related to the processes of problem solving and decision making, and consideration of ways to ensure effective planning begins with surveys of the purposes and processes of the planning function. Accordingly, the principal needs to analyze and look at the major types of plans (strategic and operational) in use by most organizations, and determine which, if used, will facilitate his or her awareness the barriers to effective planning and how to overcome them.

The effective principal is fully aware that in order to organize, lead, or control, he or she must develop plans that give purpose and direction to the school, deciding *what* needs to be done, *when* and *how* it needs to be

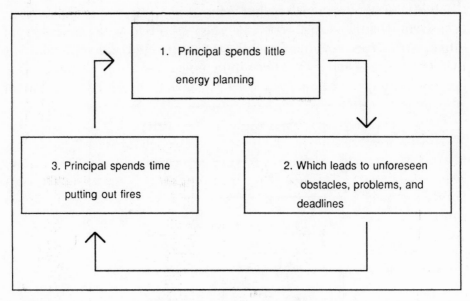

Figure 6 : Cycle of the non-planner

done, and *who* is to do it. Planning is direct and often presented in simple steps which are adaptable to all planning activities, at all organizational levels.

Step 1: Establish a goal or set of goals. Planning begins with decisions about what the school wants or needs. By clearly defining its goals, the school is able to focus its resources directly, identify its priorities, and maintain a specificity of aims.

Step 2: Define the present situation. How far is the school from its goals? What resources are available for reaching the goals? After analyzing the school's current conditions, plans are created to give direction to further progress.

Step 3: Identify the aids and barriers to the goals. In what manner or form can the school's internal and external environments help? Where are there apt to be problems? Although the future is never clear, anticipating future situations, problems, and opportunities is essential to planning.

Step 4: Develop a plan or set of actions for reaching the goal(s). Finally, the planning process evolves into developing alternative courses of action for reaching the desired goal(s), evaluating these alternatives, and choosing from among them the most appropriate alternative. It is here that decisions about future actions appear and where guidelines for decision making become relevant (Stoner and Wankel, 1986, p. 88).

There are barriers that must be overcome if effective planning is to occur. One of these is the would-be planner's internal resistance to establishing goals and planning to achieve them, an unwillingness or inability to engage in meaningful goal-oriented activities. Another, may appear beyond the planner in the form of reluctant school personnel who, for various reasons, oppose change.

Those principals who are unable to establish meaningful goals are also unable to make effective plans. These principals are seen as hesitating, or failing, to set organizational goals because (Kolb, Rubin and McIntyre, 1984): of their unwillingness to give up alternative goals, of their fear of failure, of their lack of organizational knowledge, and of their lack of confidence.

STRATEGIC PLANNING

Leadership requires the principal to act as a catalyst or spark in forming, communicating and implementing a shared vision on which strategic planning can build to develop a plan. The best answers always rest within the organization; they just have to be brought to the surface and stated clearly. The strategic planning process depends on the willingness of the school and school system to solve problems and the leadership being able to take risks and see things through.

Strategic planning is a powerful tool, if used honestly and objectively to guide the principal in the management of his or her school.

Today's world is a world in transition. The industrial age is gone and the new information age originally present in the economic environment, now appears throughout our society, bringing with it changes in how our educational product is delivered, and the basic nature of our children and youth. These children and youth come from a socioeconomic environment considerably different from the one that shaped and molded this author and the students of his day. Those basic premises upon which we planned are no longer considered totally valid by a substantial segment of today's society.

Today, planning is increasingly complex and difficult. A wide variety of options within our personal and professional lives are now available that were once not even considered possible. These conditions call for logical and systematic planning in order that frustrations and indecisiveness are reduced.

As the leaders of the education profession, we must move from the philosophy of reactive administration to one of inticipatory administration. We must begin to

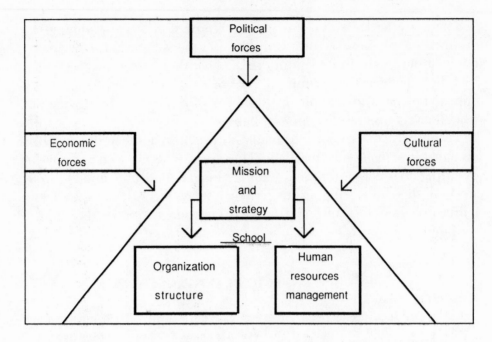

Figure 7 : Strategy management and environmental pressures

consciously look for potential problem areas in both our schools and the community at large (Bradley and Vrettas, 1990).

What are the basic essentials for the practicing principal when he or she is involved in the strategic planning process? In order to respond to this question one must first determine what strategic planning is not. Strategic planning is not a computer program into which basic data is entered and, in turn, receives answers to all possibilities. Rather, strategic planning is a process which assists the principal and school in their efforts to anticipate the future and also suggests procedures and practices needed to achieve that future.

Strategic planners are convinced that making schools more effective means more than reorganizing the traditional practices of the past. The improvement of the schools calls for a restructuring of those schools, significant changes from earlier procedures and practices for delivering instruction to the school's clients, its students. It is responsive to changes in the external environments that continue to affect the school, and permits significant moves from past practices. Restructuring may bring with it a change in the school's educational goals, management structures,

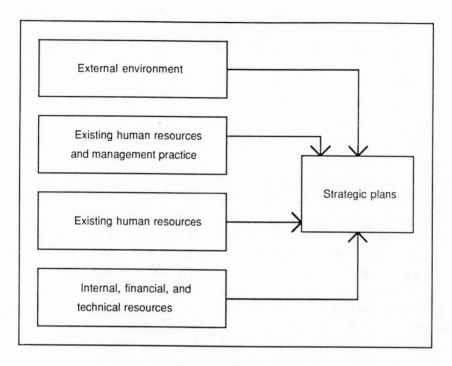

Figure 8 : Constraints on strategic planning

evaluation and accountability practices, school funding, and school and community relationships and communications.

Strategic planning is then (Bradley and Vrettas, 1990):

1. A management process for changing and transforming the school
2. A management philosophy
3. A way of thinking about and solving problems
4. An educational experience and developmental activity
5. A school-community education and involvement process

The organization for strategic planning is seen to follow a logical sequential order. Initial preparatory measures include a review of the school's current organizational structure. Components of the school and school system, such as present academic programs, staff, and school-community interest groups (internal and external environments), do contribute to and often control not only the school's program and service offerings, they affect the school's delivery systems.

This preliminary review appears to fall into two distinct groupings, individual and organizational questions, such as:

1. How is the school preparing its clients (students) for the future?
2. What are we actually doing?
3. What are the consequences of societal changes to me personally and professionally.
4. What does all this mean to my future?

This preliminary review provides the planner(s) with a clearer definition of needs and clearly establishes the nature and level of resistance that may be anticipated. This is a creative management process that is powered by basic human drives to solve problems and reduce discrepancies between what is and what should be. Strategic planning is of real value therefore because it requires that individuals and schools reexamine, refocus, and seek out new means for satisfying their requirements.

Next, strategic planning calls for the sequencing of tasks to be completed and the approval of timelines for the satisfaction of each of these tasks. This sequence of tasks and timeline must of necessity account for the uniqueness of the school and maintain a reasonable flexibility. This is followed by the selection of a representative body, to provide assurances to the entire school-community of the seriousness of purpose of this effort, assurances that purposeful and effective discussions are to occur.

What should follow is the gathering of information that is determined necessary if the strategic plan is to be developed. Such data might include a scanning of the external environments, a scanning of internals environments, and appropriate interactive scannings. This external environmental scanning is to include: trend analysis, pattern analysis, and scenario decision locations. The internal organizational scanning draws upon the school's academic offerings, staff utilization, physical facilities, support services, and stakeholders perceptions and expectations. The interactive scanning seeks to determine just how effective the school's program have been in preparing students who have left the school system (McCune, 1986). Once this data is gathered the strategic plan, plus a mission statement and supporting policy statements, for the school and school system are then developed and approved.

Strategic planning does impact upon the staff and community, accordingly throughout the process an extensive communication system is in order. Also, the strategic plan should be presented as a concise document that details the desired future of the school and school system, thereby providing increased assurances of community understanding and support.

The strategic plan sets forth the mission and goals of the school and system and provides for understandings of the relationships between the various elements and buildings of the district. The plan's outline includes the goals, objectives, timelines, responsibilities, specific activities, and planned results.

The implementation plan that follows should contain sequential short-term goals and proposals and the focus should now shift to incorporating the plan into the daily activities of the school and system. The inservicing of staff is vitally important to further the strategic plan goals and to building understandings and shaping the school's and system's cultures, and regular progress reports to the plan's progress must be made to all elements of the school-community.

Finally, the strategic and implementation plans should undergo an annual review and evaluation. Where appropriate, adjustments in the mission statement and goals to retain their relevance may be in order and determinations made as to how the implementation plans are addressing the school's objectives. This evaluation should be communicated to the school-community, thereby assuring the school system's commitments to its shareholders and stakeholders.

Effective school planning does not occur in isolation. Today's educational needs and social change force planners to acknowledge that schools are related to other institutions and affected by societal conditions. Therefore, users are involved in planning because schools exist to serve their communities, and members of the community deserve a voice in school-related decisions. This input is appropriate and valuable since new and creative insights are brought to the task and ownership of the final product is widened, thereby increasing the potential for the plan's success.

Clearly, strategic planning reaches beyond traditional and outmoded planning forms and procedures. Its strength is its ability to change old and established positions held, identify new possibilities, and introduce new questions. Evaluation and renewal of the strategic plan provide the dynamic nature of strategic planning. Strategic planning anticipates new understandings of the changing school environments thereby encouraging an awareness of necessary changes and opportunities, a sense of direction and purpose, and an organization tasks and activities designed to satisfy the school's goals. Such information, participation and anticipation, properly used, do provide for the future of our children and youth.

ENVISIONING THROUGH STRATEGIC PLANNING

Strategic planning is not long-range or comprehensive planning. Strategic planning defines the desired outcome through its own planning function and develops
strategies to achieve these outcomes. Strategic planning puts greater emphasis on
vision, leadership, and broad-based involvement than other planning functions.
There is no model only a process that sets direction and finds solutions from
within.

If you as the principal of a school, accept the premise that change is
inevitable, the future must be prepared for in the present, and can
respond in the affirmative to any of the following questions, strategic
planning may help you deal more effectively with the future and the
changes which it brings.

1. Is change leaving your school without control or accountability.
2. Do you know your school's philosophy regarding education?
3. Do you want and desparately need community and staff support for
    educational success?
4. Does your school, school system, and community, and its leaders lack
    vision?

Leadership requires principals to act as catalysts or sparks in the
forming, communicating and implementing a shared vision on which
strategic planning can be built. Peter Drucker, former professor, author
and management authority, refers to vision as the task of thinking
through the mission of the business or asking what is our business and
what should it be? In this instance, the business is the school and
strategic planning can be defined as developing the appropriate actions
to understand and establish the role the school and school system will
play in today's and tomorrow's community. For this to occur, according
to a 1988 Allstate Forum on Public Issues of Labor Force 2000, key
activities must occur in the school-community:

1. Active involvement of key school-community leaders.
2. Development of a vertical and horizontal vision that raises the level of
    effectiveness of the school-community.
3. Enabling a bottom-up implementation of the vision.
4. Creating of a formal, ongoing investment and management process
    within the school-community.

These requirements evolve into three key elements in the strategic
planning process:

1. Initial planning carried out by a leadership planning team (with representation from across the whole organization), that establishes some basic truths and directions for the process. This group, through careful articulation, usually develops: beliefs, values cultural analysis, demographic factors, competition, basic strategies mission statements, goals, strengths and weaknesses, resource identification, leadership resources, and data collection.

Development of these elements of the plan is important because vision ownership and commitment unfold during this process. The eventual definition of business, solutions, action plans, and success factors all are germinated in this function.

This initial phase requires the ability to scan broadly what exists, while pinpointing raw facts and articulating concepts that must be understood in some depth. All of this must be communicated through one concise document that clearly reflects the consensus of the planning phase group.

2. The process now spreads to all entities of the organization for the *development of action plans* that flow out of and directly back to the planning phase document. Here the *best* thinking of the entire staff seeks the *best* solutions. The best answers rest within the organization; they just have to be brought to the surface and stated clearly.

3. Evaluation, the final key element, again draws from a broad base to develop standards and a sense of quantitative targets. This accountability factor is the way the organization knows it is accomplishing what it has set out to do. Evaluation is ongoing and provides accurate and timely feedback.

Such planning is extremely helpful in finding the focus. Purposes are identified and these are known to take form as: maintaining a clear focus for the school, matching goals with available resources, and managing change, among other. Throughout this planning process participants grapple with their fundamental beliefs, beliefs which are identified and included within the agreed upon statements developed within the group. Later, formal, simply stated values and convictions of the school emerge; they are questioned, challenged, and restated until agreement is reached. When concluded, these statements now describe the fundamental beliefs of the school. Next, the group develops a *mission statement,* a brief, often one sentence description of the purpose and functions of the school. This statement which describes the uniqueness of the school is formally adopted eventually by the entire school-community.

Now that a firm foundation and sense of purpose has been attained, the group identifies the school's strengths and weaknesses. Each team member brings his or her list of these strengths and weaknesses to the table. All issues of concern are discussed, however, these are limited to those recognized, presented, and of concern at that particular time.

Every effort is made to avoid the introduction of new agendas or the stonewalling of discussion. However, consensus is not sought in this part of the process because strengths and weaknesses are, at this level of discussion, a matter of perception, not fact. The intent at this time is to raise the awareness level of issues, and differences tend to fall by the wayside as the group focuses in on the larger vision for education. Finally, there is an emergence of agreed upon strengths and weaknesses of the school.

The next phase in the process includes a comparative analysis of the schools within the school system and neighboring schools and school systems, and a review of those internal and external factors affecting the school. This analysis includes advantages and disadvantages of other schools, information on economic trends, demographics, social and political trends, and the impact of technological and educational changes.

The group then identifies factors that are assumed to impact on the school, and issues determined to have significant impact are addressed in the plan. The greatest threats and opportunities facing the school are flagged and the group is now ready to develop objectives and strategies, again through the process of research. Measurable objectives are shared with the entire group and these are focused on student outcomes and public support, and respond to critical issues within the school and school system. Group consensus is expected and a limited number of school objectives are identified.

Finally, the group turns its energies toward developing strategies. Background information, research and teamwork offer valuable benefits during this period in the planning process. A select group of strategies will have been produced and a final discussion will have provided for methods of communicating the plan to the entire school-community, as well as a review of the remaining parts in the strategic planning process.

The implementation of the strategies now follows. Action leaders are selected and commissioned to identify how the strategies can and will be implemented within the school.

MANAGEMENT BY OBJECTIVES

There are as many definitions of management by objectives (MBO) as there are writers, practitioners, and theoreticians who have concerned themselves with the subject. Definitions run the gamut from two or three lines of oversimplification to many paragraphs of over-sophistication. The following definition represents a balance between the two extremes.

> MBO is a systems approach to managing an organization—any organization. It is not a technique, or just another program, or a narrow area of the process of managing. Above all, it goes far beyond mere budgeting even though it does encompass budgets in one form or another.
>
> First, those accountable for directing the organization determine where they want to take the organization or what they want it to achieve during a particular period (establishing the overall objectives and priorities).
>
> Second, all key managerial, professional, and administrative personnel are required, permitted, and encouraged to contribute their maximum efforts to achieving the overall objectives.
>
> Third, the planned achievement (results) of all key personnel is blended and balanced to promote and realize the greater total results for the organization as a whole.
>
> Fourth, a control mechanism is established to monitor progress compared to objectives and feed the results back to those accountable at all levels.

Contrary to popular thought, the key word in the term management by objectives is not the word objectives but the word management. Failure to recognize this distinction has been at the root of management's failures in attempting to practice MBO. The successful MBO manager views objectives as only one part, admittedly an important part, of a total system. This manager insures that the management system is in place so that he or she can position objectives into the system rather than have them stand on their own. This manager first masters the system, determines what it is, what it isn't, its rationale, the prerequisites to be met, the pitfalls to be wary of, the mechanics of the system, the components. It is then that he or she addresses the objective proper.

MBO is adaptable to any type of organization as long as that organization has a mission to perform. Differences appear in the type and content of the objectives. In a police department, the objective may be to lower the crime rate to a predetermined level. In a school system, the objective might be to reduce the dropout rate by a certain percentage, or provide specific educational services at particular cost levels.

Once the objectives have been approved, they are then translated into the principal's actions within his or her school. This objective-setting process is complete when all stakeholders within the school system have objectives that, when added up, equal the overall objectives of the school system. MBO is the full, in-depth delegation of elements of the overall organizational objectives so that each stakeholder is accountable for accomplishing part of the higher-level objectives.

MBO is a systems approach to managing the school. It is a combination of plans and actions (or components) that, when acting as a whole, cause something to happen. It is time-limited, clearly delineated, and measurable. These plans and actions are concrete. This system comprises: objectives, plans, managerial direction and action, control (monitoring), and feedback. The absence of any one of these key components will render it inoperative.

The managerial direction and action assumes that the manager is given proper direction and takes action to accomplish what the school wishes to achieve to carry out the school's objectives and plans. This component includes such functions as: organizing, communicating, motivating, coordinating, and developing fellow staff members. It brings to life the objectives and plans established by the school; it's the action vehicle of MBO. Controlling (monitoring) is tailored to measure the specific objective and each manager has controls for each of the responsibilities for which he or she is responsible, and these controls are tailored to particular needs. Each control must include the objective being measured, the method of measuring, the frequency of measuring, and to whom the control information is to be sent. Finally, we arrive at the feedback and its role in the MBO system, and this is accomplished when each manager receives the type of information, in the right form and at the right frequency, that he or she requires to carry out the accountabilities of the assignment.

Management by objectives is much more than a goal-setting and review procedure tacked onto existing traditional processes of management. Instead MBO is seen as a way to realize a totally new kind of organizational life, one that is characterized by:

1. A climate of mutual trust, respect for the dignity and worth of others, frankness, candor, and collaboration;
2. An environment wherein each principal knows what is expected of him or her, wherein delegation, freedom to act, and authority to make decisions (and mistakes) are the norm, and wherein the principal is prepared to be accountable for results;
3. A spirit of vigor, venture, creativity, and innovation; and
4. A systems approach in which the management process is viewed as a total system, in which the smallest subsystems are integrated with the whole, in which the functions of management (planning, organizing, directing, and controlling) are systemitized, and in which the system's technology of modern management science is employed to maximum advantage.

THE PRINCIPAL AND PRODUCTIVE MANAGEMENT

Hall, Rutherford, Hord, and Huling (1984), in their description of the effects of principal styles on school improvement, presented an integrated view of management for effective school leadership. Regardless of the style being considered (initiator, manager, responder), indicators of success in facilitating change were broad-based dimensions/behaviors of principals: vision and goal setting, structuring the school as a workplace, managing change, collaborating and delegating, decision making, and guiding and supporting. Understood in these dimensions/behaviors related to school improvement is the importance of the general administrative, albeit clearly focused, nature of the principalship.

Snyder and Johnson (1985) proposed a school management productivity model for the principal's role. In this model, the principal is seen as coordinating many activities designed to effect school improvement. This model suggests a cyclic process which focuses on four managerial phases: organizational planning, developing staff, developing program, and assessing school productivity.

In keeping with this productivity model, the Illinois Administrator's Academy (Illinois State Board of Education, 1986) published a well-conceived triad of responsibilities for the principal as the school's institutional leader

1. *Defines the mission* — frames goals and communicates goals
2. *Manages curriculum and instruction* — knows curriculum and instruction coordinates instructional programs, supervises and evaluates, and monitors student progress
3. *Promotes school climate* — sets standards focusing on achievement, sets expectations, protects time and provides orderly atmosphere, creates productive working environment and promotes instructional improvement and staff development, and cultivates supportive external environment.

The well-run school enhances learning opportunities and this is key to understanding the role fulfilled by the principalship in productive schools. It is within this concept of school management that principals contribute to the productive learning environment of the organization.

The principal's managerial role is indispensible to productive schools. One way of summarizing the principal's general management function on productive schools is to view the role through the eyes of students.

Kojimoto (1987) reported from interviews with school children that the important functions of the principal were seen as: being visible and meeting the school's needs for safety and order, functions that are squarely within the managerial realm of the principalship.

THE COMPUTER REVOLUTION AND THE SCHOOL

The computer revolution is here and traditional management concepts are being obsoleted rapidly. In the age of the computer, it is clear that managers (principals) will be subject to change, with little notice and less choice.

The efficiency of the typical practical manager today may be impaired by the rational behavior of the computer. Computer competition may lead the manager to frustrations unless he or she is able to divert his or her energies into more creative channels.

The future school system may exchange the practical administrator for a new model, one with a creative imagination and a broad outlook. The specialist with narrow-gauged skills will be less in demand since the computer will take over many of such specialized functions.

The computer is transforming the nature and practice of management. Even management's basis philosophy is being put to the test. Management values, attitudes and life styles are undergoing change as computer technology permeates organizations. Organizations themselves are being restructured in the process. It is evident already that traditional organizational structures, management philosophy and practices require radical adaptations to meet the new conditions. The longer the delay in making changes, the greater the expected disturbance of the equilibrium of the organization and disruption of the management social system.

Computers and the management sciences have done much more than place new tools in the hands of managers. They have also created a new way of thinking. No single concept has emerged in recent times which has had a more powerful impact upon management than the systems approach. No longer can we view things piecemeal. To understand how things work, we must understand how various sub-systems link to others to form a total system. All are interdependent. A breakdown in a subsystem immediately affects the whole system.

Thoughtful school administrators have come to realize the implications of the systems approach for their school systems. To function at optimum levels, school system and school management must find linkage towards common goals.

THE MANAGEMENT OF TIME

The varied pressures on administrative effectiveness have made administrative time a most strategic and crucial asset. There are three different approaches to effective time-management.

1. Increasing the amount of available time.
2. Doing more work in the available time.
3. Doing only the important work in the available time.

The first approach suggests that the administrator stretch his or her working hours as far as possible. This could result in severe depression, fatigue and lack of efficiency. The second approach is work and methods oriented. It requires a mechanically oriented mind. There is absolutely no limit to this type of training. The third approach suggests that a scale of priority be assigned to the management of time. It also denotes a commitment toward only essential and conceptual matters, rather than toward massive details of an operational nature, which may be delegated elsewhere. This approach necessitates an action-oriented strategy. In order to be functional it requires a preparatory phase, educational training and a generally enlightened organizational climate.

The preparatory phase requires the establishment of key guidelines to identify both internal and external pressures, and to determine the best means of coping with them. The second phase of educational training prepares administrators to effectively reorganize their time by exposing them to: modern administration concepts, behavioral and social science approaches, training in areas such as better interpersonal relations, awareness of time and its value, and visits by outside speakers and consultants.

Employees on all levels within the organization will benefit from the third phase of enlightened organization environment, which should consider the following: a generally sympathetic and understanding central administration, a quality and quantity conscious administration, an administration willing and ready to adapt to change, and a personal atmosphere, rather than one which is highly artificial and paternalistic.

The planning and control of administrative time, is done in much the same way for any organizational goal. It is a method that can be used effectively to optimize any of three approaches to time management. Planning increases the amount of time by foreseeing how much time will be needed in particular areas. It most certainly optimizes the amount of work that can be done in a span of time because the needs are projected and arranged to the administrator's best advantage. Further, the control aspect of a time plan will help insure that the projected amounts of time are indeed spent on the most important subjects.

Management of time is an important administrative objective. This concept is relatively new since the frequency and severity of administrative pressures and tensions are in themselves relatively new phenomenon. It should be assumed as a high priority by the school administrator, since its proper treatment can increase the overall effectiveness for the principal, broaden the principal's involvement insignificant school issues, and create the makings for an overall integrated organizational environment.

SCHOOL-BASED MANAGEMENT

A current and important issue in educational policy and practice is school-based management. This school-based management (SBM) refers to a program and philosophy assumed by schools and school systems to improve education by increasing the autonomy of the school and its staff to make decisions at the school site.

Researchers, practitioners, and policymakers are known to hold differing views regarding SBM, for SBM is interpreted by a certain degree of vagueness and uncertainty. Schools and school systems are observed as introducing variations concerning the levels of authority, the stakeholders involved, and the areas of control. Although decentralization is broadly viewed as the delegation of decision-making authority to smaller internal units of the organization, SBM is a design of decentralization in which authority is shared by the central office administration and the school site. SBM school systems tend to allocate greater decision-making authority to principals and further this decentralizing emphasis by increasing the authority of teachers, students, parents, and community members (Clune and White, 1988; Pierce, 1980).

SBM differs from earlier decentralization efforts because it introduces changes in the entire school system and organization, and restructures most roles in the district (David, Purkey, and White 1988). Its purpose extends beyond the reorganization of administrative responsibilities, it makes changes in traditional structures of authority by encouraging new relationships among teachers, administrators, parents, and students.

The sources for support for SBM comes from state and local policymakers, teachers, administrators, and school board members who believe that the closer a decision is made to those served by the decision, the better it will serve those affected. Both of the nation's major teacher organizations, the National Educational Association and the American Federation of Teacher, and the National Governors' Association, have encouraged an increase in school site flexibility and limitations on state mandates and regulations so as to insure local autonomy. The ultimate goal of SBM is to improve the teaching and learning environments available to students.

Three areas of decision making most often decentralized under SBM are: budget, curriculum, and staffing. School site budgeting permits principals, with the advice of teachers and community representatives, to allocate funds in accordance with priorities determined at the building level. Those who support SBM argue that school personnel are more suited to meet the needs of their students by purchasing instructional supplies and equipment designed for students' specific learning needs (Gideonse, Holm, and Westheimer, 1981; Pierce, 1978).

School site curriculum development permits school site staff to create the instructional program, to select instructional materials and textbooks, and to design inservice training and staff development programs. School site personnel are afforded greater freedom to choose the directions to be taken during curriculum development, the choice of school instructional materials and methods and the unfolding of curricula that are most appropriate to the needs of their students (Knight, 1984). This involvement in staffing decisions permits principals, teachers, and other school staff to determine the number and distribution of positions within at each school site. It also permits the school staff to employ personnel with specific skills, thereby assuring their increased responsiveness to students' needs.

One of the central objectives of SBM is increased community participation and involvement. Such groups as school site councils engage community members, in cooperation with the principal, teachers, and students, in share decision making regarding school issues. As local conditions dictate the selection, composition, and responsibilities of the council varies from school to school, and they are known to be involved in such activities as: interviewing and recommending candidates for staff positions, establishing school priorities, making school budget recommendations, and assessing the effectiveness of school programs (Lindelow, 1981; Marburger, 1985).

SBA provides for increased flexibility, increased participation of school staff in school decisions, and opportunities that assure more appropriate programs and services in response to defined student needs. Some research suggests that SBM may produce another benefit, that of student achievement. It is difficult however to draw a cause and effect relationship between SBM and student achievement since this is complicated by other trends within the school's internal and external environments. Also, increased involvement and feeling of personal ownership is seen as improving self-esteem, morale, and efficiency of school personnel.

According to Rosenholtz (1987, p. 540), autonomy enhances performance:

> Jobs that give people autonomy and discretion require that they exercise judgement and choice; in doing so, they become aware of themselves as causal agents in their own performance. Loss of the capacity to control terms of work or to determine what work is to be done, how the work is to be done, or what its aim is to be, widens the gap between the knowledge of one's unique contributions to work and any performance efficacy that can be derived from it.

Conflict may appear when administrative tasks are assigned to teachers and the school staff is engaged in decisions that may be in discord with the system's collective bargaining agreements. This is so because SBM often provides for diversity and differentiation; in procedures, while collective bargaining often results in the standardization of procedures.

In earlier and current experiences researchers have identified a number of essential ingredients in initiating SBM (Lindelow, 1981; Marburger, 1985; Parker, 1979):

1. *Training.* SBM brings to bear new lines of communication among its various stakeholders and select training is in order for this to occur effectively.

2. *A gradual transition.* Successful SBM programs experience a gradual transition process that limits implementation problems.

3. *Financial support.* An SBM program is not necessarily more expensive, however, to be effective, school staff must have flexibility over the use of funds. Costs are bound to appeal within the curriculum development process and the provision for training and released time for staff in order that they meet.

4. *Shared goals.* The participation of all stakeholders in the development of school goals strengthens their commitment to them.

5. ***Administrators willing to share authority.*** If SBM is to work, admin-

istrators must allocate authority to principals and principals must be prepared to allocate authority to teachers, parents and students.

    6. Support from the school-community. SBM cannot be imposed on schools, but rather must acquire the support of the entire school and its community.

It is logical that those who are most affected by such decisions as: curriculum development, textbook selection, staffing structure, and allocation of school resources should have a voice in making those decisions. What is needed is systematic comparisons of the allocation of authority to different stakeholders. Also, research is needed on the more effective methods of training the various actors for their new roles and the degree of school improvement after the implementing of SBM.

FOCUS GROUPS, A SOURCE FOR COMMUNITY VIEWS

An extremely effective means of communicating with the school-community and learning what is really thought of the school can take the form of focus groups, a cross-section-representation of the community.

It is important for the principal to learn what the school's community thinks periodically and regularly because:

1. Demographics change.
2. Public opinion is fluid, Communities and their thinking change. School administrators need to be aware and keep pace with that change.
3. Administrators need information from constituents to make informed decisions.
4. When we take time to ask, we tell our publics we are interested in their opinions.

Principals who seek community input, early and often, from a broad cross-section of their community, can make decisions with confidence, confidence that the decisions they make are in sync with their community's priorities and expectations.

The standard means of seeking community input or opinion is to conduct a survey. This is usually done through the mails. However, responses are known to be rather limiting and limited, and therefore often unreliable. Surveys have been conducted by phone, however, for this to be reliable expert help is needed. This is oftentimes costly. An alternative is the focus group.

Focus groups allow the principal to communicate with a large cross-section of the community in a short time. Unlike the survey, the focus group permits people to talk about what's important to them, not what the principal thinks ought to be important. Such groups often are used by research firms or advertising agencies to gather information that can later be used to develop questionnaires for more formal research methods. Schools can use focus groups to explore people's reactions to school issues and problems.

The organization of focus groups can range from something resembling town meetings, to highly structured, videotaped sessions commonly used by advertisers for market research. Focus groups are considered structured nonprobability sampling, a research method that provides directional rather than quantitative data. Although the responses cannot be statistically validated, as they can be for a survey of a randomly selected sampling of the entire community.

Principals have used focus groups to assess community thinking on a particular topic or issue, and to determine if there is a pattern to the responses that can offer direction or help in the decision making that might follow. The focus group's success depends on the moderator. That person must be an effective facilitator, able to put people at ease and encourage them to respond without interjecting any bias into the discussion. This person need not be the principal. Success also depends on the moderator's ability to record comments as close to verbatim as possible, and then to work with the group to assign priorities for their responses.

The principal needs to know what his or her community thinks and the focus group offers one means of learning of this. Focus groups bring with them an added bonus, community-wide dialogue about schools.

SUMMARY

Today's principal-practitioner and current research regarding the role of the principalship leaves little room for debate: principals are found to be primarily oriented toward their managerial roles in the educational hierarchy. What is also becoming even more clear is the value, or the importance, of the principal's managerial role for supporting effective schools.

The educational reform, school restructuring, and school renewal programs of the eighties and early nineties did rightly focus in on and draw attention to the principal's instructional leadership function. This is as it should be because of its importance throughout the effective schools programs. However, while developing and supporting high quality learning environments should be a fundamental goal of principals, the managerial function and instructional leadership are not mutually exclusive. At issue within the school improvement program is not the role of the principal as the school manager versus instructional leadership; rather the focus must be managing productive schools.

From its inception in American education, the principalship has undergone a transition from that of principal-teacher to that of general administrative agent. In Goodlad's (1978) analysis of the principal's role, the principal's work was characterized, prior to 1950, by an orientation toward; instructional management. Since 1950 there has appeared an increased propensity toward management of non-instructional activities. The reasons for this increased emphasis on general administration were offered by McDaniel (1982): increased size of school; increased and specialized expertise requirements in the content and process of instruction; greater need for specialized management skills, more complex legal procedures; and increased state mandated programs.

One example of this increased emphasis on general administration of schools and school systems occurred during this author's earliest teaching experience. In 1948, I was employed by a New York State Board of Cooperative Educational Services as an itinerant teacher, servicing five school districts, one day per week in each school system.

One of these school districts, the Commack Public Schools, prided itself with one Kindergarten through Eighth Grade elementary school (built in the late 1800s) and housing less than 100 students. The limited number of high school students from this district were tuitioned-off to a neighboring school system that maintained a secondary school program. During that year, a four room addition to this, the Marian Carle School, was proposed, and the district's voters rejected this, claiming that there would never be a need for four additional classrooms. By 1973, the student enrollment of the Commack Public Schools had increased to 16,000 students, and the school system now sported 18 school buildings (two of which were high schools). Further, during the ten year period that followed, because of substantial declines in the birth rate and demographic changes, the students enrolled in the Commack Schools dropped to 8,000 and 9 of its 18 schools were either closed and/or sold.

The complexity of this situation was further increased with the numerous state legislated laws, programs and courses of study to be implemented in the elementary and secondary schools of that period, ranging from the teaching of traditional academic curricula to special emphasis programs, the collective bargaining laws of the early 60s, changing directions in student and personnel rights and responsibilities, and mandated improvements and changes to facilities, ranging from facilities for the handicapped to the removal of asbestos.

Clearly, the principalship has moved from a focus primarily on instruction to one of board-based administrative responsibilities. The effective principal does not abdicate his or her role as an educational leader and is responsive to changing environments with leadership styles that are adaptable to varying situations and circumstances.

Personal experiences of successful principals and effective leadership literature have helped identify four key areas of principal leadership: goals and production emphasis, power and decision making, organization/coordination, and human relations. By engaging in these broad areas of responsibility, principal management behavior improves the school climate and instructional organization, and, in turn, facilitates student learning. This global view of the educational enterprise provides further assurances that the school will be operated effectively and efficiently.

In the school management productivity model for the principal's role suggested by Snyder and Johnson (1985), the principal is perceived as coordinating many activities designed to effect school improvement. This model focuses on four managerial phases: organizational planning, developing staff, developing program and assessing school productivity.

Consistent with this productivity model, the Illinois Administrators Academy (Illinois State Board of Education, 1986) published a well-conceived triad of responsibilities for the principal as institutional leader:

1. *Defines the mission* — frames and communicates goals
2. *Manages curriculum and instruction* —knows curriculum and instruction, coordinates instructional programs, supervises and evaluates, and monitors student progress
3. *Promotes school climate* —sets standards focusing on achievement, sets expectations, protects time and provides orderly atmosphere, creates productive working environment and promotes instructional improvement and staff development, and cultivates supportive external environment.

The effective principal recognizes the vitality of a well-run school in enhancing learning opportunities as a key to understanding the role of the principalship in productive schools. These principals contribute to these productive learning environments through the breadth of the management genre.

The principal's managerial role is indispensible to productive schools, and the recognition of it's importance is not license to fill the role with meaningless adversarial argumentation, management versus instructional leadership. General management diversity will continue to characterize the contemporary role of the effective principal.

DISCUSSION QUESTIONS

1. What environmental factors enhanced the growth and development of each of the three major schools of management thought?
2. What is the major task of the principal, as school manager, according to the contingency approach?
3. Which approach or school of management thought makes the more sense to you? Why?
4. Why is flexibility a characteristic of a good management plan?
5. How can a principal be helped to overcome difficulties in setting goals?
6. How will strategic planning help a school take the great leaps needed to catch up with a world that keeps moving at breakneck speed?
7. How and in what way is the management of the school office vital to the well-being of the organization?
8. What is the difference between *accounting* and *accountability*?
9. Do you agree with the author that today the dominant factor of the effective and productive school is change? Why?
10. What is it about the *contingency approach* to school management that would or would not encourage you, as the school's principal, to approach school management in this manner?

REFERENCES

Beaubier, E. and Thayer, A. (Eds.): *Participative Management—Decentralized Decision Making: Working Models.* Burlingame, California Association of School Administrators, 1973.

Bradley, Larry G. and Vrettas, Arthur T.: Strategic planning and the secondary principal—the key approach to success. *NAASP Bulletin,* March 1990, pp. 30–37.

Clune, W. H. and White, P. A.: *School-Based Management: Institutional Variation, Implementation, and Issues for Further Research.* New Brunswick, Center for Policy Research in Education, 1988.

David, J., Purkey, S. and White, P.: Restructuring in progress: lessons from pioneering districts. Paper prepared for the National Governors' Association. Washington, 1988.

Gideonse, H., Holm, D. and Westheimer, R.: *School Site Budgeting: Abstracting the*

Literature. A project for the Educational Panel of the Cincinnatus Association, 1981.

Goodlad, J. I.: Educational leadership: toward the third era. *Educational Leadership, 35:* 1978, pp. 322–31.

Hall, G., Rutherford, W.L., Hord, M., and Huling, L.L.: Effects of three principal styles on school environment. *Educational Leadership, 5:* 1984, pp. 22–29.

Hofsteade, G.: *Culture's Consequences: International Differences in Work-Related Values.* Beverly Hills, Sage, 1980.

Hostrup, Richard W.: *The Effective Principal Administrator.* Palm Springs, ETC, 1990.

Johnson, William L. and Snyder, Karolyn, J.: *Managing Productive Schools,* Austin, Southwest Educational Research Association Paper Presented at Annual Meeting, January 1990, pp. 25–27.

Joyce, Bruce R.: *The Structure of School Improvement.* New York, Longman, 1988.

Kanter, Rosabeth Moss: Power failure in management circuits. *Harvard Business Review. 57:*4, July–August 1979, pp. 65–75.

Kaufman, Roger and Herman, Jerry.: Strategic planning for a better society. *Educational Leadership, 48:*7, April 1991, pp. 4–8.

Knight, P.: The practice of school-based curriculum development. *Journal of Curriculum Studies. I,* 1984, pp. 37–48.

Kolb, David A., Rubin, Irwin M. and McIntyre, James M.: *Organizational Psychology: An Experiential Approach to Organizational Behavior, 4th ed.,* Englewood Cliffs, Prentice Hall, 1984, p. 102.

Kojimoto, C.: The kid's eye view of effective principals. *Educational Leadership. 1,* 1987, pp. 69–74.

Lindelow, J.: School based management. *In School Leadership: Handbook for Survival.* edited by S. C. Smith, et. al. Columbia, National Committee for Citizens in Education, 1981.

Marburger, C.: *One School at a Time: School Based Management a Process for Change.* Columbia, National Committee for Citizens in Education, 1985.

McCune, Shirley D.: *Guide to Strategic Planning for Educators.* Alexandria, Association for Supervision and Curriculum Development, 1986.

McDaniel, T. R.: What's your P. Q. (principal quotient)? A quiz on improving instruction. *Phi Delta Kappan. 63:* 1982, pp. 464–68.

Nyberg, D. and Farber, P.: Authority in education. *Teachers College Record. 88:* 1986, pp. 4–14.

Parker, B.: School based management: improve education by giving parents, principals more control of your schools. *The American School Board Journal. 7:* 1979, pp. 20–24.

Patterson, Jerry L., Stewart, C, Purkey and Parker, Jackson V.: *Productive School Systems for a Nontraditional World.* Alexandria, Association for Supervision and Curriculum Development, 1986, pp. 7–8.

Peters, T. J. and Waterman, R. H.: *In Search of Excellence: Lessons from America's Best-Run Companies.* New York, Harper and Row, 1982.

Pierce, L. C.: Decentralization and educational reform in Florida. Paper presented at the American Educational Research Association, Toronto, 1978.

Pfeiffer, J. William, et al.: *Understanding Applied Strategic Planning: A Manager's Guide.* San Diego, University Associates, 1985.

Rosenholtz, S. J.: Education reform strategies: will they increase teacher commitment? *American Journal of Education. 4 :* 1987, pp. 534–562.

Schaefer, R.: *School as a Center of Inquiry.* John Dewey Society Lecture No. 9, New York, Harper and Row, 1967.

Snyder, K. J. and Johnson, W. L.: Retraining principals for productive school management. *Educational Research Quarterly. 3 :* 1985, pp. 19–27.

Stoner, James A. F. and Wankel, Charles: *Management.* Englewood Cliffs, Prentice Hall, 1986, pp. 85–90.

Stronge, Jame H.: Managing for productive schools: the principal's role in contemporary education. *NASSP Bulletin. 74 :* 1990, pp. 1–5.

Taylor, Frederick.: *Scientific Management.* New York, Harper and Row, 1911. *The Principal as Instructional Leader: A Research Synthesis.* Monograph Series Paper No. 1.

Springfield, Illinois State Board of Education, 1986.

Uttal, B.: The corporate culture vultures. *Fortune.* October 17, 1983, pp. 66–72.

White, P. A.: *Resource Materials on School Based Management.* New Brunswick, Center for Policy Research in Education, 1988.

Chapter IV

EFFECTING A
PRODUCTIVE SCHOOL ORGANIZATION

INTRODUCTION

The creative organization is one dominated by new ideas that are implemented and, as a result, is characterized by change. The creative organization may undertake problems that are different from traditional ones in standard fields and disciplines. It may attack these problems in original or interdisciplinary ways that do not respect conventional classifications of knowledge. It is difficult to characterize innovation, almost by definition, but it is clear that the creative organization looks for new means to achieve old goals.

Richard M. Cyert, *President,*
Carnegie-Mellon University

Today's society has often been characterized by an apparent propensity to grow and prosper through the establishment of more and larger organizations. Although the emphasis on the human being behind any achievement continues to receive the attention it deserves, the realization also continues to grow that it is the organization behind the achievement and the human being that helps determine the extent of success in each case. More significantly, it is the leadership exercised within each organization that enables it to meet its challenges, absorb its inevitable changes, and produce benefits. This chapter is focused on these two entities: the organization and the leadership within, the school and its principal.

The central concerns of this chapter are: how organizations are created, how they evolve, how they work, how they change, why they succeed or fail, and what their components and functions are that determine their progress. All organizations, the public organization and the private, for service or for profit, have certain constants. They all have their reasons for existence, their missions, and their needs. They all require leadership, structure and resources in order to function. This chapter is focused on the school, its evolution, its internal and external impacts, and its synergistic relationships with its internal and external environments, including the rest of society.

99

From $\longrightarrow$	To
Closed systems	Open systems
Materialistic orientation	Human orientation
Centralized power	Distributed power
Extrinsic motivation	Intrinsic motivation
Negative attitudes about people	Positive attitudes about people
Balanced focus on employee	Balanced focus on employee and organizational needs
Imposed discipline	Managerial discipline
Authoritative managerial role	Managerial role of leadership and team support

Figure 9 : Trends in organizational behavior

Leadership in organizations has many styles and manifestations. It also changes and adapts to new situations and circumstances. Although it has frequently been said that leaders are born, and not made, it is important to recognize that leaders also grow and excel if the preparation is there to meet the challenges. This chapter focuses on various aspects of leadership challenges within the context of the school.

Research on leader effectiveness indicates that clarity of organization vision, ability to communicate that vision, commitment to empowering others, and ability to cultivate trust in the organization's functioning are distinguishing characteristics of effective leaders (Bennis and Nanus, 1985; Hickman and Silva, 1984). Of these, the central characteristic is vision: that is, the presence of a clear image of the future state of the organization.

The purpose of this chapter then is to propose a number of procedures and practices that will help principals:

1. Develop a precisely stated school vision
2. Foster faculty ownership of the vision

3. Communicate the vision to concerned constituents
4. Develop organizational trust in the vision through ongoing reinforcement of its major emphases.

To bring organizational behavior to a point consistent with the vision is a long-term process. That process can be facilitated if the staff's orientation and the organization's commitments are basically similar.

AN OVERVIEW

Organization represents an attempt to define duties, responsibilities, power, and authority in a manner that best realizes the purposes of the school. It is one of the many functions of the principal that generally precedes the other steps in the administrative process. It is the design of the operation, based upon institutional purposes, through which individuals can work together to achieve personal and institutional goals and objectives, and as a function, it is continuous.

The formal organization of an institution are those definable characteristics of its structured design which can be clearly set down on paper. Its characteristics, as stated by Dale (1955) appear as follows:

1. Organization is a planning process. It is concerned with setting up, developing, and maintaining a structure or pattern of working relationships of the people within an enterprise. It is carried on continuously as changes in events, personalities and environment require. Thus organization is dynamic. However, the resulting structure is static, i.e., it reflects the organization only as of a given moment of time.

2. Organization is the determination and assignment of duties to people so as to obtain the advantages of fixing responsibility and specialization through the subdivision of work.

3. Organization is a plan for integrating or coordinating most effectively the activities of each part of the enterprise so that proper relationships are established and maintain among different work units and so that the total effort of all people in the enterprise will help accomplish its objectives.

4. Organization is a means to an end. Good organization should be one of the tools for accomplishing the school's objectives, but it should not become an objective in itself.

The nature and character of the education function in American democracy may be expressed through the following four general principles:

1. the relation of the education function to the total culture,
2. the constancy of the function and the transitory character of organizational forms,
3. its idealistic and dynamic character, and
4. its reflection of the democratic state.

DEFINITIONS OF ORGANIZATION

Organization is that function of administration which attempts to relate and ultimately fuse the purposes of an institution and the people who comprise its working parts. It is the continuously developing plan which defines the job and shows how it can be efficiently and effectively accomplished by people functioning in particular social environments. Organization is the process (or result) of arranging interdependent elements into a function or logical whole.

School organization takes many forms: curricula, departmental, divisional, formal, functional, grade, horizontal, informal, internal, line-and-staff, radial, secondary school, student, unit, vertical, and by cycles.

The structure and techniques through which the education function operates should be determined by purpose. Organization has no validity per se, but should simply be a means through which a given objective is attained. In practice, unfortunately, organization is frequently adjusted to personalities and the result rationalized as functional.

The approach has been through the orientation of the education function within the democratic state and through the manner of institutional operation. These discussions form the background from which an organic or functional attack upon the entire problem of administration may be made. Principles through which the organization and operation of the education function must be analyzed and appraised, and some of these principles are basic to any culture, but others are limited distinctly to the operation of education within a democratic state. They represent an attempt to gather into logical continuity many concepts that have had wide popular and professional acceptance, and to clarify others as yet imperfectly recognized.

COMMONLY ACCEPTED PRINCIPLES OF ORGANIZATION

There are those commonly accepted principles which are considered basic in the field of organization and administration. Attempts have been made to differentiate between the principles of organization and administration however, because of an overlapping, this has not been done satisfactorily. These principles have been equally applicable to all forms of government regardless of political philosophy.

Generally, authoritarian and democratic administrators agree on statements of principles of organizational process even though the organizational structure varies considerably when the decision-makers differ in philosophy. There are however, assumptions underlying traditional or authoritarian administrations and those underlying democratic or decentralized administrations. These assumptions provide the rationale for the particular kind of administration.

Principles do not constitute a theory of organization because many accepted principles of organization are in conflict with one another. Campbell and Gregg (1957), and Simon (1951) are among those who have directed attention to these contradictions. For example, many authorities on administration accept the principles of adaptability and stability as applied to organization. Adaptability and stability are certainly mutually contradictory. In actuality, many commonly accepted principles of organization are valid only within certain limits, and these limits have seldom, if ever, been defined. Most principles lack a certain degree of validity and should not be considered as scientifically determined but rather as operating principles that have been developed primarily from experience and response to changing internal and external environments. They are primarily useful as points of departure.

SYMPTOMS OF ORGANIZATIONAL DEFICIENCIES

The fact that symptoms of organizational deficiencies can be easily identified emphasizes the importance of this function. The end effect of such lack of attention to organization leads to an organization administered through a series of crises. The administrators involved seem to have lost control of their own situations and face one emergency after another, each seemingly unrelated to the preceding one. They lose not only the concept of their own jobs, but a concept of the purpose of the school or school system which employs them.

Each school administrator should periodically raise the following questions concerning himself or herself and his or her administrative and teaching staffs (Modern Practices, 1956):

1. Is a large proportion of administrative time spent in handling emergencies and dealing with spontaneous conflicts?
2. Do different members of the administrative and teaching staffs often make conflicting decisions on the same problems?
3. Do decisions result in unexplained delays in carrying out plans?
4. Are there frequent complaints that, *No one told me, I didn't know who was responsible for it,* or *You should have sent it to me?*
5. Must members of the administrative staff work inordinately long hours and suffer frequent interruptions of their leisure time?
6. Does it seem that there is never enough time to develop long range plans for the school or school system or to think of and experiment with new ideas?
7. Are there frequent personality clashes among members of the administrative and teaching staffs?

These are symptoms of organizational deficiencies. They do not describe the serious effects such deficiencies impose upon the school, its personnel, and its clients.

EVADING THE PROBLEMS OF ORGANIZATION

Despite the need for administrators to understand the vital function of organization, there are many who offer all forms of rationalizations and assume the attitude expressed by Alexander Pope in his *An Essay on Man:*

> For forms of government let fools contest; whatever is best administered is best.

One contention deemphasizes the importance of organization as the organizational patterns on the individuals in administrative positions. Most managerial individuals are neither strong enough to raise their organizations substantially above their organized potentiality nor weak or perverse enough to destroy the organizational structures. Therefore, a sound organizational structure is bound to encourage greater achievement by most people.

A rationalization which is prevalent finds the organizer with people who are already in jobs. This lament is attacked in this fashion:

> If the principal has not got a clean sheet, there is no earthly reason why he or she should not make the slight effort of imagination required to assume that he or she has a clean sheet. He or she should never for a moment pretend that these difficulties don't exist. They do exist; they are realities. Nor, when he or she has drawn up an ideal plan for organization, is it likely that it will be able to fit into all the existing human material perfectly. But these adjustments can be made

without harm, provided they are conscious adjustments, deliberate and temporary deviations form patterns in order to deal with idiosyncrasy.

Another rationalization takes the form of gang administration, we're all good fellows, and we work on all our problems together. Under these conditions no one assumes or feels an individual responsibility for anything other than the strictly routine and as a result large areas of administrative functions are virtually untouched since they fail to represent the problem of the moment.

Rationalizations have been known to take yet another form, one that suggests the *practical man fallacy.* Here we find a rationalization for evading serious consideration of organization as an administrative function.

> There is a very general feeling that to be hazy and opportunist about organization is in some mysterious way *practical,* while to try to draw up proper charts and procedures is somehow theoretical.

It is impractical to ignore a sound approach to the function of organization because of the toll in time, money, and personal frustration are common results from such procedures. Since the function of theory in the social sciences is to predict behavior, the practical value of good theory is immediately apparent. If theory is not practical, the theory is simply not sound.

BASIC ELEMENTS AND PATTERNS OF ORGANIZATION

When surveys are made of school administrative staff, a multiplicity of positions emerge. These positions are arranged in a hierarchial order or chain of command. Each has certain duties, responsibilities, power, and authority which are defined as follows (Griffiths, 1956, p. 96):

> *Duties* are the functions that an individual is required to perform by the structure of the organizations in order to maintain his or her individual place in the organization.
>
> *Responsibilities* represent the functions for which the individual is accountable.
>
> *Power* is the ability to employ force or produce action.
>
> *Authority* is the outward manifestation of power.

These are often implied in the official title and thereby assume a form of authority as suggested in a job description or organization chart. The chain of command is formed by the interrelationships of these positions.

The grouping of school administrative positions provides for the creation of patterns of organization. In public school administration two patterns of organization have generally been recognized on the basis of the distribution of duties and responsibilities. One has been referred to as horizontal, and the other vertical.

The horizontal pattern suggests that the organization is broad at the top in such a way that a horizontal line could be used to connect two or more positions of first echelon responsibility and authority. In these types of organizations lines of authority extend in a general horizontal pattern. As an example, an assistant superintendent would probably be in charge of secondary education instead of all instruction. Likewise, supervision under this plan would deal with a particular level, rather than have one individual's authority extend throughout. This horizontal type of organization followed the period of the 1800's when special supervision and specialization were in the forefront.

The vertical plan of organization is one in which lines of authority and responsibility extend more or less vertically from the top down through the entire organization. The assistant superintendent is in charge of instruction and has responsibility for both elementary and secondary instruction. This plan provides for a greater simplicity and yet it is felt by many administrators that this has gained popularity at the expense of over-all efficiency.

Generally, one will find that upon weighing of the advantages and disadvantages of the two plans has resulted in the adoption of patterns representing some form of merger of the two.

The terms unitary and multiple are sometimes used to indicate the concentration or dispersion of authority at the top of the school organization. A unitary type of administrative organization is one in which top authority and responsibility reside in one official, usually the superintendent of schools. In the multiple type of organization, top responsibility is dispersed to reside with two or more administrators who are approximately co-ordinate in authority and responsibility. The areas for which each is responsible are defined. There are few of the multiple arrangements and for some time the trend has been away from this type of organization. And yet, there is some movement, or at least interest, toward the co-principal arrangement.

Other organization patterns which may be found include the tall organization in which the number of authority levels between the classroom teacher and the chief school administrator are numerous. It is the distance between these two extremes within the organization that characterize the pattern as a tall organization. The flat organization differs in that it provides generally for only one authority level between the teacher and the chief school administrator. The short distance between lowest and highest level employees characterizes this pattern as a flat organization.

Each pattern is presented out of context and as mere descriptions for they bear little real relation to the true purpose of the organization. This purpose must form the criterion against which the efficacy of each pattern can be measured. All of these patterns fall within a conceptual framework of organization which is generally referred to as line and staff. Although line and staff is a method by which most school districts are organized, other models will be presented and considered later in this chapter. This is being done so that the informal aspects and understandings of organization within which school personnel work are presented. Contacts with superiors, peers, and subordinates will be seen as a means of recognizing that the informal organization of the school is supplemented and complemented by informal channels.

LINE AND STAFF

Besides borrowing from the public service and from industry, school administration also borrowed at least one significant practice in organization from the military. This is the practice of designating relationships within the personnel organization as either line or staff.

The distinction made in the true line and staff organization is based upon the location of a position with reference to the line of command. All positions within the direct line are line positions, and positions transmit the line authority through one step of the organization. Normally, in a public school the line of authority extends from the board of education through the superintendent, assistant superintendent, principals, and to the teachers.

Staff positions are advisory and do not carry what may be called command authority. The position in school organization most often designated as a staff position is that of supervisor. Staff positions provide specialists who have wide discretion in working with and for people.

In actual operation it is difficult to find a school position that operates wholly as a staff or as a line position. Present-day planning has enabled the establishment of organizations that maintain some of the line concept as well as some of the staff concept in their functioning. An attempt to reconcile current practices and older theoretical concepts produces some interesting situations. These have caused the creation of some of the country's best administrative plans.

AN EMERGING ADMINISTRATIVE PATTERN

The trend in organization is clearly in the direction of the unitary and limited vertical pattern with certain positions having staff relationships. A limited vertical pattern has the features of a vertical organization but with a limited number of steps or stages from the top positions to the lowest ones. This may be partly explained by the fact that within present-day school organizations there are numbers of highly specialized positions. Most of the need that at one time emphasized the worth of the horizontal and multiple-head patterns not only still exists but has been accentuated.

A principal reason for the adaptability of modern organization has been an emerging concept of administration which advocates sharing rather than delegating authority. Wiles (1950) was especially clear in his explanation of this concept of sharing authority as the democratic replacement for delegating authority.

The school administration that accepts shared authority as a concept of management is in a position to derive all the benefits of a horizontal organization and at the same time to retain the flexibility and specificity of the vertical organization where needed. Multiple-head administration is a direct contradiction of shared authority, since authority is split on an assignment basis rather than being shared. Thus it is apparent that the emerging pattern of organization and administration is positive, flexible in its operation, but at the same time can be democratic and efficient.

MODIFYING THE PYRAMID

The pyramid, a most popular organizational structure, must undergo modifications so that management needs of the schools may be met and more effectively satisfied.

A *beehive*, a *doughnut*, a *bell*, a *super griddle*, and a *ladder* are all organizational structures that are being used to overcome the inadequacies of the pyramid. Various experts who have cited the limitations of the pyramid and who believe it embodies outmoded concepts have had this to say:

In a time of rapid market and technological change, growing complexity, and a shift of emphasis to individual aspirations, administration can no longer rely exclusively on the pyramid. The pyramid only shows the static picture. What really matters are the dynamic aspects of how an organization works and the personnel inter-relationships. In today's technologically dominated world, pyramidal concepts no longer have any credence.

As school systems increasingly experiment with new strategies to answer the challenges of the school renewal, reform and restructuring movements, as well as the swiftly moving and changing education scene, the need grows to find ways to modify and supplement the pyramid design.

For centuries the pyramid has been regarded as the ideal command structure. There appeared to be no better way to pass orders from the one person at the top to the subordinates below. The Egyptians viewed its perfect symmetry for it symbolized the pharaohs' autocratic rule. The church and the military were quick to recognize its advantages. There appeared no better way of getting the general's battle orders to his many foot soldiers. However, new developments are revealing limitations which are beginning to outweigh the pyramid's advantages, particularly as related to such public service organizations as the schools.

Current trends do not seek to eliminate the pyramid, they offer approaches to modifying it, to alter the downward pyramid in favor of something that moves in other directions, or gives scope for sideways relationships. The result is a variety of variations on the pyramid theme which have been dubbed as the *behive, doughnut,* and other such titles. They help to visualize in a simple and evocative way something which is more complex.

These variations aim primarily at toning down the strict autocratic nature of the pyramid which is accentuated by its sharply defined apex. The *bell* depicts the idea of collegial management since the apex of this kind of pyramid is broadened by a top of management leaders. The *behive* structure also softens the pinnacle of the pyramid, however the beehive is designed to do more than accommodate the trend away from autocracy. It views the problems of human relationships that do not appear in the pyramid.

The three-dimensional beehive, consisting of concentric circles, overcomes this pyramidal inadequacy. The innermost circle represents the apex of the management hierarchy. The surrounding bands constitute the supervisory echelons and correspond to the various levels of management. Pie-shaped segments represent the principal operating divisions or functions. The chief administrator's symbol is placed in the middle of the circle, but not necessarily in the exact center. If he or she tends, for example, to favor one particular division perhaps because he or she was promoted out of it, his or her symbol is placed closer to it. A similar system is used at lower administrative levels. If an administrator is close to the chief school administrator, his or her symbol is placed near the inner rim of the band. Where the reverse is true, it is placed at the outer rim.

A circular organization structure similar to the one adopted by CIT Financial Corporation has been dubbed a *doughnut.* At the center are the top administrators. In the outside ring are the sub-administrators such as department chairpersons. However, these sub-administrators are not subordinate to any particular one of the top administrators in the center circle. Outside of this ring are the various teachers and specialists who are not connected to any operating department. This circular organization emphasizes the close physical relationship of the administrators. Furthermore, it demonstrates a way of achieving a high degree of rapport among administrators of every level thru the freer flow of communications throughout the system.

The *ladder* is also seen as the answer to the problem by some. This arrangement suggests lifting all the management services out of the pyramid and placing them in a neutral ladder apart from the hierarchy. This provides for the freedom of administrators to call for the advice and assistance of any specialist without having to go through the hierarchical channels. It also releases the administrative communication network from the obstruction of specialist departments. The specialists, on the other hand, are left to their specialty instead of being required to climb to positions in the system that they are ill-prepared to fulfill. This may be likened to the gantry supporting a space vehicle on the launch pad. The engineers can move up and down the gantry, servicing the space vehicles at whatever level is necessary. Similarly, a system's support staff should be able to pass up and down the ladder, temporarily entering the main system's structure at various levels whenever their services are required within. Since the ladder does not solve the problem of how to accommodate project administrators who are assigned to guide new projects through from start to finish, a matrix, or a grid-like structure that criss-crosses the lines of authority is provided.

A three dimensional matrix may be utilized to solve different problems.

A primary advantage of super griddle is that it allows for personnel to function in those areas or subjects they do and know best.

This system is also designed to ensure that teachers are not advanced into jobs for which they are unsuited. There is no pressure on them to become administrators and in some instances they are capable of earning more than the administrator. This is seen as differentiated staffing.

Most of the attempts to modify the pyramid reflect a growing trend towards more democratic forms of management. Staff participation and job enrichment are highly fashionable, and the growing complexity of school system operations is forcing the delegation of authority to lower reaches of the hierarchy.

Bottom-up management suggests a participative and supportive management which creates the inverted pyramid. Administrators are charged not so much with directing and supervising as with offering assistance to those reporting to them.

ORGANIZATIONAL THEORY, PERSPECTIVES AND DESIGN

Theory evolves from research, testing, and practice and should: offer useful working ideas of how people act in organizations, and provide useful methods, strategies and tactics for bringing about concrete organizational change, development and improvement.

Theories aid the practitioner in attending to what is important and fits pieces of information into concepts, categories and patterns of meaning. Any new paradigm which reflects our beliefs and assumptions about the human condition impacts on organizational theory development and observable shifts in the following assumptions are in evidence:

1. from a probablistic world view to one that is complex and diverse,
2. from a hierarchically ordered world to one of heterarchy (interactive simultaneous and mutual influence),
3. from mechanistic to holographic (interconnected network patterns),
4. from assumption of direct causality to mutual causality, and
5. from pure objectivity to a perspective or multiple viewpoint model (Lincoln 1985).

Organizational theory looks at the outcomes and actions of organizations as well as the behavior of individuals and groups within an organizational setting. It is the study of the organization, both internally and externally. Internally, we view the organization at three levels:

structurally (macro), technically (micro), and behaviorally (organization behavior). In organization theory we look at these components separately and as a whole, as a system. Organizational theory also views the systems impact on its own environment, as well as the impact the environment has on it.

THE CONCEPT OF ORGANIZATION DEVELOPMENT

Organization development is a broad label which includes many activities through which the administrator makes better use of his or her human resources. These activities can be both problem-solving and developmental in nature, in that they aim to mesh people and their work in ways which best meet organization objectives. Although they may be pursued in a low-keyed fashion at times or thought of as isolated activities within an overall effort, collectively they have a sustaining effect in improving the performance of the organizational unit.

In organization development activity, the focus is more on the group than on the individual performers. It is best viewed as an on-going process of working with the problems of the existing organization in order to handle them more effectively. It is a deliberate attempt to use developmental and analytical methods in order to solve problems of the moment, while increasing the capability of the group for solving future problems.

Viewed as a process, organization development aims at achieving the following typical objectives:

1. to create an open, problem-solving climate throughout the organization.
2. to build and maintain systems and procedures which lead to sound decisions about the work itself.
3. to locate decision-making and problem-solving responsibilities as close to the information sources as possible.
4. to build trust among individuals and groups throughout the organization.
5. to make competition more relevant to work goals and to maximize collaborative efforts.
6. to develop a reward system which recognizes both the achievement of the organization's mission and organization development.
7. to increase the sense of ownership of organization objectives throughout the workforce.

8. to develop managers to manage according to relevant objectives through-out the workforce.

9. to increase self-control and self-direction by getting people to perform in a more responsible manner within the organization.

ORGANIZATION-ORIENTED MODELS

The major types of organization-oriented models are:

1. social system models;
2. economic models;
3. decision-rendering, or power models;
4. communication models;
5. service models;
6. structural models; and
7. dynamic models.

Some overlap exists among these types and a miscellaneous category is needed for those models that fit in none of the other classes.

Social-System Models. Such models view the school as an organization of human behaviors that promote the attainment of social goals. They concentrate on factors related to describing, analyzing, or predicting human behavior in a given system. They may identify individual needs as aided or inhibited by the demands of the organized institution. The underlying assumption is that it is difficult if not impossible to compre-hend what goes on in an organized society without looking at how human beings are relating to each other and how they behave in the face of given constraints. Many models begin by describing the institutional dimension as expressed by roles and expectations, and the individual dimension, as evinced by personal needs predispositions. Interaction between these two fundamental dimensions of the organizational and cultural matrix produces social behavior. In a sense, the individual actualizes himself or herself through the organization and simultaneously, the organization realizes goals through the individual's behavior.

Other models analyze the organization as a social system, not in terms of individuals resolving personal needs within institutional demands, but rather as coalitions of individuals pursuing conflicting goals. How the organization copes with its internal and external coalitions is signifi-cant to its productivity.

Still other models emphasize conflict between those who have access to the power and control the reward system of the organization and those

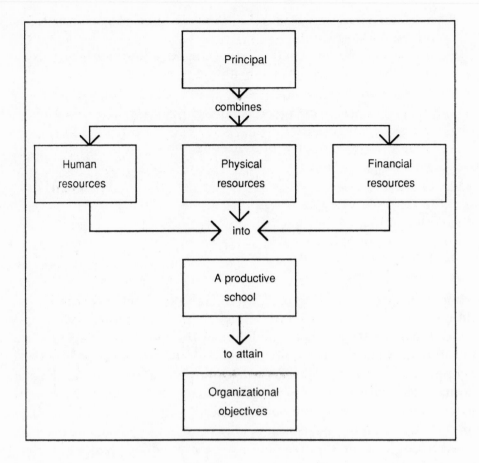

Figure 10 : Principal coordinates the school's resources

who do not have formal and legal access to power but strive to control the reward-distribution system. Collective bargaining is the classic model, that is, how a social system manages human conflict.

Human relations models, coalition models, and conflict resolution models are other examples of social system models. In short, models of this type view the organization as a social system in which human behavior is the result of the many forces within the system and determines to a large degree the productivity of the system. Individual needs, institutional demands, role behavior, coalitions, and resolution of conflicts are key factors within the system.

Economic Models. These models focus on those aspects of an organization concerned with procuring, allocating, and utilizing resources. In other words, the emphasis is on what is done with the resources to fulfill the productivity goals of the organization. Economics can be defined as the study of how persons and society allocate scarce resources or means among competing ends. Few organizations have all the resources required to satisfy competing purposes. How human and material resources of a school system are obtained, made available to meet the various objectives of education, and effectively managed, constitutes the economics of school administration. Specific examples are the finance models and the logistical models. Logistical models can be further subdivided into budgeting and accounting models, personnel allocation models, transportation models, and school-facilities models. Efficiency and the production function of education are rather vaguely defined at present, but future models may suggest a defensible measuring stick. Certain mathematical techniques such as linear programming can be used to attack such allocation problems as the scheduling of transportation facilities.

Decision-Rendering or Power Models. These models examine the organization in terms of the locus and flow of decisions on policy and administrative matters. They may be called political models to distinguish them from the previously discussed social and economic models. People and positions are categorized in terms of formal and informal decision points or power levels. The formal chart of organization is an iconic model of key decision points. Within such models a flow diagram of the decisional processes within large multifunctional, and hence, complicated organizations can be developed. Identifying key factors which will determine how formal or informal power and authority are distributed within the establishment becomes germane. What happens when a decision reaches another level can be part of such models as well. They can be sharpened to predict where in the organization a certain type of decision can be made. While it can be argued that decision-rendering models should be separate from power and authority models, their combination is also valid because power can be measured in terms of its effect on the decision-making process.

Communication Models. These represent the organization as a giant processor of information or a vast network wherein data are generated, transmitted, and received by various positions. Without communication, coordination would be all but impossible and prudent decision would be the result of pure chance. Each position in the hierarchy becomes a kind of switchboard with varying degrees of influence. Models of this type stress how an organization secures information, how the communication reaches its various parts, or what is done with the data. Structural and functional relations are developed in terms of the communication function.

Service Models. These models focus on the instructional and allied functions of a school organization. Teaching models, learning models, counseling models, welfare models, student-body-activity models, and curriculum models are all connected with the service function of an educational organization. The opportunity for overlapping with other types is most evident. The emphasis determines the basis for select models.

Structural Models. These models analyze the structure of an organization, with less emphasis on decisions, communications, and social relations, and more emphasis on line-and-staff relations, tall and flat patterns, departmentation, and span of control. Overlap with other types of organization oriented models is a distinct possibility.

Dynamic Models. These models view the organization as evolving, living and thriving, and possibly dying. More recently these types have been referred to as general systems models. The word dynamic is used in the sense of a moving force or energy that affects equilibrium. The dynamic model is an adaptation of the biological models. It is closely related to innovation and how it is met, resisted, or encouraged in the organization deserves consideration. To illustrate, some key factors in an organizational-change model might be the organization's sensitivity to its clientele and or environments, ability to design in operational terms new services, ability to identify alternative solutions to change, feasibility and speed of developing new organizational arrangements, and ability to rid itself of old practices.

What disturbances do to the system is of prime concern in the dynamic model. It suggests ecological problems as the organization copes with its environments. This is sometimes called the boundary maintenance concerns of a system. The organization may live through a cold war with certain elements in its community or hot or open war with self-appointed critics of the system. How it meets those factors which create disequilibrium is a subject of concern for dynamic models. The organization is seen as a viable entity, interacting with its environments and carrying built-in mechanisms of varying degrees of effectiveness to meet challenges. Change, planned or unplanned, is a significant theme in such models. How crises are faced as the organization develops is of concern in related models. For example, Lippitt and Schmidt (1967) developed the thesis that *certain recognizable nonfinancial crises occur in the life cycle of an organization.*

MOTIVATION PROGRAM: A CHANGE IN PHILOSOPHY

In the business field, employee motivation programs stressing a do it right the first time attitude have undergone changes in their basic philosophy. The conceptual basis of zero defects remained relatively constant since 1961. The purpose of the zero defects program was to motivate people to accept the challenge of doing their jobs right the first time.

New employee motivational programs differ from zero defects in methods and concepts. Though these new programs are derived somewhat from the original zero defects programs and are seriously limiting in the school district framework, here too there is potential for movement. In place of the hard sell method directed at the employee, in this case the teacher, we note a change in the attitude of the administrator concerning defects and the teacher is indirectly influenced. The administrator should provide the experience and the knowledge to solve problems arising from defects and be prepared to respond to the usual questions that arise.

The conceptual difference between the two types of programs are easily analyzed and unquestionably the latter provides results which are more effective and in the long run less threatening to all personnel concerned, therefore bound to produce more positive and long term results.

Perhaps even more notable is the high premium placed on autonomy. Individuals want to have more and more impact on their work and environment, to control it, not to be controlled by it. Acceptance of the status quo is being replaced by comparing oneself or the organization to its potential. The result, is a kind of giant dissatisfaction with what is versus what could be.

These shifts in values affect the philosophies and assumptions under which organizations operate, their styles of management, policies and procedures, administrator-teacher relationships, employment compensation practices, and even the kinds of school system organizations.

This increased interdependence of organizations and their relation to society require a broader knowledge base of the behavioral, social, and political sciences. Further, keeping up with technological developments is more critical than ever before, and administrators must also understand that the nature of power is changing. The new administrator must behave differently for we see collaborative and more democratic styles replacing coercive and bureaucratic tactics. Administrators are becoming more participative, they work toward consensus and seek to gain personal commitment to tasks. The task is to create an environment which prizes and nourishes ideas of all people, encourages attentive listening, and rewards personal involvement and commitment to the work being done.

We are today in a period when the development of theory within the social sciences will permit innovations which are at present inconceivable. The capacities of the average human being for creativity, for growth, for collaboration, and for productivity are far greater than we have recognized (Douglas McGregor 1960).

We are coming to recognize with increasing clarity that the capacity of an organization to function well depends both upon the quality of its decision-making processes and upon the adequacy and accuracy of the information used. In diagnosing its problems, every organization needs to understand the fundamental nature of its system, the way in which its component parts function, and the adaptive responses it makes to its environment (Rensis Likert 1961).

RENEWING THE ORGANIZATION

The whole purpose of creating an open, problem-solving climate within the organization unit is to encourage that process which must take place from time to time to *renew the organization,* otherwise it suffers a continuing deterioration.

Organizations have a predictable life cycle in which decline is ever occurring and must be offset by a struggle for renewal. To be capable of this renewal, the organization needs to have built-in provisions for self-criticism. It must create an atmosphere in which uncomfortable questions can be asked. Further the organization needs a method whereby it can question its own procedures in order to lay aside those that are no longer pertinent, and to challenge those that are protected by vested interests.

The organization development process, therefore, is basically a people-oriented problem-solving system with its activity focused more on the group than the individual performers. As a process, it deliberately attempts to develop effective group interaction.

THINK TANKS

One approach used in organizing for innovation is the *Think Tank.* Think tankers think today in order to produce innovations for tomorrow. The name of their game is inventing the future. It is a game played along a time axis. The past is given fairly short shrift, while the future is what commands attention. The future is not yet created and there is a chance yet to mold it and shape it. It can, to a degree, be invented, and made to be more of what we would like.

The innovator is naturally interested in keeping abreast of new techniques for creativity. One technique that is easy to learn and apply is *forced relationships.* The purpose of the forced relationship technique is to deliberately break down habitual associations and forcibly establish new ones. For creativity to occur, we need fresh, different, useful, and new combinations. The forced relationship technique is designed to help break down the rutes of habitual thinking and pave the way into fresh territory.

The ways of organizing think tanks and the methods for conducting them are fairly numerous and various, however, they all are reduced to bringing people together to think, searchingly, critically and creatively about their school and school system. The first step in setting up a think tank is selecting the appropriate people participants. This is followed by expressing and stating as clearly as possible what its goal is or what specific concern or problem is to dealt with or resolved. The creative work in a think tank takes place when its members face one another, interact, and exchange views. They cross-stimulate and cross-fertilize one another, and meet sufficiently often to assure that idea pollination, germination, and flowering processes have assurances of occurring.

The think tank is fascinating in that it often results in motivating the creative thinking abilities of its participants. This decentralization of thinking requires that the school administrator accept this new style or technique of arriving at answers to questions and concerns appearing within the school's internal and external environments. This type of experience introduces a new consciousness of contemporary realities and assists the principal in discovering, profoundly and personally, a vision of a creative style of thinking.

AGENTS OF CHANGE

Rapid and drastic changes have taken place in society and technology. These transformations necessitate significant changes in the nature of organizations, the demands placed on school administrators, and the needs and motivations of organization members. In order to survive, organizations must learn to cope effectively with the accelerated pace of change. Successful administrators will be those who learn to understand and cope with this change.

Those who are not successful will have relinquished the initiative and merely reacted to change. If today's and tomorrow's administrators are to truly function as agents of change, rather than reactors to change, they must fully understand the critical changes occurring and their implications for management strategies.

Of the major pressures affecting organizations today, which underlie administrators' challenges to change, three deserve special note:

1. the organization's role as an involved, concerned element of society,
2. the growing complexities of today's organization, and
3. the ongoing shifts in professional values of individuals.

Schools are becoming increasingly involved in society's larger problems because of society's growing awareness of its problems and recognition of the school's capacity, and obligation, to provide solutions. Trends affecting the role of school systems in society make it clear that administrators will need a broader perspective, and will be viewing themselves as persons with increased responsibility who function within an organization which, in turn, draws its fundamental support from that particular society.

Diversification will continue to pervade organization life. Large scale, complex organizations will tend to replace smaller scale enterprises. Tasks will become more technical, complicated, automated, and shorter lived. There is evidence to suggest that the rate of technological innovation can cause scientists' and engineers' knowledge to be obsolete in ten years if further education and research is not pursued.

These increased complexities and technological changes will create continued inefficiencies in the traditional bureaucratic organization. Temporary and short-term projects will become more common. Individuals from various specialties will be brought together from different parts of the organization to accomplish tasks and then be dispersed. The traditional mode of operation will become less able to quickly pull together the necessary resources to get a job done.

A most significant and fast moving change facing organizations is the shift in individual values. Traditional values and ideals appear threatened. Commitment is more in terms of the task, job, or profession rather than loyalty to the school system. New criterion beyond pay and job content determine job choice.

RISK TAKERS

New ideas are everywhere. All they need is the environment to make them happen.

It has often been quipped that there are three types of people found in organizations: Risk takers, caretakers, and undertakers. Truthfully, most of us play each of these roles from time to time, even though there may be a dominant mode in which we usually operate. In this chapter we ignore the undertakers, people involved with burying programs and projects. We briefly discuss the caretakers, persons working to preserve existing resources. Our focus is on the risk takers.

Creativity involves the act of producing a new and novel response to a task that cannot be solved in a clear and straightforward manner. Since creativity is connected with the new, the unknown, or the untried, it almost always involves risk, especially in education. Risk takers are organizational innovators.

How do we encourage individuals within organizations (schools) to take risks? Should we try to turn everyone into an experimenter? How can we encourage a risk-taking pattern that will be in a school's best interests? In order to promote organizational innovation we must understand why people choose and refuse to take risks. We must understand how to design an organizational environment that fosters the risk-taking behavior the school-community desires or needs to be encouraged to consider.

Caretakers play an important stabilizing role in schools. Their mission is to preserve existing programs, resources and services. They tend to see environmental changes as threats, not opportunities. Caretakers respond predictably to change by advocating strategies that guard current practices, the status quo.

There are times however when caretakers realize that the usual defensive means of preserving current school practices, programs and services will not hold. Sometimes threats to the status quo are so ominous that riskiest strategy would be to stay in a maintenance mode. Not wanting to turn into a risk taker, the caretaker in these inverted circumstances supports innovation and change. However, the caretaker's statement of the school's mission remains basically the same: *This outside threat forces us to take aggressive action in order that overall organizational resources can be maintained.*

Risk takers view their environments from a different perspective. Changes and challenges are seen by risk takers as opportunities as opposed to threats. Furthermore, risk takers view the environment as something they should actively shape. The organizational risk taker develops and introduces program and services that anticipate and create further programs and services.

> This author assumed the post of superintendent of schools of the East Stroudsburg Area School District, in East Stroudsburg, Pennsylvania, in 1973. He established as one of his missions an increase and improvement of the academic offerings of the system, the reduction of its pupil-teacher ratios, and provision for such increased facilities as might be required by these changes. In this school district such a change implied some risk taking since this would necessitate substantial budgetary increases and major adjustments in the taxing of its resident taxpayers. One immediate change included the provision for a full year experience in science education for all students in grades seven and eight. Until that time, the instruction for these students was limited to a one half year course offering for each of these grades. This change represented a doubling of both the seventh and eighth grade science teaching staffs and facilities (classrooms), and the related substantial increase in instructional and operational costs. What with an historic resistance to increases in taxes, this was in fact a major risk taking experience by this new superintendent of schools, particularly since it was common knowledge that the average length of service of the superintendents in the 501 Commonwealth of Pennsylvania school systems, during this period was limited to approximately three (3) years. A major reason for the termination of many of these superintendent's contracts was budget increases, a factor which appeared to receive increased local emphasis when one resident of the community petitioned for election to the school board with the termination of the superintendent's contract as his platform, all because the budget had been increased.
> It is worthy of note that the faculty of the East Stroudsburg Area School District increased by 30% (from 140 to 182), while there were *no* increases in the student population during the 14 year tenure of this superintendent.

Successful risk takers are *not* wildly passionate about risks per se. Before venturing out on a course of action, most innovators seek first to understand and contain the risks. Doing so increases their confidence as they move forward, and they do so aggressively. They are confident of obtaining necessary human, financial and physical resources. They have the drive to propose a forging of the new, and at the same time respect for the old. Pure risk takers emerge when circumstances do not allow the odds of success to be determined with reasonable accuracy.

Risk taking and innovation generally appear more frequently in small school settings. Promoting an innovation with unmeasurable risk is less common in large organizations because in these latter situations the caretakers influences are often too great and the bureaucracies often serve as a roadblock to change.

Risk taking, whether measured and contained or not, is linked to creativity and innovation. Newly positioned principals, in newly situate schools, may be more prone to take high risks than continuing principals in established organizational environments. The question remains: What can a school do to encourage a desirable degree of risk taking, a level conducive to needed creativity and innovation? Here are but some thoughts and suggestions:

Tension. A principal must appreciate that a certain level of tension between school risk takers and caretakers is not only inevitable but desirable. It is a fundamental dynamic to preserve the best of the old while developing new. For a school to maintain its stability, it must have some *unloseables,* a core from its history that is protected and preserved. Yet, if the school is to be vibrant, it cannot ossify into its past. There must be some venturesomeness in responding to the school's environments. Organizational integrity and unity demands a general consensus among the school's personnel as to how aggressive the innovative thrust should be. Resolving this tension is the starting place in developing organizational policy toward risk taking.

Assessment. In areas in which the school seeks to be innovative, risks need to be assessed and contained where possible. This will increase the confidence level of the principal as he or she ventures forth. However, not all innovation can provide these assurances, but the potential gain is of such substance that you take your chances.

Diversification. It is advisable to diversify away as much risk as possible. In the efficient risk portfolio, the school needs to explore options for the diversification or sharing of the project or program risk (and gains) from a variety of perspectives or joint ventures. The school must then concentrate on succeeding in the areas of nondiversifiable risk to which it has chosen to expose itself.

Leadership and support. Select project leaders to head innovative projects and provide them with organizational support that encourages risk taking behavior on their part. A project leader should be free to select project team members and team access to information relating to project success is vital. Mental and material support is vital for creating productivity.

Promotion. To cultivate creativity in organizations does not mean that school policy should encourage all employees to be as unrestrained as free-form poets. However, in project areas in which the central office wants risk taking to occur, it must promote risk as well as understand the failure that frequently accompanies it. Failure in the context of working toward project success must meet with social acceptance.

Commitment. Work to keep innovative people committed to the school and to the specific projects on which they are working. If innovative success is to occur within organizations, individuals must be willing to make enormous psychological investments in school projects. Unless the employee is wholly dedicated to organizational and project goals it is highly unlikely that the intensity of effort required for creativity will be reached.

Appreciation. To promote organizational innovation, the mechanisms that encourage and support individual and group risk taking must be in place. In order to prevent risk takers from evolving into school caretakers, the central role that risk taking plays in successful innovation must be appreciated. Such appreciation applies across the entire risk spectrum, from showing overt recognition of risk takers (not just the successful ones) to understanding how risk exerts its subtle influence on every new idea or venture.

LONG RANGE PLANNING

Long-Range Planning (LRP) is a method which helps answer three basic questions: Where are we going? Where should we be going? How do we get there? School systems cannot afford the luxury of running blindly into the future, and this requires the organization to master the techniques of long-range planning.

LRP is a comprehensive mobilization of relevant data about a school or school system and its environment, past, present, future, and its organization in a coordinated way for the attainment of specific goals. LRP probably takes in a wider time span and generally includes a review of the operations of the past several years and the setting of goals for several years ahead.

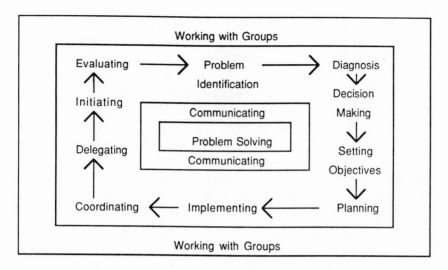

Figure 11 : Administrative process

Long-range planning has been known to be divided into five phases although, in practice, the activities of each phase overlap and recur.

Phase I. Orientation. Planning must result in something more than words on paper. It has to influence behavior; just winding up a planner and turning him or her loose is not sufficient. Planners need data and the administrator is the one to provide this and assurances that the plan will succeed. Accordingly, there are two preconditions to successful planning in addition to having a good planner: (1) absolute support of central administration, and (2) a clear understanding of the plan, and enthusiasm for it on the part of the principal, with key administrators participating in the process from the outset.

Phase II. Position Analysis. This is the data gathering phase. It is also the germinating phase for many of the creative ideas that come from planning. The school system's image, how it views its purpose and place in the community, and its principal concerns are considered at this time. The school must examine fully both its internal and external environments. Further, consideration is given to the happenings within other systems and new technologies. Questions containing the fundamental challenges of planning, specifying school and school system purposes and opportunities, and consideration of success potentials occupy the agenda of this phase.

Phase III. Determining Objectives. This is the decision phase. It is during this phase that decisions bring the administration to a confrontation with hard choices and realities. This availability of choices test not only creativity and ingenuity but also judgment and strength.

Phase IV. Implementation. It is during this phase that the administrator determines how and when the plans strategic objectives are to be achieved. Arriving at these provides for the further process of decision-making at the building level. Implementation is perhaps the most difficult part of planning since it here that concensus or agreement is required, because it is at this point that administrators must commit themselves to specific performance goals. It is here that the administrator makes his or her commitment to the plan and estimates the probability of its success.

Phase V. Feedback. Planning does not eliminate risk and uncertainty although it does reduce the potential for each of these to occur. Inevitably, actual results will deviate from the planned results, and the longer the interval between checks and corrective action, the wider the deviation. Systematic assessments of progress and results are essential here.

To succeed, the planner must generate a personal, and general conviction and commitment by all of the stakeholders because meaningful change is a long-term process.

CREATIVITY AND INNOVATION

Creativity isn't limited to special people, places, or times. Given shared goals and an enabling environment, everyone can contribute.

The school or school system that wishes to be innovative and creative must make this a deliberate objective and conscious policy. In management, the single most important factor influencing creative activity is the organizational climate, and it must be recognized that organizational climate can turn off or turn on creative output with equal ease.

Such conditions within the school's organizational climate which appear conducive to the release of ingenuity and creativity are: scepticism toward existing policies and practices, decision making which is future-oriented, a planning and objectives management style, relative indifference to minor errors, and an appetite for constructive novelty.

The ability to converge logically and to diverge imaginatively do not appear to necessarily go together. Organizations include logical and analytical persons who often do not share the creativity and imaginative skills of others within the same organization. The innovative organization makes sure that the divergent thinkers play an important role in determining the school's future goals and objectives.

This conspicuous trend toward increased management by innovation brings with it subtle but profound changes in the criteria used for administrative advancement and personnel and behavioral changes. This change process involves unfreezing (casting doubt at existing modes of operation), changing (trying new behaviors or modes of operation), and refreezing (reinforcing the new, more desirable changes). Human systems interact in ways which make them hard to change, let alone change rapidly. However, there are numerous recommendations for managing change and creating healthy organizations.

1. Organizations should consider the in-house training or employment of organization development or organization improvement specialists.
2. Compensation, in its broadest sense is a fundamental aspect of change. To be really effective, compensation systems should be analyzed periodically in terms of policy, philosophy and application.
3. Goal-setting, or management by objectives, as a management tool is received by some with mixed reactions, however, this tool may be used for integrated planning, the channeling of energies, and the evaluation of performance based on results.
4. The use of vertical or horizontal or perhaps random sampling techniques is a means for administrators to gather data on their organizations. This data may be related to general school problems, interschool questions, or specific areas of concern.
5. Administrators need to train and educate themselves in change and change techniques just as they learn of budget preparation, the dynamics of forecasts, and other controls. Training programs and seminars should provide insights into interpersonal and intergroup relations, the nature of change, related demands on administrators, the use and misuse of competition and collaboration, appraisals, understanding managerial styles, and the impact of new technologies.
6. Many organizations do not know how to pull together or apply the creative problem-solving ability they have within their own systems. Properly prepared interdisciplinary task teams can supply the integration of thinking and creativity necessary for quantum leaps on organization effectiveness.
7. The focus, in permanent or temporary work teams, is on the identification and solution of work group problems, particularly across interpersonal and organization barriers.
8. Increased job mobility is a prime means for keeping personnel challenged. Policies and mechanisms need to be established which facilitate career movement.

9. When problems between work groups become acute and there is mutual commitment to deal with them, intergroup meetings are a relevant change suggestion.

10. Use of knowledgeable and skilled third persons for diagnosis and problem resolution can be a highly effective way to bring about constructive change.

11. Administrators can improve their work units by collaboratively changing job content to better suit the unique skills of their subordinates or by changing job tasks to provide for greater satisfactions of individual needs.

12. Individual contributors need to be more initiating and aggressive in developing their own development programs.

SUMMARY

Change, as related to school organization, is not easy to come by. Schools are surprisingly resilient in maintaining and retaining their existing organizational structures.

Today's schools face innumerable new and complex challenges: how to reorganize in such fashion as to increase their ability to enhance the learning of their students and still maintain their productivity, efficiency, and effectiveness. Site-based management, properly conceived, is an approach to school organization that is seen as having real merit. Whatever the approach to school organization, there is an increased likelihood that they will benefit teachers and students, if they are arrived at through a decentralized, cooperative and democratic bureaucracy and if they are responsive to the principles of cooperation, empowerment, responsibility, accountability, and purposefulness.

We find that regardless of the organizational structure used, certain characteristics are identified as common to many of the organizations which exhibit high productivity. Foremost among these is:

Management levels, consistent with effective operations, are maintained at a minimum. This enhances direction, decision-making, and communication; provides less fragmented responsibilities; minimizes proliferation of overhead activities, and helps prevent personnel from feeling buried under excessive layers of organization.

In this chapter the author conceptualizes that schools are more effective and productive at performing their designed roles when they are organizationally responsive to their various internal and external concerns and issues, when they become more intelligent and organize for success.

DISCUSSION QUESTIONS

1. Discuss factors a principal should consider in regard to the human aspects of organization.
2. What are the symptoms of a poorly functioning organization plan?
3. What is meant by: a systems analysis is a very useful way for the principal to understand how the school operates within a social setting?
4. Discuss the merits (advantages) of publicly stating the school's discipline procedures and code.
5. Through their vision and practicality, principals articulate for their schools a collective ideology that defines an organization's identity and purposes. The principals who do this make these schools coherent, binding philosophy to goals, goals to programs, and programs to practices. Discuss this.
6. In the successful school the principal is a driven, energetic worker, committed to establishing the best possible school environment for the school's clients, its students. Do you believe this?
7. As the principal of a school, how would you determine its organizational deficiencies?
8. As the principal of the school, how will you deal with the tensions that are bound to arise between the *caretakers* and the *risk takers?*
9. Many studies support the premise that the principal who has a clarity of organizational vision and is able to clearly communicate this vision is an effective principal. Discuss this.
10. Is there a relationship between the development and growth of school organization's perception, reasoning and motivation, and similar characteristics in the organizational functioning of that school's classrooms?

REFERENCES

Bennis, W. and Nanus, B.: *Leaders: The Strategies for Taking Charge.* New York, Harper and Row, 1985.
Campbell, Roald F. and Gregg, Russell T.: *Administrative Behavior in Education.* New York, Harper and Row, 1957, p. 367.
Dale, Ernest.: *Planning and Developing the Company Organization.* New York, American Management Association, 1955, p. 14.
Griffiths, Daniel E.: *Human Relations in School Administration.* New York, Appleton-Century-Crofts, 1956, pp. 96–121.

Hickman, C. R. and Silva, M. A.: *Creating Excellence: Managing Corporate Culture, Strategy, and Change in the New Age.* New York, New American Library, 1984.

Knezevich, Stephen J.: *Administration of Public Education.* New York, Harper and Row, 1969.

Likert, Rensis.: *New Patterns in Management.* New York, McGraw-Hill, 1961, p. 20.

Lippitt, G.L. and Schmidt, W. T.: Crisis in developing organizations. *Harvard Business Review. 45:* 6, November–December 1967, pp. 102–112.

McGregor, Douglas.: *The Human Side of Enterprise.* New York, McGraw-Hill, 1960, p. 15.

Modern Practices and Concepts of Staffing Schools. Albany, Cooperative Development of Public School Administration, 1956, p. 12.

Morphet, Edgar L., Johns, Rose L. and Reller, Theordore L.: *Educational Organization and Administration.* Englewood Cliffs, Prentice Hall, 1967.

Simon, Herbert A.: *Administrative Behavior.* New York, Macmillan, 1951.

Wiles, Kindall: *Supervision for Better Schools.* New York, Prentice Hall, 1950, p. 133.

Chapter V

LEADERSHIP AND
THE SCHOOL'S HUMAN RESOURCES

INTRODUCTION

Today, more than ever before, democracy depends upon the development of efficient forms of democratic social management and upon the spreading of the skill in such management to the common man.

Kurt Lewin (1947)

C reative and effective human resource management is critical in productive school. Changing governmental and legal requirements, increasing demands for a more skilled and better motivated work force, intensifying external and internal environmental factors and pressures, a more demanding work force, changes in the work force, and new technologies are just a few of the elements that have contributed to the increasing importance of human resource management in today's schools. Human resource management has expanded and moved beyond mere administration of the traditional activities of employment, labor relations, compensation, and benefits. Today, human resource management, in order to have meaning and purpose, is much more integrated into all of the functions of the school because the school's organizational climate has become much more complex and challenging, it is more sophisticated. With this expanding role, that human resource management must fill, it is essential that the principal be integrally involved in the organization's strategic and policy making activities. This chapter is designed to emphasize all of this by bringing both the theoretical and practical aspects of human resource management to the attention of the reader.

Every aspect of a firm's (school's) activities is determined by the competence, motivation, and general effectiveness of its human organization. Of all the tasks of management, managing the human component is the central and most important task, because all else depends upon how well it is done.

Rensis Likert, *1967.*

In addition to the many recognized concerns and needs facing the principal and the school's personnel, another has gained prominence despite the national education movement, school reform, of this past decade. According to a sweeping survey by the Carnegie Foundation for the Advancement of Teaching, released in 1990, teachers continue to evidence morale problems and mounting frustrations in their work. According to a spokesman for the National Education Association, this study is characterized as a cry for more teacher participation.

The problem of alienation facing today's schools has much of its roots in American society itself. Heightened mobility, urbanization, population density, poverty, religious decay, family decay, etc., all influence the alienated condition of today's citizen. While disquieting, there is little that today's principal personally can do to alter these states of affairs. However, there are numerous school-specific factors, conditions and actions which can magnify or abate some of these societal influences.

To deny alienation in teaching as a problem in our society today is to ignore personal and societal changes which have superimposed upon what are for the most part archaic and unyielding school organizational forms and practices. To be sure, they were efficient in the technical sense and appropriate to satisfy the growing needs of a young nation. However, whether the externalities generated by such organizational forms and practices remain acceptable, or are indeed necessary, in an affluent and highly educated, socially concerned society remains a vital and controversial question.

Organizations (the schools) were created by humans and can be changed by them. It is time for the principal to reclaim responsibility and personal power, and to nurture self-courage and pursue uncertain paths. The alternative is to continue to be locked into dehumanizing structures which have been around for a long time, which schools have become used to.

This chapter presents the *compleat* principal's leadership role in the management of the school's human resources. In addition to personnel planning, recruiting, screening, selecting, inservicing, inducting, assessing, and staff development, we introduce: theory based decision making, participatory management, empowerment, and site based management. The considered affect, of external and internal influences, and special interest groups, upon the principal's mission are expressed as they impact upon: organizational design, collective bargaining, regulations and laws governing human interaction, participatory consultation, and shared leadership.

The author is convinced that the quality of personnel and human resources management leadership provided by the principal contributes to the creation of the effective and productive school. The principal is seen as a proactive leader who: views supervision and empowerment as compatable concepts, increasing personnel effectiveness as a primary human resources management function, and one who understands the linkage between structure and process. Practical messages from research and personal experiences of the author, in support of the ideas and thoughts appear throughout the chapter.

DEFINITIONS OF HUMAN RESOURCES MANAGEMENT

An educational system is no broader, no deeper, no more humane, no more dynamic, no more qualitative in its aspects than the people who are its architects and leaders. In the last analysis, one quality of education is the quality of each of us.

                                                                Samuel Gould

Personnel and human resources management is concerned with: obtaining, organizing, assessing, developing, and motivating the human resources of the school; developing the organization climate and management style to promote effective effort, cooperation, and trust between all persons in it; and helping the school meet its legal, moral, and social responsibilities toward its employees with regard to the conditions of work and their quality of life. It is the process of planning, organizing, staffing, directing, and democratizing school staff to accomplish organizational goals through the coordinated use of the school's resources. (Armstrong and Lorentzen, 1982, p. 3).

THE SCHOOL'S HUMAN RESOURCES OBJECTIVES

Planning for and managing or directing the school's human resources are major determinants of organizational effectiveness. Viewed broadly, human resource planning is the process intended to provide those capabilities and commitments essential to the school's self-renewal and sustained vitality. Such planning requires the integration of strategic and on-site planning, and permits the appropriate positioning of personnel within the school organization.

Human resources planning includes:

1. Reviewing the present human resources capabilities of the school.
2. Projecting these capabilities in terms of future planning, including likely turnover of personnel, and potential development of current personnel.
3. Projecting capabilities of present personnel in terms of the school's mission, goals and objectives.
4. Determining the capability gap between the school's needs and potential of the present and continuing personnel pool.
5. Planning for filling the gap, recruiting, screening and selecting personnel, evaluation procedures, and staff development programs.
6. Preparing and organizing for teacher empowerment and shared decision making.

The politics of education in America is a complex arrangement of relationships, various power elements, and continuous effort and pressures by a multitude of *parties in interest,* for control of the school system and its schools. Evidence of this is best seen when one observes the actual performance of the school administrators as they direct their energies towards effective personnel or human resources management practices. This political structure is best described as a struggle within each of the elements which comprise, or exercise control, over the total school-community and its environs.

All organizations have a continuing need for human resources planning. This need becomes increasingly more apparent because of the emergence of new technologies, new and changing governmental requirements, and new techniques drawn mainly from research and new knowledge. Such experiences, technologies, and requirements make human resource planning less subjective, more precise and scientific. Another equally important reason for devoting time and energy on human resources planning is its strategic impact on the school, its mission, goals, and objectives, and the increasing academic and social demands being placed upon it. The school's mission and demands have implications on the way the school is to be structured, and the nature and quantity of personnel needed to fulfill this task. It is the strategic planning of the principal, not simply administrative style, that generates the school's personnel and human resource requirements. This provides further assurances of the school's effectiveness and productivity.

STRATEGIC PLANNING

In its most powerful use, strategic planning identifies results, based upon an ideal vision, to be achieved at three levels: individual, organizational, and societal.

Strategic planning, without considering the opportunities and constraints within the school's human resources is a mistake. Also, changes in school strategy require the total commitment of the principal. Major changes in strategy are rarely developed, implemented, and successful without the expectation of an appropriate timeline. Further, it requires a massive redeployment of assets, change in organization and systems, and continued commitment to the new direction to achieve success. There is a myriad of actions that must take place within a school to effect change. These actions must all be delineated and must support the strategy. It takes time for the principal to develop a personal commitment, first to any change, and second, to the direction of change. It then takes time and effort to educate the school organization both to the change and to management's (administration's) commitment to change. (Albert, 1980, 18).

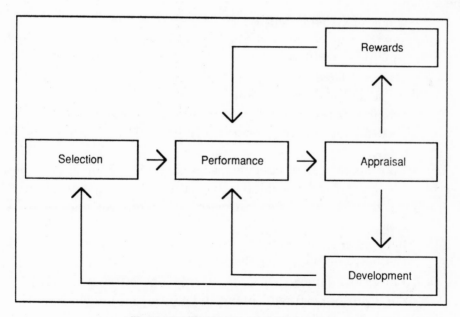

Figure 12 : The human resources cycle

While planning, the principal must assess the opportunities and constraints in his or her school-community environments, match these with the interests and expectations of the school district administration, and then decide what is to be done and how to do it. Similarly, human resources planning without reference to strategic planning is also seriously limiting. Strategic planning should provide a blueprint of a school that is changing, adapting, and developing through time.

The school assesses opportunities and constraints, first by articulating its mission, goals, and objectives. It is of utmost importance that the guidelines under which the school and staff will operate and the objectives that they strive for are clearly defined, communicated and understood. These missions, objectives, and goal statements provide the structure within which the principal will prepare his or her detailed strategies and plans. Further, these statements should be modified and reaffirmed as changes in the administration's data base occur and, or as a result of new information or approaches that come to light during the ongoing planning process.

Strategic planning requires the preparation of separate but related documents.

1. Statement of Mission. This is a broad statement of the purpose of the school.

2. Statement of General Policies. Policies are intended to establish the school's general philosophy and to clarify further the means by which the mission will be fulfilled.

3. Statement of Goals. Goals are statements of the overall long-term intent of the school's administration.

4. Statement of Objectives. Objectives are statements of what the principal wishes to achieve in areas related to or affected by the school and its community.

The school needs a firm concept of its educational function to best perceive the opportunities open to it by virtue of its unique capabilities. These goals should define relative degrees of emphasis and areas for concentration.

The school must then assess its external and internal environments. The external environment is analyzed in terms of pertinent economic, political and social characteristics, and trends. The internal strengths are analyzed; in terms of pertinent financial, facility, and human resources. The principal must seek to achieve an optimal fit between environmental opportunities and constraints and organizational strengths and weaknesses, consistent with his or her personal values, the school's mission, and the school system's academic and social commitments. By matching external opportunities with internal strengths, the principal drafts a strategic purpose and direction, or mission.

ORGANIZATIONAL PLANNING IMPACTS ON HUMAN RESOURCES

Strategic direction is translated into sequential and successive organizational designs. These sequential organizational designs are structured to anticipate changes that occur as the school passes from the developmental phase to a mature one. Schools change for a variety of reasons and in various ways, and these changes often seriously impact on the school's human resource planning.

In what direction should I take my school? Simply stated, this question expressed the essence of school strategy. The principal has a myriad of concerns and, at any given time, immediate problem solving or decision making may be paramount. Fundamentally, the principal's mark on a school will be set by the direction chosen for the (school), the strategies developed to get there, and the success experiences in reaching goals. (Albert, 1980, 3).

GENERAL SYSTEMS THEORY

The genesis of modern general systems theory was developed years ago, however only recently has it been applied in the study of organizations. Its purpose is to bring order to increasingly diverse approaches to organizational theory. Simply stated, the general systems theory emphasizes that components or subsystems of a system are related and dependent upon one another.

Each organizational system must accomplish essential tasks or functions that promote or detract from the productivity or lack of productivity, of the entire organization each systems has its own boundary and transforms inputs from other systems into outputs.

DYNAMICS OF ORGANIZATION

Modern society has frequently been characterized by an apparent propensity to grow and become productive through the establishment of organizations. Although the emphasis on the human being behind any achievement continues to receive the attention it deserves, the realization also continues to grow that it is the organization behind the achievement and the human being that helps determine the extent of success in each case. More significantly, it is the leadership exercised within each organization that enables it to meet its challenges, absorb its inevitable changes, and produce benefits. Accordingly, the principal needs to focus on these two entities: the organization (school), and the leadership within.

The central concerns of the principal are: how the school organization is created, how it evolves, how it works, how it changes, why it succeeds or fails, and what are those components and functions that determine its effectiveness and productivity. All organizations, from the urban school system to the small rural school have certain constants. They all have their reasons for existence, their mission and their needs. They all require leadership, structure and resources in order to function. The dynamics of organization, in this instance, focuses in on the school, its evolution, its internal and external impact, and its synergistic relationships with the rest of the school-community.

Leadership in schools evidence many styles and manifestations. It also changes and adapts to new situations and circumstances. Although, it has been frequently said that leaders are born, and not made, it is important to recognize that leaders, in this case principals, also grow and excel if the preparation is there to meet the challenges. The dynamics of organization focuses in on all the various aspects of leadership challenges within organizational contexts.

The dynamics of organization, is not one of developmental planning nor one of organizational theory, it is a program which focuses on the qualitative aspects of the school, on the development of its leadership, and of organizational development and adaptation within our complex and ever-changing society.

HUMAN RESOURCES PLANNING

Leadership appears to be the art of getting others to want to do something you are convinced should be done

(Vance Packard).

Human resources planning requires the collection and analysis of basic data that describes and evaluates jobs and estimates the capacities and potentials of employees. The combined data are applied as measures of person/job fit, and provide the basis for formulating action plans for the personnel development of the individuals involved. Human resources planning follows a sequence which includes describing

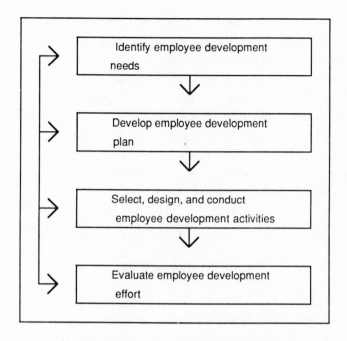

Figure 13 : Employee Development Process

the position, evaluating the position, and generating developmental actions.

A common error of many principals is to focus on the school's short-term replacement needs. Any human resource plan, if it is to be effective, must be derived from the long-range plans and strategies of the school.

The school's human resources planning normally consists of four basic steps:

1. determining the impact of the school's objectives on specific organizational needs;
2. defining the skills and expertise and the total number of employees necessary to achieve the school's objectives;
3. determining the additional (net) requirements; and
4. developing action plans to meet the anticipated human resources needs.

HUMAN RESOURCES AND THEORY Z

We must create conditions in schools that will nurture talented teachers.
Larry Cuban

Theory Z is applicable to the human resources planning of the school principal. Although Theory Z means many things to different people, depending upon the environment within which they function, most agree that the basic ingredients are: clearly defined organizational goals and objectives that are determined and worked towards in a participative atmosphere.

Some of the more popular characteristics of Theory Z include:

1. Organization objectives are known and communicated to all levels, a management by objectives approach.
2. Primary information flows from the bottom up, not the reverse.
3. Few levels of management exist.
4. The emphasis is on team rather than individual effort, the we concept.
5. Employees are involved in problem solving and decision making.

POSITION DESCRIPTION

Position guides or job descriptions define the general purposes and responsibilities of individual assignments. Each position is analyzed so that the principal can understand and anticipate the results expected from each job through time, and the context and methods for achieving results. Since strategy planning is a dynamic process, as is human resources planning, instead of merely describing jobs as they presently are or appear, the human resources planning process analyzes each school's design to determine those specific job requirements that will be required to fulfill the planned school strategy. This analysis translates human resource plans into specific job accountabilities and selective knowledge and skills.

POSITION EVALUATION

Once described, positions are evaluated for their relative importance and potential contribution to the school's mission, goals and objectives. An approach to job evaluation should give consideration to such critical dimensions as:

1. Each position should clearly offer solutions to the unique and general problems anticipated by the principal when he or she relates the position to the school's mission, goals and objectives.
2. Each position is assured of relative degrees of freedom to think, to be creative and encouraged in risk-taking.
3. Each position is answerable for specific mid-term and end results.

Accountability is accompanied by a well-defined freedom to act. Measuring job content within this dimension aid in determining how the position impacts on the school's mission, goals, and objectives.

A position evaluation should specify such requirements as:

1. Specialized knowledge.
2. Managerial skills.
3. Human relations skills.
4. Self-starting skills.
5. Original and creative thinking.
6. Capacity for accepting accountability.
7. Capacity for taking risks.

There are major themes to be considered during position evaluations.

1. We hunger for a community work place, that is, for a workplace where people can use their talents and find personal growth along with mutual security and satisfaction and the need to belong.
2. The world is changing too fast for experts, and it is hard to solve one problem without creating many others. The main tension in working with others is derived from conflict within each of us, between authority, individuality, and the need to belong. Dignity and meaning can be gained by restructuring work places to resolve tensions.

RECRUITMENT OF PERSONNEL

The education of children is the central purpose of any school, and the teacher is the most important single source in producing a quality education.

(Davis and Nickerson, 1968, p. 17)

The principal is to distinguish, as a primary goal, the taking of those measures that will assure the improvement of the professional staff of the school. To begin with, the principal of the effective school occupies a contributing role in the school system's recruitment program. The workings of the school system's recruitment and selection of personnel program is a fundamental and important area for personal involvement of the principal. Although the recruitment portion of this function is often assigned to a central office administrator, the principal can provide guidance and direction, and seek assurances that candidates being recruited satisfy the expectations and demands of the school's human resources plan and mission. The principal's message to the total school-community should be clear. *I seek teachers who can assure the school-community that this school will be effective and productive, and will strategically participate in the recruitment and selection of the personnel who are to staff this school so that the school's mission is in fact realistic.*

The principal exercises leadership in and through a social system comprised of formal and informal groups with interpersonal relations, leadership hierarchies, patterns of interactions, social norms, and so forth. The effective principal creates such change as may be required in order to become a contributing force in the district's recruitment plan.

The recruitment of staff personnel represents a continuing and aggressive search for candidates to fill current and anticipated openings in the school. The purpose is to attract the most suitable and desirable candidates available, and encourage them to make application in the school system. A creative and aggressive school system recruitment plan will normally actively search for candidates, particularly in the hard to fill teaching posts and attract the most qualified people to the school system.

DETERMINING NEEDS

Leadership involves remembering past mistakes, an analysis of today's achievements, and a well-grounded imagination in visualizing the problems of the future.

Stanley C. Allyn

The principal can be more assured of success in this effort by clearly defining the staffing needs of the school. This is accomplished by carefully preparing data in support of the determined staff needs and furthering this with a restatement of the school's mission and how this staffing program will provide assurances that the school will satisfy the expectations of the mission.

Data prepared by the principal include:

1. Changes and projected modifications in student enrollments creating adjustments in staffing requirements.
2. Education and program changes which necessitate additional or specially trained personnel.
3. Staff resignations, transfers, and various leaves of absence which impact upon the school's personnel requirements.
4. The relationship of the school's mission, goals and objective to the stated staffing needs.

The principal, consistent with his or her human resources plan, responds and supports these staffing needs with estimates of school and school district student enrollment estimates and projections, secures similar information from any feeder schools, should there be any, studies the school system's census information, and maintains an awareness of anticipated student turnover and the drop-out experience of the school. The principal also develops profiles of the student body, the school's culture, and inventories the continuing staff.

AVOIDANCE OF EMPLOYMENT DISCRIMINATION

Federal laws, regulations, and court cases regarding discrimination in employment is an important consideration within the school district's personnel and recruitment policies and procedures. This includes the creation of an appropriate *affirmative action plan*, and a clear statement regarding equal employment opportunities within the schools of the system.

The federal government has defined affirmative action as employer initiated development of a set of specific results-oriented procedures to ensure that job applicants and employees are treated without regard to race, color, religion, sex, or national origin. This affirmative action plan should include a statement of policy and purpose, procedures for identification and modification of present procedures and practices which may have a discriminatory impact or which perpetuate past discrimination, and a statement outlining affirmative action goals and timetables. Guidelines for developing affirmative action plans are available through various federal offices.

The primary purpose of an affirmative action plan, as it is related to staff recruitment and selection, is to ascertain the need to correct past discrimination in employment, and if such discrimination is determined to be present, to take corrective measures to aggressively correct these concerns. Further, attention must be directed toward monitoring the actual manner in which the policy and plan implemented. Regardless of the various changes which periodically appear in legislation regarding this question, it would serve the best purposes of the school administrator to aggressively and vigorously eliminate any practices which represent employment discrimination in any form.

Equal Pay Act. 1963	Equal pay for men and women performing the same work
Title VII, Section 703A - Civil Rights Act as amended by Equal Employment Opportunity Act, 1972	Prohibits employment discrimination that is based upon race, religion, color, sex, or national origin
Executive Order 11246, 1965; 11375, 1967; 11478, 1979	Federal contractors and subcontactors must utilize affirmative action plans to eliminate discrimination practices
Age Discrimination in Employment Act, 1967, amended 1978	Outlaws discrimination against any person 40-70 and prevents the use of mandatory retirement standards
Pregnancy Discrimination Act 1978	Prohibits discrimination against women affected by pregnancy, childbirth, or related medical conditions
Vocational Rehabilitation Act, 1973 and 1974	Outlaws discrimination against handicapped individuals
Vietnam-Era Veterans Readjustment Act, 1974	Requires affirmative action plans for and outlaws discrimination against Vietnam era veterans

Figure 14 : EEO Legislation and Executive Regulations

THE SELECTION OF TEACHERS

Why has teacher-effectiveness research failed to provide definitive procedures for the selection of the *best* teachers from among the applicants for each position? This issue was explored by Ornstein and Levine

(1981) when they reviewed the literature on teacher behavior research. They suggested that because teaching is so varied and complex, that the tools with which to determine potential effectiveness do not exist. However, a number of studies have highlighted those conditions that contribute significantly to the teaching/learning process. Among these appear the personal characteristics of the teacher.

It was Barr (1961) who placed considerable emphasis on teacher-pupil interactions. In his summarization of twenty years of research, the interaction of teachers and pupils were noted as critical factors in teaching affectiveness. In David Ryan's (1960) Teacher Characteristics Study of some 6,000 teachers, the following description was offered for those who experienced the highest ratings. They have a tendency to be extremely generous in appraisals of behavior and motives of other persons; possess strong interest in reading and literary affairs; interested in music, painting, and the arts in general; participate in social groups; enjoy pupil relationships, manifest superior verbal intelligence; and are superior with respect to emotional adjustment.

These studies, and others provided by (McNeil and Popham, 1973, Good, 1975, Getzles and Jackson, 1963, Whitehall and Lewis, 1963), support the view that classroom teaching requires talented, spontaneous persons who are emotionally stable and socially integrated. These teachers are the *self-actualized* people according to the hierarchy of needs model developed by psychologist Abraham Maslow. His famous, often studied, theory contends that human needs are arranged in a hierarchy of priority and potency. It is when the lower needs, including the physiological, safety, love and belonging, and self-esteem needs are relatively well-satisfied will people be motivated to self-actualize or try to achieve what they are capable of doing (Maslow 1970).

Ringness (1968) defined self-actualization as the need to live up to one's potential to become what one has in him to become and to utilize one's energies to live fully as possible. Accordingly, the selection process would indeed be best served if the schools are staffed with teachers who are motivated and psychologically healthy. Teachers who are confident, and achievement oriented are likely to provide positive working relationships with students, communicate and interact meaningfully with them, and stimulate productive learnings. Henjum (1983) added further to this contention in his study, which included the following summary. *Self-actualizing related traits such as: enthusiastic, participating, emotionally stable, self-assured, venturesome, strong will-power, and unfrustrated were apparently related to teacher effectiveness.*

This study further supports the hypothesis that a healthy social adjustment and positive mental health are related to teaching effectiveness. When selecting teachers for the classroom it would be prudent to give strong consideration to anyone who exhibited that they are motivated, enthusiastic, self-assured, emotionally stable, participating, unfrustrated, and have strong willpower. These people can be identified by noting the extent and quality of their accomplishments and involvement in teacher related activities. Practical examples would include good grades, experience with youth groups, work in community organizations, participation in co-curricular and extra-curricular high school and college activities, and well-developed hobbies and jobs.

Our society desperately needs these self-actualizing teachers who are mature and developed, and whose basic personal needs have been met. These qualitative characteristics reflect their readiness to effectively carry out the demanding activities inherent in teaching and the teaching profession.

TEACHER PERFORMANCE EVALUATION

There are four instructional leadership functions of the principal: curriculum development, staff development, clinical development, and teacher performance, appraisal, and evaluation has received increased attention and review during the current educational reform and accountability movement.

In its review of exemplary teacher evaluation systems Research for Better Schools declared that forward looking school systems have lead the way in such substantial personnel appraisal changes as:

1. linking evaluation systems to research on effective practices,
2. providing improved training for evaluators,
3. holding administrators accountable for conducting evaluations,
4. using evaluation-identified teacher deficiencies to focus on staff development,
5. making teachers active partners in the evaluation process. (Buttram, 1987, p. 5).

Currently, much time and energy is directed toward the evaluation of student progress in most school systems. Detailed record-keeping programs trace student learning, per teacher prepared tests and standardized testing programs, and this data is monitored. However, teacher appraisal has been, at best, seldom used to join classroom performance with instructional practices and for the most part there are questions now being raised as to whether test scores do actually measure student learning. Many ongoing evaluation programs of teachers are in place to simply support tenure recommendations, and seldom satisfy boards of education and other interested persons and groups within the school-community. Others are done so poorly that they are meaningless, and point to the fact that certain principals either lack the skills required to prepare satisfactory teacher evaluations or they are unable to commit themselves to the considered purpose for teacher appraisal.

An example of such limitation appeared as a result of one principal's lack of commitment to or understanding of the purpose and value of the process in a school system in which the author had had considerable experience. In this instance the principal was expected to observe an approved Policy and Procedure for Evaluation. One of the requirements outlined in the policy specifically referred to time schedules to be observed in the performance of principal observations and evaluations of the teachers within his school. Further, the numbers of such observations and evaluations to be completed by the principal during each school year, for tenured and probationary personnel, were also specifically spelled out. Also, the nature and content of the observations and evaluations were clearly detailed in the policy. This principal failed to complete the observations and evaluations, conferences, and reports required, within the policy. When pressed by the central administration for these reports, the principal simply completed each evaluation report with the following statement, *I have nothing to recommend at this time.* It should be noted that the staff was represented and participated in the development of this school system's evaluation policy. The value and purpose of this approved process was seriously questioned by members of the principal's staff and future efforts to include personnel of that school in the creation of other procedures and policies were seriously limited. There were, as would be expected, additional problems now appearing between the principal and those central office administrators who were also included in the school systems teacher evaluation process (Appendix C—Teacher Evaluation Program).

No one single template for teacher evaluation is totally satisfactory or meets the differing organizational traditions, management principles, and governing values or practices. While goals espoused for teacher evaluation in each school district are similar, accountability and improvement upon examination, we find differences among all design parameters, the role of the principal, the role of teachers, the frequency of evaluation, evaluation instrumentation, and institutional responses to evaluation. School system evaluation programs define different elements as the linchpins on which each process turns. For example:

1. In a North Carolina school district, success of the system depends on the ability of the advisory/assistance teams to support the teacher through the evaluation process and ultimately to make a summative decision regarding the teacher's status. In addition, the presence of district-wide observer/evaluators who serve as a mechanism to insure quality control represents a central feature.
2. In a New York school district, joint training received by teachers and administrators coupled with clinical supervision techniques rests at the heart of the program.
3. In a California school district, multiple sources of information an evaluation portfolio, including direct observation, samples of student work, results of student surveys, grading distributions, and teacher-made materials, characterize the district's approach to evaluation.
4. In a New Jersey school system, a peer-based remediation process for teachers judged to be at risk is the system's defining feature. Peers work with teachers for a period of sixty days independently of administrators in an attempt to improve teacher performance or counsel them out of the profession.

Despite this diversity, several distinct features emerge at all locations as pivotal. In these systems, teacher evaluation activities have the support of teachers and administrators and achieve their objectives. These common features are:

1. joint training for administrators and teachers
2. systems of checks and balances
3. accountability structure for evaluation
4. effective feedback procedures, and
5. flexible instrumentation
6. integration of evaluation and development resources

Teacher performance evaluation is similar to clinical supervision in that it strives to improve instruction, but goes beyond clinical supervision in that it serves as a record of accomplishment, provides a quality control mechanism, examines how teachers are delivering instruction, and calls to the teacher's attention the school's mission and student achievement data while stressing the functional school and classroom curriculum.

Enabling teacher performance evaluation begins with the process of unfreezing, reexamining understandings, beliefs, and practices fundamental to the school system and school. A proactive leadership is necessary to turn the school district and school from standard operating procedures and sanction significant organizational and operational change. Teachers and administrators will realistically and professionally approach the matter of improved and qualitative teacher, expressed and strong commitment of the superintendent to the program.

EMPOWERMENT

Clearly, people are more committed to goals they have formulated themselves than to those which are imposed upon them. Creativity isn't limited to special people, places or times. Given shared goals and an enabling environment, everyone can contribute.

Empowerment is defined as a process in which individuals or groups of individuals are encouraged to take risks and to compete without repercussions of failure. In education, this is a process that provides teachers and principals with the opportunities and the resources to enable them to better understand their world the power to change it. These professionals experience greater autonomy and independence in decision making. Empowerment means loosening control over what people do, and at the same time gaining a wider span of control over information and outcomes.

Such important themes emerge with the onset of empowerment as:

1. the language of shared governance, growth and empowerment
2. readiness for professional growth and empowerment

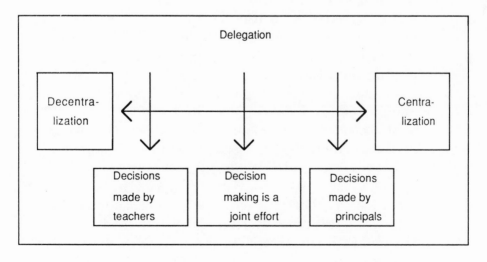

Figure 15 : Decentralization and centralization affecting delegation

3. the importance of the superintendent's leadership on empowerment
4. time as a key resource for empowerment
5. boundary spanning for school principals
6. enhancing of teachers' and principals' professional image
7. the importance of hearing teachers' voices
8. shared professional thinking, and
9. dealing with power through empowerment.

Empowerment awakens individual and collective potential, and significant breakthroughs in schools can occur when revitalized teachers and principals develop and nurture powerful networks of collegial relationships. Empowered individuals are alive and living in the organization, and make a difference; are learning and growing on the job; and are part of a community with a common purpose, the school's mission. Linkage occurs between empowerment and the effective and productive school.

Schools are assured of increased effectiveness and productivity when teachers know more about their subjects and disciplines, and how to teach them. Empowerment gives teachers this opportunity.

Traditional theory in the administration of schools, the principalship, provides for the principal to make decisions regarding school policy and determine the framework for the school's operation. Naisbitt, in his book *Megatrends,* signalled the beginning of the reform movement in organizational structure and management style by identifying a shift from a representative democracy to a participatory democracy. Naisbitt claimed that people whose lives are affected by a decision must be part of the process of arriving at the decision. In an educational setting, teachers and students are *most* affected by decisions, therefore their participation in the decision making process signals a shift to the empowerment of these personnel.

This theme, *empowerment,* now appearing in school management writings, discussions, and practices has gained considerable popularity and support. It is praised because it encourages teachers, parents, principals, and others to become part of the decision making process, to gain a degree of ownership in the decisions that affect them and in the school's vision, mission, and programs. This shift to decentralized decision making signals a shift to the empowerment of all professional personnel.

New ideas are everywhere. All they need is the environment to make them happen.

Advantages	Disadvantages
1. Provide principal with broader range of information on the problems, alternatives, and recommend solutions.	1. Hold principal accountable for group's decisions.
2. A more creative approach to solving problems since ideas maybe piggybacked.	2. Takes work group's time away from other aspects of their jobs.
3. Improves communication in school because work groups become aware of issues facing the principal.	3. May result in choosing sides and and cause morale problems over differing opinions.
4. Creates a higher morale in the work place.	4. Allows strong personalities to dominate work group and decisions may not reflect whole group opinion.
5. Stresses a stronger commitment to the decision once it is made since the work group helped make it.	5. Requires more supervisory skills in communicating and clarifying group's role in a given decision.
	6. Is difficult to use if the decision must be made quickly.

Figure 16 : Group decision making

Empowerment is a necessary ingredient for schools striving for excellence, and excellence can only be permanent achievements if educators and their clients become part of the change process. The principals of schools that accept the concept of empowerment are expected to modify their methods of operation, beliefs, and attitudes toward school organization, administration, supervision, and operation. The enlightened principal is himself or herself empowered so that conditions are ripe for the empowerment of teachers.

Empowerment, in the form of shared decision making is a major force for enhancing the position of educational professionals. As strategic planners, long-term planning to achieve a vision, the empowered arrive at consensus beliefs, develop a vision, create a mission statement, conduct internal and external data scans, and identify factors critical to the effectiveness and productivity of the school. As operational planners, the empowered develop yearly action plans, designed and directed toward the desired outcomes stated in the school's mission and vision statements. These action plans detail individual responsibilities, define expected accomplishments, clarify timelines for the satisfaction of goals, assure the availability of those resources necessary to accomplish the desired outputs or outcomes, the means by which these are to be accomplished, and the manner(s) in which desired outputs and outcomes are to be measured.

The guiding principles to empowerment are knowledge, status, and access to decision making. The poorly informed or misinformed are not likely to serve as responsible professionals. Knowledge for teachers is vital to the success of this change, this decentralization of the decision making process. It is reasonable to anticipate teachers exerting greater and responsible authority, not only because they are permitted and encouraged to do so, but also because they have been equipped to do so. Surely, the teacher who has been helped to more fully understand the school's curriculum or the school's administration, may be expected to make more meaningful contributions to each of these processes.

Excellent and effective school-based empowered communications-governance committees allow a broader base of discussion and information sharing in the strategic (long-term with a vision) decision making and operational (short-term action planning) decision making that takes place at the building level. This broad based dialogue permits and encourages the varied human elements of the school's educational community to work more cooperatively and positively together with the end result being improved quality and quantity of instructional programs for the school's clients, the students.

In the schools of America, there is generally a disincentive for risk taking. Teachers and principal are often discouraged, either intentionally or unintentionally, from risk taking and being creative while on the job. Empowerment provides that ingredient that encourages risk taking and the potential for school change.

Empowerment does not mean the abdication of authority or the relinquishing of leadership; leadership is essential to the implementation of significant innovations and change. Empowerment does mean, however, giving others the opportunity and responsibility to gain and wield influence. Teacher empowerment can be better appreciated if it is viewed as professionalization rather than an exercise in worrying about who is boss (Maeroff 1988).

Empowerment brings with it group decision making and there are both advantages and disadvantages that are known to accompany the process.

TRAINING TEACHERS TO TAKE RISKS

Teachers' beliefs may be best modified while they are in the thick of change, taking risks, and facing uncertainty. At the effective and productive school new ideas are constantly happening, because creativity is constantly being encouraged.

The school traditionally has not been noted for its risk taking capability, it is not been a natural occurrence in our culture. The training of principals traditionally included ways: to maintain employee self-esteem, to offer employees help without their assuming their ownership or responsibility for the task, to listen to employees with empathy and compassion, and to ask employees for help to solve problems. It is necessary to train and encourage educators to take risks, and at the same time assure those educators that they will not be placed *at risk* for having become part of *school change.*

For example, there is the instance of this junior high school principal who entered the superintendent's office and promptly announced, *We* have a problem. The superintendent in turn responded with, *We* don't have a problem, *you* have a problem. Tell *me* what *your* problem is, and then *we* will decide if this is *our* problem. In this instance, the principal, although empowered to deal personally with the issue, was in need of training to take risks.

Another example of this need appeared during a school experience which dealt with the expressions and creativity of a junior high school social studies teacher. The teacher, because of his creative teaching methods, upset the principal of the school. The teacher sought to encourage his students in the workings and understanding of local government and the significance of special interest groups and his overt activities proved to be upsetting to the principal of that school.

An unprotected railroad crossing, within the community, was the site of a tragic accident. Local government and parents were unable to persuade the railroad officials to make corrections or improvements to this hazardous condition.

The teacher encouraged his students to be participants in this project. He arranged for the students to study, survey and report upon the nature and quantity of traffic at all of the railroad crossings within the community. In addition, the students participated in a letter writing campaign and developed a community-wide petition, all demanding that immediate corrective action be taken by the railroad. Further, the students requested and were invited to a personal meeting with the president of the railroad. All of this, naturally, filled the local media with some interesting and provocative editorials, articles, and letters to the editors.

The principal had not empowered this teacher to pursue such overt and provocative methods for the teaching of government and the operations of special interest groups. In fact, the principal felt personally threatened by the actions of the teacher, and suggested the actions taken by the teacher and students fell beyond the scope of the school's social studies curriculum. It should be noted that permanent railroad crossing protections were installed at all of the railroad crossing sites located within the school district within a month after the president of the railroad received the student prepared comprehensive traffic study, the student prepared petition, and participated in the meeting with the officers of the railroad.

The key is to keep the ownership of the task with the teacher or principal through effective and continuing coaching. Teachers and principals deserve support and reinforcement when completing a task or assignment. The culture of our schools has not traditionally been fertile ground for the empowerment movement, and schools have not been on the cutting edge as risk takers. Risk takers are often viewed as threatening, and at times have been known to be fired, reprimanded, or passed over. With empowerment significant change is in the offering.

There are conditions that promote risk taking.

1. Principals must believe that teachers can identify and define their own professional development needs; and teachers have the potential to grow into expanded roles are more inquiring and contributing professionals.
2. Teachers are provided appropriate time, occasions, and space for professional work and reflection.
3. Teachers are given training, followup, and technical assistance. They also require ongoing coaching and feedback.
4. Access to resources is important, as is sufficient freedom for teachers to plan, reflect, and develop.
5. Provision for consultants and evaluators, and a budget for curriculum projects and research.
6. A commitment from teachers and the teachers' union to empowerment, and the acceptance of greater accountability for school improvement efforts.

Studies of schools practicing shared governance indicate that supervision and teacher empowerment are compatible concepts. The key to success of these practices are patience and administrator's philosophical commitment to shared decision-making.

ROLES FOR THE PRINCIPAL

Principals assume a number of different roles in the process of school improvement, effectiveness, restructuring, and productivity, including human engineering, relationship assessor, planner, facilitator, visionary, experimenter, risk taker, catalyst, model, team-builder and coach, people builder and challenger, and chaplain and reality therapist. Enlightened principals see a need to empower themselves as well as to create the conditions for teachers to empower themselves.

As human engineers, principals must understand human beings and the diverse human dimensions involved in bringing about enduring school improvement. They must be sensitive and accepting of human frailties, viewing each teacher as a human being and professional. As landscape and relationship assessors, principals must determine which approaches are best for achieving empowerment in their schools. Should they be slow and deliberate, quick, or trial and error. Consideration must be given to staff members and their relationships with each other, exist relationships between the principal and union officials, and the existing school-community climate. Principals need to identify the resisters and the supporters of change and growth experiences, and the outcomes expected. As planners, facilitators, and visionaries, the principals develop and share vision and strategic plans with their staffs (including school mission statements). These plans drive the budgets and staff development activities.

> Our understanding of the *mission* of schooling must go beyond the merely measurable to a consideration of more profound purposes.

The principals are experimenters, are risk takers, catalysts, and models, and will try different and more subtle ways in dealing with power and the frailties of initiating change. They acknowledge that teachers, as well as principals, are generators of knowledge and view them all as learners as well as responsible contributors.

As team builders and coaches, principals encourage collaborative efforts that foster trust. With teachers, principals conduct new experiences and reflective discussions where responsibilities are shared. They create the climate and opportunities for unconditional sharing to take place.

Principals, as people builders and challengers, provide for staff development activities, coordinated by the staff, and conducted to include understandings of evaluation and the application of research finding, shared decision making, situational leadership, and delegation. Other skills that need learning include: the conduct of meetings and conferences, group dynamics, consensus and team building, short and long range planning, project management and assessment, adult learning theory, conflict management, budget management, understanding the politics of education, and problem solving.

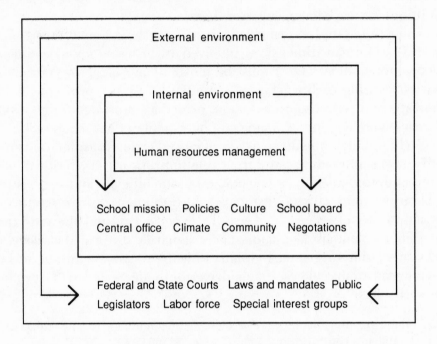

Figure 17 : The environments of human resources management

As chaplains and reality therapists, principals help staff members in understanding that change and involvement are risky, time consuming, and tiring. Perspectives are liberated in the powerment process. Staff members require new knowledge and the rethinking of previously held viewpoints. These shifts and changes can be energizing and exciting, and also turbulent, unsettling, stressful, and conflict ridden. However, with collegial support and professional assistance the negatives can be overcome.

Empowerment and risk taking are not ends in themselves, but they are essential means by which we generate and promote long-lasting and high-impact school improvement.

HUMAN RESOURCES AND COLLECTIVE BARGAINING

Collective teacher activity is no longer a new notion, it is consistent with the various labor movements throughout the country. Aside from the improvements in earnings other benefits, and various and sundry conditions of employment, collective bargaining has enabled teachers to become a more pronounced voice in the management and conduct of school matters.

Collective teacher activity has been encouraged by several social forces, and changes in employee-employer relationships is a significant one of these. Teacher power has increased and continues to grow as the various teacher organizations clamor for membership of the nation's teachers, and as these unions achieve inroads into many areas of school functioning which were once uniquely the responsibility of school boards and administrators.

Another of the social forces is the size of school systems, which brings with it their increased complexity, their many more specialized programs and services, and weakened communication systems.

These factors reduced the opportunities for teachers to belong, to participate in decisions which affect their welfare, their work, and their ideas. This size and complexity frequently caused boards of education and administrators to make decisions without thoroughly understanding or determining teacher attitudes, and to take actions which threatened job security and produced various teacher anxieties. This is furthered by the public's resistance to increased taxation for the schools, and the natural conservatism demonstrated by many who serve on school boards. An increased male teaching force, a decrease in teacher turnover, greater career commitment, and the collective bargaining *struggle* have all contributed to a *changing* school environment.

Collective bargaining is essentially an adversary relationship, a process of power accommodation, with each party having the right and ability to inflict loss on the other in the event satisfactory compromise is not reached. The resultant collective bargaining agreement is a form of joint ownership and control of the enterprise, in this instance the school system. It establishes a level playfield upon which administrators view and consider options and approaches to policy and procedure questions concerning most school matters. Understanding the contents of the negotiated agreement and managing the contract are vital to the maintenance of good human resource relationships within the school.

For many who function in the managerial-administrative areas of school operations, collective bargaining and the resultant formalized agreements (contracts) have been met with alarm. These managerial persons have viewed this new teacher-administrator relationship as one which reduces the potential for effective school leadership. Essentially, these same school administrators continue to hold that the aftermath of this power struggle in public education suggests the elimination of the school administrator as a vital, dynamic, effective and creative contributor to the educational scene. A term, often heard during the collective bargaining process is middle management, like the middle child who has a limited identity and role within the school family.

The rise of teacher political militancy has unquestionably produced a host of new, and at times difficult problems concerning the traditional role definitions of the principal. As teacher collective action increased in intensity, conflict and social distance increased between the leadership of the teachers' groups (unions) and the schools' administrations. Various pressures were placed upon school administrators who were now called upon to abandon the traditional roles that many of them had played. Many feared this new, often challenging, if not threatening relationship.

> In one of the earliest collective bargaining training films for school boards and administrators there is a scene in which teachers are shown picketing in front of a school building. The principal appears, viewing this collective activity from his office window, and while wringing his hands in anguish, he declares, *What are they doing to my school?*

On the other hand, many school administrators look upon this new relationship as a change which brings with it opportunities. They see this change as: Change requires constructive, honest, straight-forward, wise answers to the problems it presents. It is not hard to guide the affairs of a going concern along a course of previous conduct or represent people in their contented enjoyment of things as they are or have been. The demands upon today's leaders of American education is hard, challenging, and tough. Change is to be met squarely and it is to be made man's servant rather than his master. The notion that teachers, principals, central office administrators, and elected or appointed community representatives are not dependent upon one another and that each has special and totally separate functions and responsibilities is no longer a consideration (Bookbinder 1971).

School administrators must view collective bargaining as a process which places a premium on effective leadership. They must be inclined to accept the challenge, use their administrative skills and capabilities to develop procedures and practices which are responsive to and in tune with the unique nature of these current personnel management concerns and relationships. They must hold that purposeful bargaining can lead to:

1. greater acceptance of responsibility for the outcomes of education with a rise in professionalism, effectiveness, and public status,
2. increased freedom for administrators and teachers to do the things they are skilled in doing,
3. improved understanding, by boards of education and the citizenry, of the processes of schooling, and
4. community understanding and support for the school system. The are politically sophisticated.

The author, in the summary of his doctoral thesis, noted the following: The planning, actuating and coordinating, functions of the principal are only somewhat affected because of collective bargaining (Bookbinder 1971).

School principals must be prepared to accept the following thesis:

1. collective teacher action will continue in breadth and intensity, and
2. collective bargaining can be useful to a school system as a means of encouraging and using differing opinions in introducing school change and problem solving.

Essentially, the principal must anticipate personal adjustments, must search for ways in which his or her unilateral judgments are replaced by cooperative ones. This is particularly applicable in such areas as teacher evaluation and performance appraisal. The restructuring of evaluation concepts, moving from inspectional ratings to performance evaluation in terms of mutually agreed upon predetermined goals and objectives is an excellent example of such necessary change.

While the thrust for higher pay and benefits and conditions of employment are inherent in the collective bargaining process, there is adequate evidence to indicate that extrinsic gains in themselves are not all there is to job satisfaction and a sense of professional fulfillment. Factors that have been known to motivate and satisfy personnel within all job descriptions are: a sense of achievement, success in job performance, seeing the results of their work, being appreciated, having worth recognized, and better interpersonal relations with colleagues and students.

The principal is clearly responsible for effectively involving all members of his or her professional staff. This must be done without infringing upon other administrators, without violating the authority of the school board, and without ignoring the moods and educational aspirations of the community that his or her school serves. The principal's competence will be measured in the interpersonal skills he or she musters while working with the staff. This effective principal, is a social manager, a planner, and an innovator, who knows how to implement an order, how to work with people in order to accomplish common objectives, and is a successful communicator with his or her entire constituency.

> *One man with courage makes a majority.*
> Andrew Jackson

The principal must rise above the cliches and stereotypes that have led so many to believe that any legal and practical limitations on his or her authority are bad for education, for teachers, and for themselves.

DETECTING PERSONNEL PROBLEMS

Personnel problems occupy a continuing and often consuming concern for the school principal. Some of these concerns are not resolved at the beginning levels of supervision, the principal, and take the form of grievances and at time arbitrations.

It is the creative and secure principal who is able to anticipate potential personnel concerns and needs of the school. This often takes the form of counseling. While principals may be ill-prepared in terms of the technical aspects of psychology, they should understand what psychologists do, signs and symptoms of trouble, and what types of problems need special care and those that require specialized assistance.

There are any number of signals that should alert the principal that potential personnel problems are likely to present themselves and be found to be in need of help. Those primary signals that are, or should be, of real concern, often make their appearance in the following ways.

1. Absenteeism. This is one of the most serious signs of personnel problems and concerns for the school. Absenteeism may indicate severe physical, emotional, or even substance abuse problems, and job performance alone may fail to tell the total story. Absenteeism is one of the most frequent indicators of problems.

2. ***Deteriorating job performance.*** This is another obvious signal of a personnel problem. This too may involve factors other than personal problems, such as, physical, emotional, or substance abuse, however, deteriorating job performance is yet another *red flag* that requires the principal's skill and attention.

3. ***Deteriorating personal relations.*** Emotional problems are known to affect the quality of relationships. Also, it should be noted that the personal relationships (especially close ones) of persons involved in substance abuse tend to deteriorate. Depression, high anxiety, severe stress, brain tumors, or marital problems may be contributors to irritability and isolation.

4. ***Deteriorating physical appearance.*** Substantial changes in the physical appearance of a school's staff member are often signs of personal problems. This deteriorating condition may take the form of changes in facial appearances, posture, walk, and may be tied to disease. However, the existence of emotional problems or substance abuse also contribute to the appearance of physical deterioration.

STAFF INDUCTION AND ORIENTATION

The induction of personnel is a process which is standard operating procedures for most school systems. It not only responds to the needs of new staff members, but also for those who are continuing members of the faculty. Induction aids employees by orienting them to the school environment, and familiarizing them with the new and continuing programs. Included within a school's induction plan would normally be such elements as the community, the system, the teaching position, and the people with whom the new and continuing faculty member will be working with.

Orientation or induction requires sensitive planning and careful execution. It is during the orientation or induction period that new staff members gather their first impressions concerning the school's policies, objectives, leadership, and methods of operation. Moreover, it is at this time that initial acquaintance is made with colleagues and the community's inhabitants, characteristics, agencies, and services. Since first impressions are often lasting, every effort should be expended during the orientation or induction to assure that new staff members gain correct understandings of the many facets of school and community life (McCleary and Heneley, 1965, p. 28).

Induction programs within the school systems of this nation are receiving increased attention. In fact, such states as Pennsylvania now mandate the development and approval of induction programs in each of the state's 501 school districts. It is within these programs that mentors and peer coaches appear. Because of careful and thorough planning, and also a need for state approvals, these induction programs offer a much more comprehensive approach to staff orientation and development. Each new employee is teamed in the mentor program with an experienced member of the staff, who becomes that new teacher's sponsor, coach, teacher, and advocate. The purpose, is simply to ease the staff member into the new post, under the expert guidance of an experienced and successful continuing member of the school's faculty (Farren, Gray, & Kaye, 1984).

An effective mentoring program must be a community enterprise, drawing upon and fostering a collegiality within the school and developing a climate in which all participants find support from their colleagues and administrators. The roles in a comprehensive, thoroughly and carefully planned mentoring program include:

1. mentors
2. new teachers
3. principals and other supervisory personnel
4. parents
5. students
6. school district
7. community
8. colleges and universities
9. the state

The induction program process generally includes several basic principles which offer guidance to the principal and other members of the staff.

1. The induction process is a planned procedure that responds to the school district's educational goals and the expectations of its personnel.
2. Board of education approved policies guide and support the induction process, and are utilized to establish the expected goals and objectives of the program.
3. Although the primary responsibility for administering the induction program is normally assigned to a central office administrator, its execution is shared with the principal, and other related persons or groups, with each being assigned specific responsibilities in accordance with their function and skills.

4. The maximization of the school system's human resources is the primary purpose of the induction program, and its foremost goal is to increase the school's success rate by improving the instructional experiences of the school's clients, its students.

A school system's induction program begins when new personnel come into the employ of the district and continues until each new faculty member has been fully orientated and has made satisfactory adjustments to his or her new environment. The process should include:

1. The principal should communicate with new staff members before the school year gets underway. Information regarding specific teaching assignments and schedules serve as aids in orienting these personnel to the school and community, and the mentor who has been identified and assigned to help the new staff member is included in this sharing of information.
2. During the initial meeting of the faculty, new faculty members are introduced to the staff. Separate gatherings of new staff should also occur, during which the following is reviewed, explained and discussed.
   a. nature of the student body and the surrounding community
   b. school philosophy and objectives
   c. school policies and procedures
   d. the role of supportive personnel in the school and district
   e. discipline policies and procedures
   f. attendance policies and procedures
   g. requisitioning procedures

The goals and purposes of this initial workshop are to help new staff members function effectively in their new setting, and for them to become known and feel comfortable with the school faculty. The NEA publication, entitled *The Beginning Teacher: A Practical Guide to Problem Solving* could be useful in this setting. (Krajewski and Shuman, 1979).

3. The induction program is a continuous one, minimally throughout the first year of the new staff member's employment, and might include:
   a. monthly discussions with the principal and other personnel during which new staff members are able to raise questions and air problems and experiences.
   b. individual conferences with the principal, coach and mentor, as needed.
   c. inter-class and inter-school visitations to observe demonstrations and other teaching techniques.

162 6

276

2385544

   d. assistance with attendance, discipline, and grading.
4. The principal's plan includes a yearly evaluation of the induction program, which provides for assurances that new staff members have been part of the program and have been encouraged to contribute.

The East Stroudsburg Area School District of East Stroudsburg, Pennsylvania was one of the school districts to participate as a pilot in the Commonwealth's induction program. Its induction program is viewed as one of the state's exemplary programs (Appendix D: Induction Program).

STAFF DEVELOPMENT

Staff development focuses on improving personnel performance by improving attitudes, information, and morale, and raising the quality of teaching. Attention is focused on goals and objectives; the teaching and learning process; current research and changes in education; and evaluation methodologies. Consideration is also given to the role of the teacher in responding to those societal issues that impact upon them and their schools.

Faculty development provides teachers with learning experiences designed to enhance their contribution to the school's mission and goals. Among the various faculty development programs are those intended to:

1. orient new employees to the school organization and their positions; and
2. improve faculty performance in their present assignments.

Virtually all organizations engage in employee development. Private businesses and corporations invest considerable sums of their finances and human effort in their programs of employee development. For example, in 1978, AT&T spent $700 million for training; this is more than three times the 1978 budget of the Massachusetts Institute of Technology. Some large corporations, including AT&T, operate their own universities in which a wide range of subjects are taught.

Teacher development is more than training techniques. This seemingly obvious statement; is made to counteract the tendency among persons in various professions and occupations to think of employee development only in terms of the delivery systems used: lectures, seminars, programmed instruction, and the like. The excessive fascination with techniques draws attention away from the basic objectives of employee development: goal-oriented learning and behavior change.

It would appear preferable to think of employee development as a process whereby these objectives can be attained. The following employee development process model is offered by the author for review and further discussion and study.

Employee development needs may be defined as performance limitations that are important to the school's organization, that can be remedied by development activities at least as effectively and efficiently as by any other means. This definition suggests the need for responses to the following:

1. Does a performance discrepancy exist?
2. Is it important to the organization?
3. Is it correctable through employee development?
4. Is employee development the most cost-effective solution that can be applied?
5. Does the organization have the resources to offer an effective program of employee development? (Mager and Pipe, 1970).

Once employee development needs are identified, the next step normally includes the conduct of training programs, since employee development needs generally exceed available resources. It is the administrators role to determine the employee development needs, determine their order of importance, allocate the resources, and integrate surviving programs into working plans.

School administrators must balance many factors including estimates of benefits, estimates of probable program success, principals' demands, and employee desires. Once priorities are established, it is desirable to codify the division in the form of an employee development plan that shows who will be trained, major programs, time frames, persons responsible, and resources and facilities to be used. (Otto & Glaser, 1970).

Once the plan is drawn up, the next task is to design and conduct the development programs that have been decided upon. This process takes on the following appearance: first, instructional objectives are set and program content is determined; next, training methods and techniques are decided upon; and, finally, the actual training or development takes place.

Instructional objectives are statement of what employees should know, believe, be able to do, do, or accomplish when the program is over. These objectives guide the selection of program content and methods and serve as the standards against which a particular program is evaluated.

The program's content refers to the material to be included in the employee development program and the general sequence in which it is to be presented. The nature of the participants and select learning process understandings are also given due consideration.

The final step in the employee development process is evaluation, a two level process. One deals with the extent to which the staff development process has met its instructional objectives. The other is more comprehensive, and is concerned with the extent to which the overall effort is effectively and efficiently satisfying the school's employee development needs.

One program of faculty development that has experienced substantial success is the program run by the faculty of the McCallie School, a private secondary school in Chattanooga, Tennessee. Three principles guide this program:

1. the quality of the educational program is the responsibility of the entire school community
2. faculty that shares the responsibility for the educational program is empowered to act, and
3. as the educational environment improves, a sense of community evolves within the school staff.

Descriptions are given of several salient features of the development program:

1. a mentor program, which is the central component of faculty development
2. a faculty roundtable which allows individual teachers to call a one hour meeting of the faculty on any issue of concern
3. faculty members participate in interviews of all incoming teachers and determine who will be hired
4. a monthly newsletter to which any member of the school community can submit an article
5. frequent formal and/or informal inter-visitation between classrooms
6. development of a common pedagogical vocabulary

SUMMARY

Education is influenced by the societal, political, and economic concerns of the period; its human resources development (personnel management) function is not excluded. The management of the school's personnel or human resources places in proper perspective the importance of: planning;

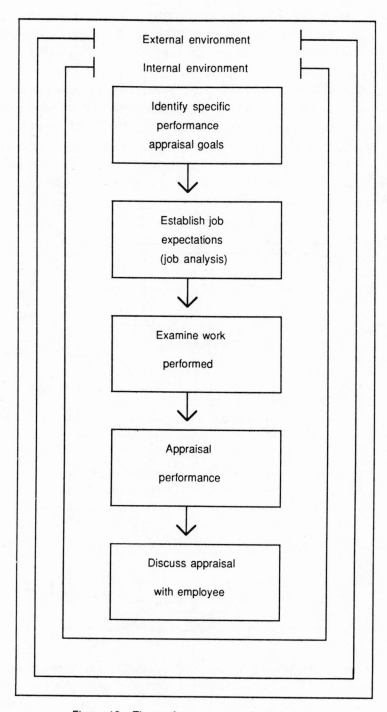

Figure 18 : The performance appraisal process

recruiting; screening; selecting; inservicing, inducting, evaluating; and developing of staff. While performing all of these responsibilities the principal must consider such external and internal influences as: organizational design; collective bargaining; staff participation and joint decision making; and communications. A familiarity and understanding of such matters as rules, regulations, laws governing human relationships, particularly as they appear within the school setting, will further enhance the effectiveness of the principal in his or her efforts to provide for a success oriented human resources program, which in turn provides increased assurances that the effective and productive school is truly realistic and achievable.

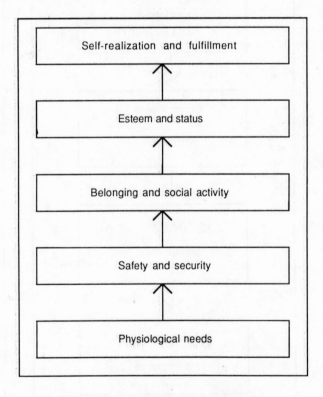

Figure 19 : Maslow's self actualization

In this chapter the author argues that a central challenge in education is to invite teachers to assume greater responsibility for the management of the school. While teachers traditionally have narrowly participated in such areas as instructional policy decisions, we urge the broadening of this to include teacher participation in the overall management of the school. School based management and teacher (first-line managers) empowerment, like their counterparts in the private sector, are being recognized more and more by school administrators and boards of education as a means of assuring their performing their functions effectively.

Literature on effective schools suggests that schools achieve close cooperation between teachers and principals, and among teachers themselves through participatory efforts. In the effective schools we see teacher participation as being associated with not only positive changes in individual attitudes, but also with enhanced group and organizational effectiveness.

DISCUSSION QUESTIONS

1. Consider several human resource planning objectives that you consider appropriate to insure the principal's effectiveness?
2. Why have teacher evaluation and appraisal programs caused such concern for all those who contribute their creation and are affected by them?
3. Have students, the school and its instructional program benefited as a result of collective bargaining?
4. What are some needs that are not addressed in this chapter's coverage of human resources development?
5. How can a good performance appraisal system help the school? What are the purposes of performance appraisal?
6. Discuss several contemporary challenges, trends and issues facing human resources management.
7. Discuss the impact of society upon the tasks of human resource planning.
8. How is a shared authority or decentralization compatible with the evaluation process?
9. Is a climate which encourages risk taking compatible with an evaluation program and compatability?
10. Discuss examples of social, economic and political problems that may impact upon the human resources of a school.
11. What are the fine distinctions between staff development and inservice education as each is viewed today?
12. Discuss how the principal separates supervision from evaluation.

REFERENCES

Albert, K. J.: *Handbook of Business Problem Solving.* New York, McGraw-Hill, 1980, pp. 1–3.

Armstrong, M. and Lorentzen, J. F.: *Handbook of Personnel Management Practice.* Englewood Cliffs, Prentice Hall, 1982, p. 3.

Barr, A.: Wisconsin studies of the measurement and prediction of teacher effectiveness: a summary of investigations. *Journal of Experimental Education. 30,* 1961, pp. 1–156.

Bookbinder, Robert M., et. al.: *Critical Issues in Education: A Guide for School Administrators.* Englewood Cliffs, Prentice Hall, 1972.

Buttram, J. L.: Effective teacher evaluation procedures. *Education Leadership.* April 1987, pp. 5–6.

Campbell, J. P.: Personnel training and development. *Annual Review of Psychology,* 1971.

Krajewski, R. J. and Shuman, R.B.: *The Beginning Teacher: A Practical Guide to Problem Solving.* Washington, National Educational Association, 1979.

Lewin, Kurt.: *Field Theory in Social Sciences.* New York, Harper & Row, 1951.

Likert, Rensis.: *The Human Organization.* New York, McGraw-Hill, 1967, p. 1.

Mager, P. and Pipe, P.: *Analyzing Performance Problems.* Belmont, Clear, Siegler, Fearson, 1978, pp. 11–16.

Maslow, Abraham H.: *Motivation and Personality.* New York, Harper and Row, 1970, p. 35.

McCleary, L. E. and Hensley, S. P.: *Secondary School Administration: Theoretical Basis for Professional Practice.* New York, Dodd-Mead, 1965, p. 28.

Naisbett, John.: *Megatrends, Ten New Directions Transforming Our Lives.* New York, Warner, 1982.

Otto, C. P. and Glaser, R. P.: How to prepare a training forecast. *Training and Development Journal, 24:* 3, 1970, pp. 24–29.

Chapter VI

THE ENVIRONMENTS OF
THE PROACTIVE PRINCIPAL

INTRODUCTION

How are they coping with the grimly urgent necessity to educate the children of the poor and the enraged as well as they educate the children of the comfortable and the satisfied? Are they equipped to elevate, or even preserve, academic standards under conflicting pressures from citizen censors, groaning taxpayers, state politicians, teachers' organizations, equipment manufacturers, and their own acquired prejudices? And are they able to get for the schools, which are their responsibility, the funds that schools require and that taxpayers so often begrudge?

(Bendiner, 1969)

Most of today's principals are motivated by critical issues in American education that surface from the school's internal and external environments. By the very nature of their roles as school-community leaders they are driven by historical, current and future issues, be they controversies, disagreements, consequences, outcomes, interests or debates, that confront both their schools and society.

Since these issues are infinite, this author has selected a limited, but significant, sampling for naming and inclusion in this, the final chapter of this book. In order to overcome this limitation, a portion of this chapter articulates the need for principals to have the faculty for vision, insight, and a sense of anticipation in identifying, among other things, the many issues that do and will confront them, their schools, and their communities.

There are numerous sources that are available to the principal in his or her search for, determining, or anticipating the school's needs. One such source is *The Annual Gallup Poll of the Public's Attitudes Toward the Public Schools.* This poll, which brings with it considerable validity and public confidence, has been produced annually for the past 22 years. It provides current information and data of extreme value to the principal. It is highlighted by one section entitled, *Biggest Problems Facing Local Public Schools.*

171

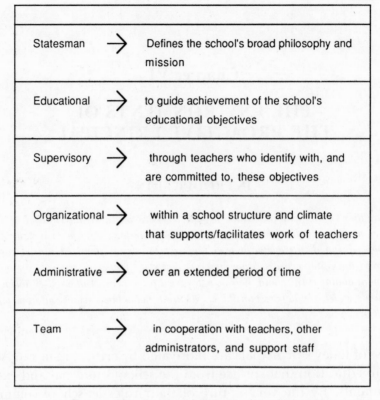

Figure   20 : Leadership roles in the principalship

Some of the data and information appearing in the most recent (1991) Gallup Poll *under biggest problems facing local public schools,* appear below:

1. use of drugs
2. lack of discipline
3. lack of proper financial support
4. large schools/overcrowding
5. poor curriculum/poor standards
6. difficulty getting good teachers
7. pupils lack of interest/truancy
8. low teacher pay
9. crime/vandalism
10. integration/busing
11. parents' lack of interest
12. drinking/alcoholism
13. teachers' lack of interest
14. moral standards (Stanley M. Elam 1991)

Some of these issues are treated in this final chapter of the text and they offer the principal some direction or possible approaches for responding to these issues, issues which are now very much a part of the school's internal and external environments.

In order for the principal to adequately respond to these pressing issues and also to anticipate new and possibly even more complex school-community related concerns, the school's leader must have a vision. He or she must be able to foresee many of those matters that are and will be faced. This view is supported by numerous management studies, writings, and also the author's personal experiences.

For example, in a recent issue of *Management Review,* the results of a six-year survey of more than 7,500 managers responded to what they admired most in leaders was published. Twenty (20) popular characteristics were included in this survey, and the one which ranked third highest, with 67 percent, was forward looking (vision). The authors of this *MR* article also made mention of a 1989 study which had determined that the ability to convey a strong sense of vision was a trait or personal characteristic most frequently described as of increased importance for leaders in the year 2000. Clearly, this study concluded, *vision* is the executive skill of the future.

In *On Becoming a Leader,* Warren Bennis wrote: The first basic ingredient of leadership is a guiding vision. The leader has a clear idea of what he or she wants to do, professionally and personally, and the strength to persist in the face of setbacks, even failures. He said that leaders manage the dream and have the capacity to create a compelling vision, one that takes people to a new place, and then to translate that vision into reality.

Principals with vision know what's happening in their school-communities, they know the economic realities, they know the social and cultural backgrounds and concerns, they can sense needs and change. Most importantly, they know how to pull information and experience together in order to provide direction to their schools and communities. They envision a mission, set achievable goals and objectives, and cause their constituents, as *participatory stakeholders* to effect and produce positive and constructive movement to occur.

This next decade will present new and difficult challenges for those who administer the schools of this nation, and the principal of today and in the future, points the direction for the educational enterprise. To the extent that this position of leadership, within the framework of the school organization, can be made more effective, the school will be improved, more productive, and the needs of our society well-served.

THE PRINCIPAL AS A LEADER

We all recognize that there are similarities between business and education, however, there are differences too. The education of a child is not the same as the production of an airplane.

> During one of the many board of education meetings that this author participated in, one boardmember, an engineer for one of the major airplane manufacturers of this nation, turned to me and stated, *Why can't you who work in education do as we do? We just built the F-14, an airplane that has limitless capabilities.* We know exactly what it is capable of doing. *Why can't you do the same with the students who travel through this school system?* Oddly enough, that day's newspapers carried a story about the crash of one of these F-14s. When I asked the board member just how this could have come about? He simply responded, *human error.*

A failed experiment in the education of a child cannot be written off as human error with the same nonchalance that business can apply to an unsuccessful or failed product line. Further, the measures of educational effectiveness are more elusive than the measures that industry can use to gauge its services. On the other hand, the leadership required to assure a quality education and learning of the school's students and the production of an industrial product does require numerous similarities and commonalities.

A consistent finding in studies of excellent businesses includes the flagging of the importance of leadership. Bennis and Nanus (1985) noted, organizations cannot be successful without effective leadership, the key factor in the ability of a business to translate its vision into reality. Peters and Waterman (1982) furthered this position when they proposed that excellent companies achieve their excellence through the efforts of ordinary people, however these very same companies have been truly blessed with unusual leadership.

The importance of this very same leadership to the organization is echoed in the effective schools research, particularly the leadership of the principal. It was Jane Eisner (1979) who concluded: The key to a school's success is the "principal principle": the strong administrator with vision and ability can make an enormous difference.

Current research findings of effective organizations (schools) and effective leaders suggest that the principal fulfill such functions and roles as:

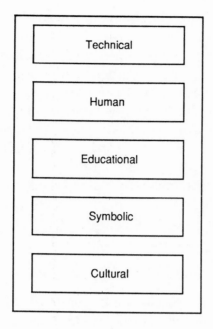

Figure 21 : Leadership forces in the principalship

values promoter and protector, teacher empowerer, instructional leader, and climate manager.

As the values promoter and protector, the principal of the excellent school is able to provide understandable statements of a vision of values. In order to influence others, the leader offers a clarity of purpose, knows what is to be accomplished, and is certain of what that vision and values require. This clarification of the school's mission reduces those barriers to school improvement which are bound to arise. This effective principal communicates this vision and values. Peters and Waterman (1982) proposed that one key to this needed communication is redundancy, a boorish consistency over long periods of time in support of one or two transcending values. Thus, the effective principal is seen as one who emphasizes, clarifies, and reemphasizes that which remains the same, the vision and values that provide for the school's direction.

The effective principal further communicates this vision and values in a continuing manner by building trust through the maintenance of a consistent position. Bennis and Nanus describe this trust as the lubricant that makes it possible for organizations to work. These effective principals are predictable, maintain positions that are consistent with the schools' values, publicize their positions, and are committed to them.

As the successful teacher empowerer, the effective principal has developed such essential skills as: delegating, stretching the abilities of others, and encouraging educated risk taking (Garfield 1986). This principal is not threatened by delegating authority and redefining his or her role from the giver of orders to the developer of human potential. He or she may consider the following as worthy areas of teacher empowerment: curriculum development, the evaluation of student achievement, the selection of instructional materials, the planning and presenting of staff development programs, determining instructional styles and strategies, scheduling, mentoring, and staff employment.

VISIONARY LEADERSHIP ON AN UNEVEN PLAYFIELD

Although the *playfield* is seldom, if ever, level, the school principal is expected to provide a clear vision of what is required, to do things right, and as a leader, to do all the right things (Ovard, 1990). He or she is expected to be imaginative and creative and build programs that are responsive, and promote excellence, while controlling entities mandate a curriculum, program, and practices with limited and limiting opportunities for creativity, choice, and change.

While serving as an elementary principal, I was also responsible for the district's transportation program, I received a call from a complaining parent. *Did you know that the bus, going up the Centerport Hill, was traveling better than sixty miles per hour?* I explained to this extremely disturbed parent that the school bus is unable to travel at that speed when making its way up a hill of this magnitude. She asked, How do you know this? I explained further, that I was aware of the limitations of the school bus and also that I had driven a bus myself over a period of years. The parent responded, Thank you, I wasn't aware of this. A few moments later my phone rang a second time. This call was from another concerned parent who called to express her complaint. Her comment went something like this. I just saw that bus traveling up the Centerport Hill and I don't think it's going to make it! These two parents had observed the very same bus, but actually saw two different things.

Also, during a school board meeting, one board member approached me and stated, *We must have that fifth grade teacher fired.* She was teaching her class about Viet Nam. Surely, this teacher is incompetent and doesn't belong in our system. A few moments later, another board member arrived at the same meeting room, approached me, and stated, *We have a fifth grade teacher who ought to be commended. She was teaching her class about Viet Nam and did such a magnificent job of it. She is without a doubt one of the district's most effective teachers.* These two board members were expressing their views of the very same teacher.

Principals have learned in an age of single, divorced and foster parents that they must not only know the parents of the school's students, they must also know who the legal guardian is, and who has custody of the student. They have also learned that one principal can be sued for not providing a delinquent student with all his legal rights and due process, while elsewhere, a principal is applauded for patrolling the school halls with a loudspeaker and a baseball bat. They now know that student records must be open to parents; however, the of-age student can prohibit a parent from seeing them. How does the principal maintain a vision under such conditions and circumstances? It is suggested that the stability of a vision for the future accompanies a confidence that comes with holding fast to some basic values and guidelines and also a preparedness for some risk taking.

> *Progress always involves risks. You can't steal second base while keeping your foot on first.*
> Frederick Wilcox

The principal, while struggling for effectiveness and productivity must maintain sight of the value and importance of education for our society and for each individual. This country has moved from an education of the elite and education only for those who had leisure time to education for free people, education for females, education for children in grades one through eight, education through high school, education for all those desiring a college and university level opportunity, education for the blind and deaf, education for the handicapped, education for at-risk students, and education for the gifted and talented.

Principals must resist trends, the efforts of special interest groups, policies and financial restrictions that encourage elitism in education, restrictions on students in curriculum choices, restrictions in post high school opportunities, non-participation in school programs because of fee structures, and reductions in programs for handicapped or established programs that reduce the educational opportunities for *All American Youth*.

We are in error when we confuse quantity with quality. When these terms are mistaken one for the other, we confuse the issue. For example, school systems have been noted for having increased their graduation requirements and at the same time these very same school systems have done little to improve the quality of their original curricula. Another year of English for a student who cannot write well is not a solution to this limitation. *Writing* is the answer. Make adjustments in the number of students assigned to each teacher and assign writing. Or, if teacher work load cannot be reduced, find creative ways by which writing can be read and students encouraged with appropriate feedback.

New ideas are everywhere. All they need is the environment to make them happen.

Increasing quantity is not the solution to improving quality, nor is there reason to assume that more quantity in a related skill will transfer into improved education in a specific skill. The search for quality must be emphasized.

Surely, schools cannot assume responsibility for resolving all of society's problems, however, the principal must define and communicate those areas as they relate to the school's responsibility. Sex education was added to the curriculum because society had become more promiscuous, and now the school is responsible for the growing number of teenage pregnancies. Integration became the law of the land and it has become the schools' responsibility to bring solutions to this societal issue. Critics measure school success by scores on national tests, but there are no points scored on the SAT or ACT tests for combating drug use, and knowing how to manage in a society as a single parent.

SCHOOL AND COMMUNITY LINKAGE

A cooperative endeavor between a school or school district and a corporation, business, civic organization, college or university, foundation, governmental agency, or other entity where a formal arrangement is made to share resources (including human, material, or financial) with the ultimate objective of promoting the interests of the schools. From *Partnerships in Education: Trends of the Future,* U.S. Department of Education Survey

Community groups, businesses, corporations, civic organizations, foundations, governmental agencies, and colleges and universities are seen as reaching with planned, organized efforts for long-term school/ community commitments. In one community a local company lent its engineers and accounting personnel to schools that were seeking additional help in preparing their students for the state-mandated math proficiency examination. Nationally, the Chamber of Commerce launched regional workshops on business involvement in schools and published a comprehensive book, *Business and Education: Partners for the Future.* There are mounting examples where partnerships in education are appearing, at all levels, and will all kinds of groups. Private group and individual contributions to public schools is one of today's most significant connections in American education.

> In the East Stroudsburg Area School District, scholarship money for post secondary and college education of its students grew from less then $2,000 in 1973 to more than $30,000 in 1987. The funds for these ongoing scholarships and student loans were derived primarily through this author's efforts to link the school system with individuals and foundations within the community.

Business interests in schools have advanced in many arenas for obvious reasons. Individual schools have adoptive businesses and corporations, and chambers of commerce are increasing their interest in linking up with the schools.

> The Pocono Mountains Chamber of Commerce elected this author (who was then one of the county superintendents of schools) to its post as president. This same chamber of commerce repeated this effort to link itself with the local schools when it again elected one of the local educators (another county superintendent) to its post of president, just four years after the earlier election had occurred).

Although business leaders are becoming the strongest allies of school reform, other community groups have increasingly impacted upon the schools. This broader society connection is seen as another means of achieving a common goal, better and more effective schools.

Although many national and state partnership ventures in school-community partnerships have been of note, such arrangements at the local level is where it really is happening. Here is where relationships between neighbors are developed. Here is where the reestablishment of a sense of community, a truly great need today, has a chance for some success. It is here that relationships are developed and nourished between the school and its business-industrial-professional community. This linkage binds the school and its community.

Most urban school systems have experienced substantive and creative partnerships that have contributed to their school-community relationships. Although smaller school systems throughout the nation have fewer active partnerships, it does appear that rural schools that do have partnerships have more of their schools participating in such arrangements, percentage-wise, than urban districts.

This may be partially due to the kinds and numbers of resources available to the urban school system, there are fewer large corporate resources in the rural areas, and these smaller businesses tend to be skill-specific, not lending themselves to the broader training offered in schools. Also, there is an increased tendency for rural and suburban workers to commute to their jobs in metropolitan areas thereby limiting these rural and suburban schools of the volunteers and support base they need to promote school-community ties. This is compounded by the extensive mobility of our populations, which has substantially reduced this essential element, often referred to as community.

> During my frequent visits to the district's schools, while serving as superintendent, I found upon questioning elementary school students in various classrooms, that a majority of those students were transferees from schools throughout the country. Many would note further that this was but one of several transfers they experienced because of multiple family relocations.

Because of this, and other factors, survey data collected from researchers of the U.S. Department of Education concluded, that there is need for extra efforts to encourage the smaller, more rural districts to use community resources and perhaps consider the greater need for these smaller districts to look to regional alliances and statewide efforts in organizing such partnership efforts.

It is readily apparent that the essential ingredients for purposeful and effective involvement of the economic and power influences within a community are strong, consistent communications, proactive-visionary leadership, and real effort. The untapped partnership possibilities are limitless: business, volunteer, civic, and professional and trade associations that have a contribution to make to the quality of the schools and the community around them.

The Boston City Schools, through the urging of then Superintendent Robert Spillane, was among the first formally organized programs to link an outside community resource with an individual school, a movement known as adopt-a-school that has spread coast-to-coast. The impetus behind adopt-a-school in Boston was a clear recognition by schools and business of the need to decrease the school dropout rate, improve academic achievement, and increase the percentage of students pursuing higher education and those placed in jobs. This effort was furthered by Tri-Lateral Council which layed the foundation for a unique collaboration between the schools and community, the Boston Compact, whose parties include the schools, business, higher education, labor, and the city government. Its commitments included:

1. The schools promise to improve attendance rates, lower dropout rates, and increase math and reading scores.

2. Business and higher education promise to place students in jobs or enroll them on the campuses.

In Memphis, Tennessee, because of court-ordered busing and other factors, the city's schools lost 35,000 white students within five years. Student achievement had declined, and public perception of the schools were commonly negative or apathetic.

The school administration persuaded several of the community's power brokers to serve on a school/business advisory committee. Business was encouraged to loan to the district its most successful public relations executives and the foremost community service organization was inspired to adopt the schools as its special project.

Because of this adopt the schools project:

1. a senior center adopted the kindergarten classes at one elementary school
2. a baking company, along with other projects, sponsored a field trip to the area space center for students who improved their grades
3. a hospital sponsored a student health fair with hospital staff conducting a variety of health screening tests for some 800 high school students
4. a bank provided summer intern jobs and helped with senior job interviews at the high school
5. the Welcome Wagon, promoted attendance and good behavior, by turning part of the junior high school cafeteria into a restaurant as a special treat for students with high achievement and helped compose and print a student handbook

The Memphis program, a people program, as opposed to a money program, includes these essential ingredients:

1. a strong school administrator committed to community involvement
2. a business leader with the ability to open corporate doors and willing to set up interviews with business leaders
3. a program director dedicated to the program's purpose and who articulates its needs to the business community
4. principals convinced that community involvement can be effective and enhance the education process

The Greater Wilmington Development Council was a private, nonprofit, public interest organization that identified and analyzed community problems, set priorities, and developed solutions and actions to deal with them. Its Education Project boosted community confidence by:

1. targeting a series of newsletters on public education to some 1,500 local decision makers

2. arranged a series of in-depth school tours for corporate executives and major realtors
3. prepared a thorough and sophisticated *Cultural Resources Guide* for teachers to encourage them to use community resources
4. developed business sponsorship of curriculum improvement in computer technology and mathematics
5. established a Principals' Center to improve the management skills of school administrators
6. used radio to reach the community, drive-time radio features on public education weekly and monthly talk show on specific issues
7. initiated a mini-grant program for teachers to support innovative classroom projects
8. established a School Recognition Program to provide a small grant and public recognition to the schools with the greatest improvement in attendance, student retention, and achievement
9. helped develop a project to involve volunteers in tutoring (Anne C. Lewis, 1986)

It is said that there more than 46,000 partnership projects in operation across the country, and some that appear to be the most substantive and worthy of note are:

1. The Learning Exchange in Kansas City, Missouri
2. The Cleveland Scholarship Program, Inc.
3. The Academic Internship Program in Charlotte-Mecklenburg, North Carolina.
4. Community leadership in South St. Paul, Minnesota
5. Private Initiative in Public Education (PIPE) in Seattle, Washington

THE COLLABORATIVE SCHOOL

The *collaborative school* is one in which its professional educators voluntarily seek to improve the school and their own skills through teamwork. In this school the adults observe one another, communicate, share what they know, share leadership, and talk openly about education and the quality of instruction they offer their pupils.

There is substantial evidence that the nature of relationships among the faculty who live and work in the school does influence the school's quality, character, and the level of success of its students. In spite of this knowledge, collaboration in schools does not come easily. Although the principal is identified as the one person most likely to make the school more collaborative, we find it difficult at times to determine who within the school or outside the school initiates, encourages, and sustains the collegial behavior among the teachers of that school.

> *I can think of no statement that so well captures both the importance and the difficulty of developing collaboration within a school. If we're serious about helping schools to become places characterized by cooperation, collegiality, and talking about teaching, I think we must address a number of tough questions:*
>
> 1. *How can the taboo be overcome that prevents teachers from making themselves, their ideas, and their teaching visible to other teachers, to parents, and to administrators?*
> 2. *How can principals' relationships with other principals, with teachers, and with students be transformed from adversarial and competitive to more collaborative and cooperative?*
> 3. *How can students learn to work more cooperatively when the reward system and the expectations of parents, teachers, and college admissions officers tilt toward competition?*
> 4. *What can those outside schools contribute?*
> 5. *Under what conditions will teachers, parents, students, and principals, most of whom would prefer more collaboration, come to abandon competition and isolation in favor of collaboration and cooperation?*
> 6. *Finally, once committed to collaboration, what can anyone do to interrupt the embedded, crusty culture of competitive schools and move toward the development of a lasting collaborative school culture?* Roland S. Barth

Collaboration within a school may include a range of practices and can be encouraged by such formal programs as organizational, personnel and curriculum development. The collaborative school is a composite of beliefs and practices that is best characterized by these elements:

1. The belief, based on effective schools research, that the quality of education is largely determined by what happens at the school site.
2. The conviction, also supported by research findings, that instruction is most effective in a school environments characterized by norms of collegiality and continuous improvement.
3. The belief that teachers are professionals who should be given responsibility for the instructional process and held accountable for its outcomes.
4. The use of a wide range of practices and structures that enable administrators and teachers to work together on school improvement.
5. The involvement of teachers in decisions about school goals and the means for achieving the (Smith and Scott, 1990).

The collaborative school has much in common with the school team model of staff organization described by Finn (1985):

> *An accumulating body of research about the characteristics of unusually effective schools indicates that schools in which children learn the most usually have a collegial staffing*

structure and a strong sense of common purpose among teachers and administrators. This often described in the abstract as a shared moral order or a school ethos, but what it comes down to is that the professional staff functions as a team: it has clear objectives, works together smoothly, shares goals that transcend those of individual members and shares a sense of responsibility for the mutual enterprise.

For some, the term *collaboration* means administrators sharing authority with teachers and involving them in decisions. However, *collaboration* is a more dynamic practice of teachers working together, professionally, to improve their practice of teaching. It is the informally and formally structured interaction among teachers about instruction that sets it aside from earlier models of democratic management and participative decision making, even though these elements do appear in these concepts. The collaborative school then provides a climate and structure that encourages teachers as professional to work together and with the principal to encourage school improvement and professional growth.

A STATISTICAL VIEW OF AMERICAN YOUTH

It is in the interest of the principal to have an understanding of the demographics and a population overview: past, present, and future.

There appeared an increase in this nation's birth rate during the early 1980s, thereby reversing, somewhat, the continuing decline in the numbers of children attending the nation's schools. This is but one of the more recent definite and dramatic changes appearing in the demographics of our nation's communities and school districts.

The following statistical information was excerpted from a study by the William T. Grant Foundation Commission on Youth and America's Future published in June 1987.

1. The number of American youth is shrinking dramatically. Between 1980 and 1996, this nation's population, ages 15–24, is expected to fall 21%, from approximately 43 million to 34 million. Young people as a percentage of the nation's population will also decline from 18.8% to 13%.
2. Today's youth will live longer than any other generation of Americans. A white woman aged 20 can expect to live to age 80, a white man to age 73.
3. Drug abuse peaked during the late 1970s, and except for cocaine use, has diminished significantly since then.
4. Youth today are living longer at home, marrying later, and having

fewer children. Nearly half will wait until they are 24 or older to marry. More than half of all women 22–24 years old have yet to bear their first child.

5. Of young adults ages 25–29, 86% are high school graduates, twice the percentage of 1940. Still, students from poor families, regardless of race, are three or four times more likely to drop out of school than those from more affluent households. Black youth are completing high school at nearly the same rate as whites, but Hispanic youth are twice as likely to drop out of school before graduation as white non-Hispanic teenagers.

A significant transition process engaging most youths since the ending of World War II in 1945 is the acquisition of those skills and experiences necessary to earn an adequate living during their later adult lives. This has become an increasingly difficult and uncertain task. Economic unpredictability, technological advances, growing international interdependency, and the globalization of production have created uncertainties about the future prospects of even the most powerful firms and the most crucial occupations. It is said, with considerable justification, that this nation has become a service providing one as opposed to having been an industrial leader among the nations of the world.

Social trends too, have contributed to the uncertainties. Today's young women are well aware that they will have to provide for themselves for some significant period of years, both before and after marriage.

By the late 1960s, about half of all recent high school graduates were enrolling in college within a year of high school graduation. Many found themselves ill-prepared or insufficiently motivated and dropped out. In less than 50 years, the percentage of young adults who completed high school has more than doubled, while the percentage of those who complete four or more years of college has almost quadrupled.

The high school completion rate of American youth rose steadily from the end of World War II until the late 1970s, then leveled off at about 86% of the eligible population, where it remained for a short period. An upward trend of postsecondary education enrollments continued for young women during the 1970s, however the enrollment rates for young men declined abruptly after the Vietnam War ended and then turned marginally lower into the early 1980s.

Of greatest significance, to the principal, as related to this presentation on demographics and the American youth is the matter of poverty and

dropouts. Regardless of race, students from poor families are far more
likely to drop out than those from non-poor households. The percentage
of poor white dropouts substantially exceeds that of poor blacks. Completely reversing post World War II trends, today's youth marry later,
plan smaller families, have children later in life, and have fewer children
than their parents did. These changes are observable across race, ethnic,
and socioeconomic subdivisions of the populations.

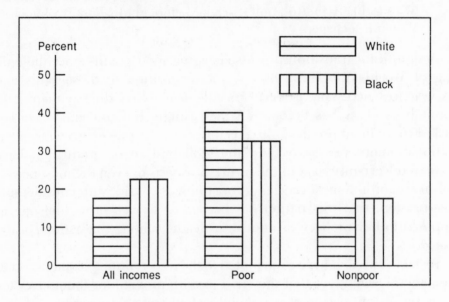

Figure 22 : Poverty and dropouts

Source: Census Bureau, unpublished OEO tabulations

Delayed marriages is unquestionably associated with increased postsecondary education of young women. Almost 60% of all current 20–24
year old women have never been married, more than double the
unmarried population at this age in 1960.

The percentage of unmarried has risen steadily, from 28% in 1960 to
58% in 1986. This reflects the fact that fewer women are marrying during
their teens and also that in 1986 almost 19 of every 20 teenage girls were
single. Because the trend to later marriage has been gradual, related
alterations in the living arrangement of young Americans have escaped
much attention. More than 1 million teenage women became pregnant in
1984 and 480,000 gave birth. Almost 10,000 births involved girls less than
15 years of age, and there were more than 450,000 pregnancies and

167,000 births to 15–17 year olds. Of the total births to teenagers, more than half were out-of-wedlock. Disadvantaged young women are three to four more times more likely to become unwed mothers than advantaged teenagers, regardless of race. Birth rates should be a concern of today's educators. Teenage pregnancy may be decreasing but this is still a significant area of concern.

PROBLEMS IN SCHOOL–COMMUNITY RELATIONS

School-community relations are *never* trouble free. Although the basic causes of problems in school-community relations are complex and may vary with the nature of the various communities and their schools, two general factors do appear to be common: (1) professional challenges to community norms, and (2) community challenges to professional norms.

The first factor deals with the efforts of educators to change the educational program or system, efforts which are at times at odds with community norms. Aids education, sex education, flexible-modular scheduling, alternative education programs, year-round education and integration are but examples of innovations that educators have introduced which challenge the norm structure of the community, thereby causing conflict in school-community relations.

The second general factor which introduces problems in school-community relations appears when the community intensifies its efforts to redirect or control what may be occurring in the schools. This may be seen to arise when the community or special interest groups within it raise objections and attack the schools' innovations.

There are also instances when, in the eyes of the community, the schools appear to be moving too slowly when responding to select school-community concerns and issues. Also, the reverse, when the schools appear to be responding too quickly to some of the issues facing it.

The principal of particular junior high school introduce *sniff dogs* as his means of attacking supposed major drug problem in that school. Nothing within the approved school district drug policy contained this method of attack upon the drug issue.

The result, was the creation of two camps within the community. One that strongly supported the action of this principal and the other which stood in opposition. Each camp, through direct communications with the board of education and letters to the editor in the local newspapers, helped create a split within the school-community that consumed the total school-community for a period of some time.

The problems in school-community relations are not easily ameliorated. However, more and effective communications between the school and its community, and greater community involvement and participation in the school's programs, services and activities can reduce the likelihood and potential for the appearance of major.

It is generally believed, and with reason, that a key to improving school-community relations is greater parent and public involvement in school affairs. Surely, there are problems associated with parental and community involvement in the schools, however these can be overcome when principals are prepared appropriately for this innovation. The school administrator needs to understand that in the final analysis, involvement is to be viewed primarily as a means rather than an end. Any involvement of others, regardless of the form it takes, should ultimately result in improving education, if the involvement is to be judged worthwhile.

Through involvement, parents and other citizens will become more knowledgeable about school affairs, and because of this they are: better informed about student-learning in the school, more understanding of the problems that the school faces, and more supportive of the school's efforts to improve the educational program. Also, through participation of this nature the school benefits by receiving ideas, expertise, and further human resources, and provides increased assurances that the school will be evaluated fairly and effectively. Meaningful citizen involvement can strengthen confidence in and commitment to the school, while making schools more responsible to citizens' diverse concerns (Don Davies, 1973).

PERSONALIZING THE SCHOOL ENVIRONMENT

Personalization is a matter of organizational design rather than of individual teachers' values and practices.

(Milbrey W. McLaughlin, et al. 1990)

In a school which prides itself with a personalized environment, relations among students, parents, teachers, and principal are founded upon close and familiar knowledge about one another. Persons in such an environment subscribe to an ethic of caring that reaches beyond the boundaries of formal, classroom-based functions (Noddings 1988).

Principals must be interested in the personalization of the school because it is a powerful means of promoting its clients' commitment to the learning that is to occur therein. Teachers who have specific knowledge of their students' learning styles and current understandings find this to be particularly important in engaging those students who are disinterested, unmotivated, alienated, and at risk. Learning is encouraged and promoted when a teacher's personal knowledge of the learner is such that associations are made between the student's life and the curriculum.

Teachers who work within a personalized school environment have traditionally rated personal contact with and the ability to get to know students as being among the most rewarding and satisfying elements of their teaching experiences. Further, according to a 1989 survey of secondary school teachers, the Center for Research on the Context of Secondary School Teaching (CRC) at Stanford University had determined that a strong relationship exists between the extent of teachers' knowledge of their students and their sense of professional efficacy.

Accountability, in its most fundamental form, is engendered in the personalized environment, for neither teachers nor students can conceal themselves within this condition. Particularly, students who are at risk or who are disengaged from schooling are bound to find this to be a significant source for their immediate need, that of motivation. This personal affirmation increases their sense of belonging or personal connection with their schools and is mirrored in their out-of-school lives.

In schools that have constructed personalized school environments we find:

1. a cheerful demeanor of students and the respect they show one another and their teachers
2. teachers recognize their students as individuals and give them personal support
3. students move from disaffection and failure toward success
4. a sense of family and of caring for each individual permeates classrooms, lunchrooms, and corridors
5. students are enthusiastic about school and attendance problems are minimal
6. predominantly positive sentiments about the school as a workplace

A personalized school environment is the product of deliberate and strategic choices about organizational structures and routines. The following features of organizational design are most critical to a strong ethos of personalization (Milbrey W. McLaughlin, et al. 1990):

1. school-level structures for communication and collective problem solving
2. broader teacher roles

3. personalized instructional strategies, and
4. strategies for revitalization and recommitment

Schools that clearly assign top priority to the task of establishing and maintaining a personalized educational environment view their function as being beyond structures, routines, and roles. In these school settings, authority is both interpersonal and institutional. In these schools there appears a vested authority in the personalized working relations among its clients and one in which students and teachers together are active participants in the enterprise of education.

THE SCHOOL AND ITS CULTURAL DIVERSITY

Schools are increasingly multicultural throughout the United States and this demographic shift raises a number of substantive issues and poses further expectations upon the leadership role of the principal.

In its *An Imperiled Generation: Saving Urban Schools,* the Carnegie Foundation's 1988 report notes:

America must confront with urgency the crisis in urban schools. Bold aggressive action is needed now to avoid leaving a huge and growing segment of the nation's youth civically unprepared and economically unempowered.

Although this report concentrates upon urban schools and the crisis they now face, this major failure of social policy reaches into the suburban and rural schools of the nation as well. It focuses on the largest minority population, African Americans, but the implications apply to all minority populations. The discussion rests upon two assumptions.

First America is still a dangerously racist, classist, and sexist society and that education as the great equalizer is an illusion; schools have for too long been relied upon as agents of social change. Secondly, cultural diversity refers to the coexistence of groups distinctive in ethnic or cultural patterns, in an atmosphere that favors the preservation of such groups within the system. In such an environment, one's own culture is not lost, repressed, or denied. Students are, instead, encouraged to hold onto their rich past and to embellish those roots with new experiences.

Studies and research that have reported upon African American students have consistently found their underachievement to be persistent, pervasive, and disproportionate. Further, there does not appear to be a region, state, city or school system that has successfully educated the majority of African American students in their charge, a factor that

underscores the importance of reviewing and reflecting upon the implications of cultural diversity in our nation's schools.

In American public schools, African American students are more
likely than other students to:

1. Be placed in special education
2. Be placed in vocational education programs

These students are less likely than other students to:

1. Be placed in gifted and talented programs
2. Be placed in academic tracks
3. Be exposed to adequate math, science, and social studies

Also, these students are often given no indication of a connection
between their schooling and their later life (The Council of the Great
City Schools, 1987).

Explanations offered that account for this condition generally fit into
four categories: (1) cultural differences theories, (2) structural inequality
theories, (3) social deficit theories, and (4) genetic deficit theories

Hale-Benson (1986) and Wilson (1987), proponents of the cultural
differences theories suggest that this widescale failure is due to a poor fit
between the curriculum and the culture of the learner. Bowles and
Gintis (1976) and Suzuki (1977) are among those who argue that there are
systemic problems within institutions in America that foster inequalities,
forcing specific groups to fit into predetermined categories in society.
Jencks et al (1972), social deficit theorists argue that this failure to
perform well academically is rooted in social conditions; inferior home
environments and low socioeconomic status. It is Jensen (1969) and
Shockley (1972) who insisted that the African American child, or Hispanic
child, cannot perform well academically because his or her parents
could not perform well; the inability has been genetically passed on.

Current scholarship posits that there are no significant differences in
the learning capacities of different racial groups. Further, the effective
schools literature demonstrates that minority students can overcome the
effects of a poor home environment and do well in school (Edmonds
1979; Willie 1987). To completely understand the problem requires a
synthesis of the *cultural differences theories* and the *structural inequality
theories,* for they offer promising means for understanding the situation.

The importance of the principal in setting the tone for the school
appears consistently in the research about school climate, principal

leadership, school culture, and effective schools (Lomotey 1987; Edmonds 1979; Leithwood and Montgomery 1982). These principals who effectively deal with this very sensitive issue:

1. believe that all students can learn and they include this belief in their goals
2. communicate these feelings to their teachers, other staff members, parents, and students
3. are concerned with the least successful students in their schools
4. are not satisfied that, on average, their students are doing above average work
5. demonstrate confidence in the ability of their students to learn
6. are committed to seeing that all students receive all that they can to ensure their success
7. are compassionate for, and understanding of the students and the communities in which they live (Lomotey 1985)
8. broaden the base of recognized achievement, including non-traditional accomplishments, good attendance or punctuality
9. emphasizes the critical role of parents in fostering the development of successful students

Minorities constitute an increasing portion of the students now in attendance in the nation's schools. In California, minorities are already in the majority in the state's public schools (*Education Week*, 1988).

Surely, it must be understood that schools are not in themselves social change agents, for they are controlled by and interdependent with other societal institutions. However, educators, in their efforts to improve the state of American education must look to providing linkages with other arenas of the society, and contribute to bringing about equity for all of their students.

THE SCHOOL AND ITS ANTI-DRUG PROGRAMS

One of the tests of leadership is the ability to recognize a problem before it becomes an emergency.

Arnold H. Glasow

There are a number of schools and school systems throughout the United States that operate comprehensive and effective drug programs. They have determined how to put wide ranging anti-drug programs in place, and how to get substantial results. These schools and school systems have produced a wide range of successful and effective ideas that are bound to prove useful to the school principal who may be looking for some direction while responding to this school-community problem.

Certain well-defined basics form the framework for each of these successful school anti-drug programs. What follows is a broad outline of those basics that have been culled from these programs.

> ***Do an assessment.*** A formal assessment of the school's drug problem is necessary because this will provide baseline data from which to design the anti-drug program. This evaluation removes the element of guesswork, pinpoints the real enemy, not just the perceived one. An effective school-community survey outlines the basics for school personnel, providing data about such things as whether alcohol use or cocaine use is more prevalent among area school children and at what ages and how youngsters are introduced to drugs. This information offers the principal an overview needed to shape an appropriate drug-education program. Periodic follow-up or benchmark surveys should also be utilized to provide school personnel with some understanding of where the school's drug-education program is succeeding and where it may require some improvements. Regular and continuous surveys provide the kind of continuous data that make the possibility of anti-drug grants more likely.

> ***Present a strong, no-drugs policy.*** An anti-drug program, to be effective, requires a clear, firm policy that is consistently enforced. This policy should provide easily understood definitions of all drugs, details what constitutes violations (possession, use, sale), and outlines sanctions and corrective measures. The policy should contain evidence within its contents that parents, students, community, legal authorities, and school are all part of an alliance, all committed to the success of this framework within which the school's anti-drug program will operate. Although the school's anti-drug policy must be tough, it cannot be purely punitive. Alternatives to student suspensions and expulsions are of importance and should be very much a part of the policy. An alternative is one that assures a therapeutic anti-drug policy that provides for the punishment of rule-breakers and also arranges for counseling and treatment. An example of this approach is the alternative consequences drug policy under which first time offenders are given the choice of suspension or remaining in school if they agree to participate (contract) in a designated counseling program. The policy provides for the consequences for various types and degrees of offenses, extends the limits to include off campus school and non-school sponsored student activities, and extends its coverage beyond the traditional school day and school year. (See Appendix 6A: Alcohol and Drug Abuse Policy)

> ***Inform the total school-community.*** Make sure that the policy is known.

To be effective, the policy must be known and fully understood by all of the school-community's stakeholders: students, parents, teachers, administrators, board of education, non-parents, businesses, community agencies, and police. Schools have been known to require teachers to review, read and discuss anti-drug policies with students in the classrooms and during parent-teacher conferences. Principals expected to share the contents of these policies in student handbooks, building newsletters, during various parent-group and task force meetings and through the various media. The superintendent, or district office, furthers this effort to inform the school system's publics by including this within the district newsletters and other printed literature such as brochures and news releases, and aggressively seeks to have its voice heard or seen in the various media.

Follow-up program. The follow-up program is really an after care program. Once the school system has created a firm drug policy and enforced it consistently, oftentimes complacency tends to set in. One should beware of this, for if students experience trouble and are still returned to the very same environment, they are likely to revert to the same trouble that got them there in the first place. In other words, some form or system of follow-up program must be in place. Informal counseling is oftentime quite appropriate for students who are just beginning to experiment with drugs, however, second and third offenders or students caught up in a continuing drug use experience may require attendance at treatment centers or be provided other special, in-depth help. A re-entry process and after-care supervision program designed to help students rethink and change those patterns that led to drug use. In a number of school systems students are trained to serve as peer counselors for students who are returning to school after treatment. Peer counseling has been found to be an effective element of an ongoing, comprehensive *safety net* program.

Drug education—the message. The school's drug education program must assure that students get the message, that the use of drugs is bad for them. The drug curriculum provides for specific classes that provide detailed drug units and assures that pertinent information is incorporated in every grade level and in every discipline. Anti-drug instruction must be tailored to the specific group of students to whom it is being taught. This instruction must also provide for the explaining why students should not use drugs and also provide training in refusal skills so that youngsters learn how to say No to drugs. In addition it should be accompanied by an ongoing staff development program designed to provide teachers and other staff members with a wide range of facts on drug abuse.

Provide alternatives to drug use. Provision is made to provide students with better things to do, such as just-for-fun activities to community service projects. Such programs are offered consistently and during traditionally off hours, including evenings, weekends, and throughout school recesses, holidays and summers. Opening the school, libraries, gymnasia, auditoriums, or even industrial arts and home economics shops during evenings and weekends can be highly effective elements in an anti-drug program. Since funding of these programs are a real concern, dual sponsorships, such as: school-business cooperatives, community service organizations, school-university partnerships, school drug abuse task forces, and school-community sharings offer solutions worthy of consideration. In fact such cooperatives provide realistic means by which the drug abuse program is able to involve the total school-community, and helps broaden community support and knowledge of school programs.

Introduce social responsibility. There is virtue in providing drug-free activities that incorporate various forms of social responsibility. These activities are action based, offer students opportunities to be proud of their actions, teach the importance of interdependence, and provide concrete opportunities for students to help others. In the process, students become less inclined to being self-absorbed and they are able to put their own concerns and problems in appropriate perspective. Further, such programs bring with them public praise and thanks, a reward experience that has true merit.

Mentor High-Risk Students. Students who are in danger of getting involved with drugs and dropping out are at risk, and generally members of the school staff know who these are. Rather than wait for the drug abuse to become a matter of fact, the school must create prevention programs that match teacher/mentors (or other appropriate adults) with students identified as being at-risk. Because mentors serve as confidants, advisers, and official in-school friends, they can play an invaluable role in the student's life. Students are helped because they are able to find someone who cares.

Involve parents and other adults. Parent involvement does represent a difficult part of an anti-drug program. This is particularly so because of the prominence of the current two-career and single parent family units. Still, a number of schools have come up with creative ways to bring parents on board in their anti-drug efforts. Such schools' approaches often have one thing in common: they extend the parent-involvement notion to include grandparents, parents of alumni, and older area residents in acting as surrogate grandparents. Also, the traditional role of the parent in the school is expanded by having the school provide these parents with training whereby they are now prepared to help teach drug-education classes.

Forge alliances and coalitions. An effective way to strengthen a anti-drug program is to forge alliances with other anti-drug efforts in the area. This combined effort has more clout than several groups working separately—and leads to shared information and resources. All sorts of alliances are possible; ones among area parent groups often are especially helpful in providing widespread community support for anti-drug efforts. An example of this coalition resulted in the printing of a pamphlet entitled *A Patient Guide to Alcohol and Drug Abuse.*

A Parent's Guide to Drug and Alcohol Abuse. This pamphlet, prepared by this author while serving as Superintendent of the East Stroudsburg Area School District, had the support of the other three superintendents within Monroe County of Pennsylvania. Accordingly, some 36,000 pamphlets were produced and mailed to *every* household in the County.

Repeat anti-drug instruction. Drug education must be an ongoing process, for school staff as well as for students. People and information change, so instruction for staff and students must be continuous, programs need repetition with regularity, and need to furnish current, up-to-the-minute information. Comprehensive drug-education programs provide for ongoing anti-substance-abuse training being woven into staff development sessions, that new teachers and staff members receive training immediately, and that new students and those who transfer in during the school year know the school's rules and its drug abuse policy from Day One.

Remember the real heroes. Like the squeaky wheels that get the grease, the at-risk students get most of the attention and concern in an anti-drug program, while the good students, the ones who are not in trouble, or in need of help, do not get their fair share of attention. It should be recognized that these students are the school's real heroes in a school's war against drugs. It is these youngsters who don't take drugs and who stand up and play a part in keeping their peers off drugs. These students should occupy a central place in the school's anti-drug efforts. These students must know the facts about substance abuse for they can advance a positive peer pressure when having them serve as peer counselors or in some other positive role model program. Be wary of glorifying former addicts by paying them substantial sums of money to appear at student assemblies. The message students often get from such sessions is that persons can survive drug addiction and at the same time capitalize on it. Ex-addicts are generally ineffective in the prevention aspects of a drug education program. Their presence, however, can be useful when schools are working with students who are recovering users.

The drug education program outlined here has helped students throughout the United States make a healthy detour around dangerous drugs. Additional suggestions can be found in the abstracts of the award-winning programs in *Profiles of Successful Drug Prevention Programs* (1988–89). available from the U.S. Department of Education, Drug-Free Schools Recognition Program, Room 510, 555 New Jersey Ave. N.W., Washington, D.C. 20208-5645; 202/357-6134.

CRISIS COMMUNICATION

Nothing is more important during a crisis than good, quick, effective, accurate communication. Effective management response is the key to credibility. One of the tests of leadership is the ability to recognize a problem before it becomes an emergency.

Arnold H. Glasow

Crisis management is no longer the unusual in school-related matters. Random violence against school children was unheard of years ago. More recently, a gunman went on a shooting rampage in Southern California. Several years ago a deranged person hijacked a school bus and its passengers. Crisis affecting schools takes many forms and most occur as unscheduled or unexpected events, and as a result of uncommon experiences. For example:

1. Tornadoes that strike unexpectedly, especially in areas that are not usually high incident storm areas.
2. Hurricanes and their devastating effect on entire communities, not just schools.
3. Evacuation and emergency procedures involving nuclear facilities.
4. Special needs resulting from teen suicide and other disruptive behavior that occur on or near the school site.
5. A fatal fire, a school strike, the arrent of a school employee, the death of a student athlete, and a myriad of other such events.

Each crisis bears its own markings and its own unique solutions, and no crisis plan can truly prepare a school for the unthinkable, but much can be done to reduce confusion, improve communication, and most importantly, care for and protect students and employees of the school.

The foremost characteristic of a crisis is surprise, if not the actual event, then its timing. The crisis differs from the problem since the problem can be on the agenda for future action while the crisis appears ahead of schedule. For example, the school system may be considering appropriate policies for dealing with AIDS victims, and before this has been completed, the media discovers a student of the system has AIDS. Another such example, a school bus crashes while on an extracurricular activity. The first reports officials receive of student injuries are from the media and police.

Although no crisis plan will work perfectly, gaining control of the information and management components is possible with a plan that is reviewed regularly, practiced, and variously tested.

There are two types of crises. One that is expected, such as a labor dispute or strike, or unexpected. An employee work stoppage permits some anticipation and planning because it generally will occur in some reasonable time. While an unexpected event, such as a bomb scare or a student being taken hostage, can be planned for; but, because of its uncertainty, response time in gaining control of the situation is much less predictable.

The five basics in crisis communication:

1. When a crisis breaks, first, get the facts. The key to credible crisis communication is the quick gathering of accurate information.
2. Once the facts are known, put together a strategic plan for managing crisis.
3. Communicate the plan, first internally, then externally.
4. Seek feedback.
5. Evaluate the plan.

The suggestions offered her focus on internal planning so as to provide the principal and school staff with reasonable guidelines to stay in front of any crisis.

(Excerpted from *Schools-Community: Guidelines for Effective Communication.* J. William Jones, PSBA, 1989.)

THE PRINCIPAL AND THE COURTS

Public schools continue to be influenced by the law. School leaders must prepare themselves by developing a basic understanding of the legal framework of public education. They also must have a working knowledge of and an appreciation for the legal rights of teachers and students.

(Sparkman, 1990, p. 59)

The legal playfield for principals has undergone dramatic changes in recent years. Each year, the Supreme Court has made major rulings on issues that have had legal implications for the schools. What with the current change toward a more philosophically conservative court, principals may anticipate some substantive and truly radical changes in that playfield.

As an example of such change, one need but review and compare the search and procedure holdings of the Court during the 1980s in T.L.O. v. New Jersey (search of student lockers) and the most recent (1991) search and seizure holding of the Court as related to the issue of police conduct of the search aboard public transportation (bus) in Florida.

Federal and state legislation has also substantially influenced the operation of the schools. There are federal laws that prohibit employment discrimination, protect the rights of handicapped students, control access to student records and more. Also, state legislation, as an aftermath of the reform movement, has created new demands on school administrators in such areas as testing, accountability, evaluation, and discipline.

There is a growing need for the school principal to have a good overview of educational governance and the constitutional principles as they relate to school law. The state departments of education, state school boards associations, and professional education organizations do recognize this and they make an effort to respond to this need by providing legal updates for school leaders. Also, there are such publications as the *School Law Bulletin* which is published monthly by the Quinlan Publishing Company, of Boston, MA, and *Legal Notes for Education* published by DataResearch, Inc. of Rosemount, Minnesota. These are but two monthly publications that respond to this need for informing principals on legal matters.

For example, the August 1991 issue of *Legal Notes for Education* provides cases and published materials which deal with such as: accidents, injuries and deaths; discrimination; employment; freedom of speech and religion; liability; state regulatory power; student rights; teachers' rights; legislation and administrative regulations; and law review articles.

Many states have introduced certification examinations for educators. For example, Texas requires prospective school administrators to pass its examination which includes questions dealing with legal issues. One sub-area of the personnel management portion of their examination deals with the rights and responsibilities of teachers, recruitment, interviewing, selecting, and assignment of staff. Another, the sub-area of educational governance, school-community relations and student affairs includes several objectives encompassing legal concerns. Florida covers federal and state constitutional principles, statutes, and regulations in the extensive legal section of its certification exam for school administrators.

Principals must develop an appreciation of the law and the legal system and the role of the Constitution in a democratic social order. Those currently in the field or aspiring to the position must not view the courts as the antagonist. The purpose of the judiciary is the peaceful resolution of conflict between individuals or between individuals and the state. The results of a court's decision may not always be our liking, however we live with it because to do otherwise would threaten the very fabric of the democracy.

Although the courts still recognize the common law doctrine of *in loco parentis,* whereby educators stand in the place of the parents in matters of authority and control, however this doctrine has been tempered with due process. Also, the courts have resisted interfering with school officials and their exercise of discretion. The courts continue to uphold the authority of school administrators in most situations. However, it is understood that school leaders cannot act beyond the limits of their authority, and they cannot abuse their authority by being unreasonable, arbitrary, or capricious in their decision making.

Finally, the principal needs that legal information necessary to operate effectively on a day-to-day basis. To a great degree this means reliance on pre-approved policies, rules and regulations of the school system.

THE TEACHING OF VALUES

The proposal to teach ethical values in the Broward County's (Florida) public schools coincides with a national trend that some experts say shows the country is healing after three decades of divisiveness. At least a dozen other states have begun either teaching values to children in the schools or developing such programs. The movement continues to gain considerable momentum (Sun-Sentinel, April 8, 1991).

The following articles appeared in South Florida newspapers in March 1991:

Values Should be Taught in Class, Task Force Says

Good students will never be good citizens without learning basic values such as tolerance, understanding and social responsibility, a school task force said.

After more than a year of study, the Broward School District's (one of the largest school districts in the nation) 100-member Challenges of Our Society task force issued its findings and said values education has a place in the classroom. It cited 18 values the community wants taught, including honesty, patience, courage and respect for the Earth.

Other values include courage, trust, respecting cultural differences and respect for authority. What's new is, we do have a community consensus on what the community values are, said the director of program evaluation for the school system.

That consensus was reached in town meetings and surveys of teachers, parents, students and school administrators. The task force also urged the Broward County School District to find a way to get parents involved in teaching the basic values, a problem that is the basis for moving values education into the classroom in the first place.

The schools need to teach this because there are a lot of parents that don't know it, said a frequent critic of the School District, also town commissioner, who served on the task force.

The recommendations represent broad proposals, such as getting parents involved in teaching values, without addressing exactly how to implement them.

While any program in values education must pass through the hands of school administrators and the Broward School Board, the county may join a nationwide trend in teaching right from wrong in school.

Around the country, school systems are adopting similar plans, saying it is the only way to cope with children who are the products of broken homes and drug-infested communities.

But some groups say these lessons have no place in the school-house. That's a parent's job, said the head of a group which advocates at-home schooling. If they don't listen to the parents and the parents haven't instilled those values, they're not going to listen to anyone else's values. The lessons are valuable, she said, just inappropriate in the classroom.

Teachers, too are concerned about how a program to teach values would be presented to them. I think the teachers need to hear that it's OK to talk about these things in the classrooms.

I think teachers need that stamp of approval. But the teachers union president said it would be best if it were not another brick in the load of classroom tasks teachers must already perform.

The task force was established in 1989 with representatives from churches, synagogues, businesses, parents' groups, social organizations and the School District.

The task force recommendations will be forwarded to the School Superintendent and then the School Board. (Sun-Sentinel, Tuesday, March 26, 1991).

DROPOUT PREVENTION

The story-behind-the-story in effective dropout programs lies in implementation, casework, and long-term follow-up activities.

Andrew Hahn

The source of the school dropout is the youngster and his or her secrets. One part consists of the public record of growth and development, the other, thoughts, feelings, hidden fears and visions of the future.

It is a given that poor children are more likely to drop out than their more advantaged counterparts. Nor does this suggest that growing up poor by itself determines school failure. However, the burden of poverty if not eased makes success all the more difficult.

Race is still another element. At best, it is difficult to break out when you are poor and white. There are valid reasons to suggest that the problem is even greater when poverty is combined with membership in a minority group. Also, in some schools there appears an unfortunate mind set that their minority students will not graduate.

Another formative element is the education, both cognitive and affective, that the dropout received while at school. There appears to be two public school systems in the United States, one endowed with resources, talent, and appropriate funding, and the other, a pauper's system. The latter system which is the one in which most poor children are educated, has been largely overlooked during the school reform movement of the 1980s and early 1990s. Whatever the reforms proposed or implemented in public education, very little has been targeted to those youngsters in greatest need, the at risk students.

There are informed estimates of how many students are dropping out. Further, profiles of the dropout population, based upon national, state, and occasionally local estimates, are readily available. This data provides answers to some central questions about the dropout population. Is the drop out rate increasing? Do more males than females drop out? Are the poor and minorities at greater risk? Is the dropout rate higher for older adolescents? Which regions of the country have the highest incidence of dropping out? Is the dropout rate highest in schools with the least resources? How do the dropout experiences of urban, suburban, and rural educational systems differ?

The U.S. Government Accounting Office reported, in 1985, 4.3 million 16–24 year olds dropped out, 13% of that age group. Of these 3.5 million were white, 700,000 were black and 100,000 were from other groups. Moreover, male dropouts outnumbered female dropouts. On a more positive note, dropout rates have declined and remained steady at about 13%, 14%. In the 1960s this percentage was at 20%.

The National Center for Education Statistics found that about 14% of the sophmores surveyed in 1980 did not complete high school. All indicators of hardship: low income, low skill wage, limited educational background, confirmed that the disadvantaged were three times more likely to be school dropouts than the advantaged. In city schools in which less than 20% of the student body were poor, the dropout rate was 13%. In schools where more than half the students lived in poverty, the dropout rates were at 30%.

The concern regarding available resources and their impact upon the dropout rate is of added concern. Former Harvard University President James B. Conant, wrote about 30 years ago that the difference in spending for suburban schools and inner-city schools challenges the concept of equality of opportunity in American public education. That inequality in spending persist today.

Some of the current researchers contend that the expenditures are less significant in affecting dropout rates than how the school is organized, the quality of teaching and administration, and innovation in the curricula. One such researcher found that teacher-student ratios correlated with the incidence of dropping out.

It is readily apparent, in all dropout literature, that with early detection, more students can be helped. Some system studies provide an identification of the grades and ages that pose the greatest risks to dropout prone youths. For example, in 1986, one third of all dropouts left school before completing the 10th grade.

Most researchers see education from preschool to high school graduation as a continuum. Therefore, the difficulties and reverses suffered by very young children, early in their school experience, can be identified and overcome as the youngsters proceed through the educational system.

The retention of select youngsters at grade levels is one such practice that brings to mind the difficulties and reverses suffered by children. Numerous primary schools have recognized this concern and have moved toward changing their grade promotion policies with the reorganization of classes into multiage groupings or ungraded programs. The stigma of overage in class assignment as related to problem youth does arise here.

Other schools permit students to make up unsatisfactory performance throughout the school year. Some have experimented with the flexible scheduling of students, and others have moved to biannual school promotions.

Since many social and economic impediments undermine the development of children, schools must provide leadership in identifying these problems and act as catalysts and proactive institutions to resolve them. One such valued effort has included the integration of education with comprehensive health and human services for young children. In one instance a council on children, youth and families has been created. In another, provision is made for reimbursement to the local school system that runs effective parent education classes and early detection, screening and remedial program for high risk 1 to 4 year olds. One state has experimented with comprehensive kindergarten intervention programs for low-income parents and children. Many school systems have looked to improve the quality and accountability of their Chapter I programs, an experience that has offered substantial benefits to underachieving poverty children.

The effective dropout prevention program is based upon elements which go beyond remedial instruction and the provision of social services. The successful dropout prevention program requires a cohesive, integrated effort that combines the following components:

1. Mentorship and intensive, sustained counseling directed toward the troubled youngster.
2. An array of social services, including health care, family planning education, and infant care facilities for the adolescent mother.
3. Concentrated remediation using individualized instruction and competency based curricula.
4. An effective school-business collaboration, providing ongoing access to the mainstream economy.
5. Improved incentives.
6. Year-round schools.
7. Heightened accountability for dropouts at all levels of the public education system.
8. Involvement of parents and community organizations in dropout prevention.

By developing elementary school risk-detection systems and tracking individual students as they progress from one level of the school system to another, the school system assumes a viable responsibility, that of identifying early warnings of school failure.

Consistent with the maintenance of a superior communication between counselors, teachers and administrators at every level of the school district, a system of accountability for following the performance and enrollment status of at-risk students is of utmost importance. Management information systems, linking all levels of the school as well as programs in the out-of-school environment, are essential elements of a comprehensive dropout prevention strategy. Reducing the number of dropouts will require a long-term commitment of resources at every level of the school system, the dedication of teachers and administrators, the concern of local, state and national officials, the active involvement of outside youth-serving agencies and institutions, and of the business community (Hahn and Danzberger 1987).

TECHNOLOGICAL ADVANCES

Technology talk among progressive administrators today includes more than just computers and VCRs. New developments in telecommunications, particularly in satellites, fiber optics, electronic bulletin boards, electronic mail, and two-way interactive delivery of instruction, are hot topics among forward-thinking educators across America

(Barker, 1990, p. 31).

Donald Ely and others (1989) summarized and discussed substantive trends and issues in educational technology as:

1. concern for the design and development of instructional products and procedures dominates the professional literature;
2. evaluation is becoming an integral part of the instructional design and development process;
3. there is increasing use of research and development knowledge to solve current problems of teaching and learning;
4. computers can be found in almost every public school in the United States;
5. interactive video is widely accepted as a research and development product, but not in schools and higher education;
6. distance education has been established as a major vehicle for instruction at all levels of education and training;
7. the definition, conduct, and status of professional education in the field continues to preoccupy practitioners;
8. the impact of technology on individuals in the society at large continues to be considered by educational professionals;
9. the applications of telecommunications used in the society at large are reflected in the schools and in postsecondary institutions;
10. the results of research do not appear to have much effect on application and operations of educational technology; and
11. the curriculum support function is an important element of educational technology programs.

TECHNOLOGY CENTERS

Centers for educational technology have made a much needed appearance on the educational scene. They are seen as serving educational agencies, foundations, coalitions, community colleges, universities, professional organizations, businesses, and school districts that are involved in developing, distributing, and using educational technology.

The activities of these centers include research and development in the following areas:

1. applying new technology in educational settings;
2. creating prototypes for educational use of technology originally developed for commercial or other purposes;
3. researching the use of technology in education; and
4. researching the use of technology for handicapped students and teachers.

In Texas, the Texas Center for Educational Technology has established research and development laboratories that will affect technology-based learning and teaching in that state. The major categories of research being studied are teacher education support, student learning, and educational systems.

Laboratory activities and their objectives cover broad educational research needs and seek to implement emerging technology. Select laboratories emphasize research on technologies originally developed for commercial purposes or on technologies yet to be developed. Briefly, the work of the labs may described as follows:

1. a study of human learning and learning activities, creating computer based methods for diagnosing students' learning and cognitive processes.
2. providing technological support of learning for learning disabled, physically handicapped, mentally retarded, and emotionally disturbed.
3. improving teacher effectiveness and efficiency in the classroom; using technology to free teachers to teach.
4. using technology to retain high quality teachers in the teaching profession; facilitating communication between master teachers.
5. using technology in curriculum areas such as mathematics, science, reading, and social science.
6. studying instructional systems and their management in the public school environment to help implement technological systems and evaluate their effectiveness.
7. studying computer-based information exchange, telecommunications, and distance learning.
8. studying ways to effectively integrate interactive multimedia into the classroom; evaluating emerging technologies and their application in education.

9. designing interactive computer technologies in relation to individual differences among learners.
10. studying the biological basis of learning, studying learning disorders.
11. using college student/classroom teacher pairs to produce instructional computing applications and utilities.

As these research centers grow and produce their findings, products, and services, they will explore additional methods of dissemination to best serve all of its clientele.

SUMMARY

The development within the young of attitudes and dispositions and progressive life of society cannot take place by direct conveyance of beliefs, emotions, and knowledge. It takes place through the intermediary of the environment. The environment consists of the sum total of conditions which are concerned in the execution of the activity characteristic of a living being. The social environment consists of all the activities of any one of its members. It is truly educative in its effect in the degree in which an individual shares or participates in some joint activity. By doing his share in the associated activity, the individual appropriates the purpose which activates it, he/she becomes familiar with its methods and subject matters, acquires needed skill and is saturated with its emotional spirit.

John Dewey

In order that the new technologies are put to productive use the user must gain a total familiarity with the tool. Although there is an abundance of literature and information now published about computers and related technologies, application and practice are essential to any skill development and this applies to today's educational technologies. When the school's faculty see their principal as being comfortable talking about and working with the new technologies, it is highly likely that they too will sense the urgency to learn and use these new skills themselves.

The public school system can and must expect to be influenced by the law and legislation. Accordingly, principals must be prepared to deal with a developing understanding of the legal framework of public education, and this must include a working knowledge of and an appreciation for the legal rights of teachers and students. The principal must anticipate that there exists an increasing trend for legal challenges against a host of program issues such as: compulsory attendance, religion in the public schools, copyright laws, special education, bilingual and special language programs, and student testing and promotion. They must also comprehend the legal concept of negligence and legal liability and the state laws regarding tort.

In this chapter the author has flagged select problems and issues which principals may expect to face. This sampling of problems and issues arises from the same sources of most: the major social dislocations affecting American society; from the rapid social changes affecting American communities which impose changes upon the schools; from cultural changes which necessitate new role definitions for principals; from individual characteristics of principals; from the rapid urbanization of our communities; and seemingly, from the persistence of traditional modes of organizational behavior and governmental structures and practices.

> *What if we gave ourselves a new set of enemies whose defeat would exalt everyone and subjugate no one? What if we declared war on ignorance, illiteracy, sickness, timidity of spirit, shallowness of vision? What if we declared not the moral equivalent of war, but war itself? Our aim in this war would be a very simple one: to cause the United States once again to be the best educated, healthiest, most productive nation in the world.*
>
> (*Carolyn Warner* 1990).

Each new decade presents new and difficult challenges for those who administer our nation's educational systems and their schools. School administrators are being required to make their schools responsive to their publics, during these periods of rapid social change. The lessons of the past do not provide complete nor satisfactory answers to these new challenges, since there are many people who are questioning many of the assumptions under which schools have operated. They appear to be calling for an increased emphasis on the qualitative aspects of life as opposed to a substantial emphasis upon material well-being as a major goal. As part of the emphasis on quality, there is a demand that society's major organizations show greater concern for people.

DISCUSSION QUESTIONS

1. Discuss some of the principal areas of misunderstanding, misinformation, and distortion about public education? Can you suggest some effective means of clarification?
2. Why is it difficult to arrive at a commonly agreed upon set of values?
3. What is meant by the following statement? Uniformity rather than individuality is the accepted concept at this school.
4. What are some of the conditions necessary for an effective school public relations program and effective school-community communication?
5. Why is it important for the school to involve parents and other citizens in school affairs? What should be the main purpose of this involvement?

6. Describe the relationship between the school and the community. List those aspects of the community about which the principal needs to be knowledgeable.

7. Why has the instructional design process received such little attention as a planning procedure for school programs.

8. The first task of restructuring, confronting our own professional knowledge, is not easy, but it is likely to produce the courage to improve, at least in a few good schools. What is meant by that statement?

9. In the past, reforms have tried to change one piece at a time, in a system of many interlocking pieces. Restructuring, however, tackles all the pieces. Discuss this!

10. Why is it that schools that have made the most progress have external conditions that support change?

11. Discuss the principal areas of misunderstanding, misinformation, and distortion about public education?

12. Identify several nonpunitive approaches to changing a student who has misbehaved. What are the advantages and disadvantages of each of these approached?

13. Under what circumstances are suspension and/or expulsion appropriate or inappropriate methods of responding to student misbehavior.

14. In what ways can the principal make a leadership and administrative contribution to the school's counseling and guidance programs?

REFERENCES

An Imperiled Generation: Saving Urban Schools. Princeton, The Carnegie Foundation, 1988.

Barker, Bruce O.: Planning, using the new technology in classrooms. *NASSP Bulletin.* 74:529, November 1990, p. 31.

Bennis, Warren and Nancus, Burt: *Leaders: The Strategies for Taking Charge.* New York, Harper and Row, 1985.

Bendiner, Robert: *The Politics of Schools.* New York, Harper & Row, 1969.

Bowles, S. and Gintis, H.: *Schooling in Capitalist America: Educational Reform and the Contradiction of Economic Life.* New York, Basic, 1976.

Brookover, Wilbur, et al.: *Creating Effective Schools.* Holmes Beach, Learning Publications, 1982.

Burns, James MacGregor. *Leadership.* New York: Harper and Row, 1978.

Bryk, Anthony S. and Thum, Yeog Meng: *The Effects of High School Organization on Dropping Out.* New Brunswick, Center for Policy Research in Education, February 1989.

Clark, R.: *Family Life and School Achievement, Why Poor Black Children Succeed or Fail.* Chicago, The University of Chicago Press, 1983.

Challenge to Urban Education: Results in the Making, A Report of the Council of the Great City Schools. Washington, The Council of the Great City Schools, 1987.

Coleman, J. et al.: *Equality in Educational Opportunity,* Washington, U.S. Government Printing Office, 1966.

Davies, Don: The emerging third force in education. *Inequalities in Education, 15 :*5, November 1973.

Dropouts in America: Enough Is Known for Action. Washington, Institute for Educational Leadership, 1987.

Edmonds, R.: Effective schools for the urban poor. *Educational Leadership, 37:* 1979.

Eisner, Jane: Good schools have quality principals. In *The Journalism Research Fellows Report: What Makes an Effective School.* edited by D. Brundage. Washington, Institute for Educational Leadership, 1979.

Elam, Stanley M.: The 22nd annual gallup poll of the public's attitudes toward the public schools. *Phi Delta Kappan,* September 1990.

Ely, Donald P. et al.: *Trends and Issues in Educational Technology.* Washington, Office of Educational Research and Improvement, 1989.

Featherstone, A.: Repeating a grade: does it help? *Harvard Education Letter.* March 1986.

Finn, Chester E., Jr.: Teacher unions and school quality: potential allies or inevitable foes? *Phi Delta Kappan,* January 1985.

Garfield, Charles: *Peak Performers: The New Heroes of American Business.* New York, William Morris, 1986.

Goodlad, John I.: *A Place Called School.* New York, McGraw-Hill, 1984.

Hahn, Andrew and Danzberger, Jacqueline: *Dropouts in America: Enough is Known for Action.* Washington, *Institute for Educational Leadership,* 1987.

Hale-Benson, J.: *Black Children: Their Roots, Culture, and Learning Styles,* rev. ed. Baltimore, The Johns Hopkins University Press, 1986.

Jencks, C. et al.: *Inequality: A Reassessment of the Effect of Family and Schooling in America.* New York, Basic, 1972.

Lefkowitz, Bernard: *Tough Change: Growing Up on Your Own in America.* New York, Free, 1987.

Lewis, Anne C.: *Partnerships: Connecting School and Community.* Arlington, American Association of School Administrators, 1986.

Lewis, James, Jr.: *Achieving Excellence in Our Schools: By Taking Lessons from America's Best-Run Companies.* Westbury, Wilkerson, 1985.

Lomotey, K.: *Black Principals in Black Elementary Schools: School Leadership and School Success.* Doctoral dissertation, Stanford University, 1985.

McLaughlin, Milbrey W., et. al.: Constructing a personalized school environment. *Phi Delta Kappan. 72:* 3, November 1990, pp. 230–235.

Peters, Thomas J. and Austen, Nancy: *A Passion for Excellence: The Leadership Difference.* New York, Random House, 1985.

Peters, Thomas and Waterman, Robert H., Jr.: *In Search of Excellence: Lessons from America's Best-Run Companies.* New York, Harper and Row, 1982.

Shockley, W.: A debate challenge: geneticity Is 80 percent for white identical twins' I.Q.s. *Phi Delta Kappan, 6:* 1972.

Shulman, Lee: Knowledge and teaching: foundations of the new reform. *Harvard Educational Review. 57:* 1987, pp. 1–22.

Smith, Stuart C. and Scott, James: *The Collaborative School: A Work Environment for Effective Instruction.* Oregon, Clearinghouse on Educational Management, 1990.

Warner, Carolyn: Wanna fight? *Phi Delta Kappan. 71:* 5, January 1990, p. 403.

Wehlage, Gary, et al.: *Reducing the Risk: Schools as Communities of Support.* New York, Falmer, 1989.

Willie, C. V.: *Effective Education: A Minority Policy Perspective.* New York, Greenwood, 1987.

Appendix A

SELECTION OF INSTRUCTIONAL MATERIALS

In fulfilling its responsibility for the selection of instruction materials for the schools of the East Stroudsburg Area School District, the Board of Education adopts this policy for the guidance of the Superintendent, and his professional staff.

The Board of Education, as the governing body of the School District, is legally responsible for the selection of instructional material. Since the Board is a policy-making body, it delegates to the professional personnel of the District authority for the selection of instructional and library materials in accordance with this policy.

Textbooks shall be adopted by the Board at regular meetings between April 1 and August 31 of each year. No adoption or change of textbooks shall be made without the recommendation of the Superintendent, except by two-thirds vote of the Board. Books, supplementary to textbooks, may be adopted and purchased for use in the schools of the district at any time. Supplementary books shall be adopted for use in the same manner as the textbooks. Textbooks and other instructional materials shall be purchased by the Board in accordance with the provisions of the School Code as amended from time to time.

Materials for the classrooms and school libraries shall be selected by the appropriate professional personnel in consultation with the administration, faculty and students. Final selection on purchases shall rest with the Superintendent or his designee.

The Board of Education believes it to be the responsibility of the professional staff to select instructional materials (library books, periodicals, textbooks, supplementary textbooks, maps, globes, charts, slides, prints, films, filmstrips and recordings) of the highest quality that will support the education philosophy of the District.

In accordance with this belief, the following policy statements will govern the selection of instructional materials in the East Stroudsburg Area School District:

1. Materials will be selected that will enrich and support the curriculum, taking into consideration the varied interests, abilities and maturity levels of the pupils.
2. Materials will be selected that will stimulate growth in factual knowledge, literary appreciation, aesthetic values and ethical standards.
3. Materials will be selected that will provide a background of information which enables pupils to make intelligent judgments in their daily lives.
4. Materials will be selected that will present a reasonable balance of opposing sides of controversial issues so that young citizens may develop, under guidance, the practice of critical reading and thinking.

213

5. Materials will be selected that will be representative of the many ethnic, cultural, and sexist groups and their contributions to our society.

6. Materials will be selected that present the many and varied aspects of our culture and society including some aspects that may be considered to be unsavory.

7. The value and impact of any literary work will be judged as a whole, taking into account the author's intent rather than individual words, phrases or incidents out of which it is made.

8. Educators, remembering the maturity level of a child, may recommend for individual reading, writings they feel will have educational significance for an individual student.

Appendix B

THE HANDLING OF COMPLAINTS ABOUT THE CURRICULUM AND INSTRUCTIONAL MATERIALS

A. Complaints about materials containing alleged seditious or disloyal material are to be handled in accordance with state law. Information relative to the conditions of the law is available at the district office.

B. Complaints about any instructional materials not covered by state law are to be made as follows:

    1. They must be submitted in writing in a signed statement containing the following information:

        a. Title, author, publisher, copyright date, and page(s) on which the alleged unsuitable materials appear;

        b. Quotations of the alleged unsuitable material with a clear statement of the writer's objection(s) to the material;

        c. Name and address of the complainant, if acting as an individual; and,

        d. If complaint is made by an organization, the name and address of the individual complainant and of the organization he or she represents and a statement of the complainant's position in the organization.

    2. They must be sent through the United States mail to the Superintendent who will forward them to the Board.

C. An investigation of the merit of any complaint, not covered by the law, will be made only at the request of the Board.

D. Upon request of the Board, the Superintendent will appoint a special review committee, at least three professional staff personnel, especially competent in the questioned field.

E. The special review committee in its determinations will consider the source, purpose and use of the material in question.

F. After due deliberation, this special review committee will submit a report of its findings to the Board through the Superintendent. The report need not be unanimous. It may be composed of separate majority and minority reports.

G. The Board will make a final decision concerning the merit of the complaint based upon:

    1. the report of the special review committee;

    2. the recommendation of the superintendent;

    3. any other additional data it may consider necessary.

H. Since the following subjects are sometimes topics of criticism these will be the district's policies concerning them:

1. *Religion* — Survey material which includes all major religions will be included in the school collections.
2. *Ideologies* — The libraries/media centers will, without making any effort to sway reader judgment make available basic factual information on the level of its reading public, on any ideology or philosophy which exerts a strong force, either favorable or unfavorably in government, current events, politics, education, or any other phase of life.
3. *Sex and Profanity* — Materials presenting accents on sex will be subjected to a stern test of literacy merit and reality by the librarian or English Department Chairperson who takes into consideration his or her reading public and accepted public moral standards. While the literature must not in any case include the sensational or over-dramatic, the fact of sexual incidents or profanity appearing will automatically disqualify instructional material. Rather the decision will be made on the basis of whether the instructional material presents life in its true proportion whether circumstances are realistically dealt with, and whether the material is of literary value. Factual material of an educational nature on the level of the read public will be included in the library collections.

I. The Board endorses and accepts the principles incorporated in the School Library Bill of Rights of the American Association of School Librarians as criteria for the instructional materials to be used in the Harborfields Schools.
These principles are:

To provide materials that will enrich and support the curriculum, taking in consideration the varied interests, abilities and maturity levels of the pupils served.

To provide materials that will stimulate growth in factual knowledge, literary appreciation, aesthetic values and ethical standards.

To provide a background of information which will enable students to make intelligent judgments in their daily lives.

To provide materials on opposing sides of controversial issues so that young citizens may develop under guidance the practice of critical reading and thinking.

To provide materials representative of the many religious, ethnic and cultural grounds, and their contributions to our American heritage.

To place principle above personal opinion and reason above prejudice in the selection of materials.

J. Suggestions from faculty, pupils and parents regarding purchase of materials will be encouraged and will be included in the collection on the basis of such factors as interest, traditional recognition and importance to the students' understandings of their world.

K. Individuals or groups objecting to materials will be offered copies of this written statement, requesting clarification of their objections and the course of action they recommend.

Controversial Issues

Criticism of school practices or procedures should be taken up initially with the principal of the school where the student, parent, or citizen first became aware of such practices or procedures. When the criticism relates to the action of a school employee, the criticism or complaint should be taken up first with the individual and if unresolved, with his or her immediate supervisor and/or the principal of the appropriate building. If the complaint remains unsolved, it may be taken up with the superintendent or his or her designee. Matters not resolved at the superintendent's level may be appealed to the Board.

Such appeals must be submitted in writing. Any employee who is the subject of such criticism or complaint will be fully informed thereof and will have the opportunity to present his or her case at each level of appeal. Every opportunity will be afforded to all parties involved to present their respective positions and to have a fair and impartial hearing on the matter in question. Every effort will be made to maintain the confidentiality of such matters.

Appendix C

TEACHER EVALUATION PROGRAM

The primary purpose of the evaluation of teachers shall be to ensure the highest quality of education being offered to students. This requires the development of a process whereby all staff members may increase the effectiveness of their services to the educational program. A broader purpose of the evaluation process is to assess teacher competence, to make decisions regarding the assignment and employment of staff, and to verify that district educational goals are being implemented and achieved.

I. Program Assumption

The Teacher Evaluation Program is based upon the following assumptions:

A. Teachers and other instructional personnel have a responsibility to demonstrate interest in their own development by acquiring new knowledge and skills.

B. Teachers and other instructional personnel have a commitment to work effectively with their colleagues and want regular feedback about the quality of their work.

C. Teachers know what is expected of them and understand the responsibilities and key functions of the position.

D. A proper climate exists to encourage the self-development of each teacher.

E. Professional goals of teachers shall be compatible with organizational goals.

II. Responsibility for Supervision and Evaluation

All staff members will be evaluated on an annual basis. It is the responsibility of the building principal to inform each staff member of this policy and to review with staff the procedures for evaluation. The primary responsibility for teacher supervision and evaluation is held by the building principal. Principals are assisted in this function by supervisors, department chairpersons, coordinators, directors, assistant principals, and additional administrative/supervisory personnel as designated by the superintendent of schools. Annual evaluation reports are the responsibility of the building principal(s), with input from other administrative/supervisory personnel. Classroom observation reports are the responsibility of the administrator or supervisor observing the lesson.

III. The Process of Evaluation

A. Planning Conference and Setting Objectives

The building principal and/or the principal's designee shall hold an individual conference with all teachers at the beginning of the school year (*September*

218

1–October 15). The purpose of this conference is to review general evaluation procedures, assess responsibilities of the position, and review district, building and individual objectives.

B. Classroom Observations

Classroom observations will be conducted by building principals and others who are responsible for supervision and evaluation.

Regular substitute and probationary teachers shall be observed at least *five* (5) times each during each full year of employment. A minimum of *two* (2) of these observations are to be performed by the building principal(s) and at least *two* (2) observations shall be made by *December 1.*

Part-time and tenured teachers shall be observed *at least once* during the year.

Formal classroom observations will be followed by a post-observation conference normally within five (5) school days of the observation. As soon as practicable, following the conference, a *Classroom Observation Report* form shall be completed by the evaluator (Form included with policy). The teacher shall be provided a copy of the report, and will sign an original indicating receipt of a copy.

C. *Mid-Year Review Conference*

A mid-year conference will be held with the teacher by *February 15.* The primary purpose of this conference is to review the teacher's overall performance.

D. *End-of-Year Conference*

A year-end conference will be held with each teacher by *June 15,* of each year. This conference should be viewed as a summation of the entire evaluation process. The primary purpose of this conference is to review performance relative to the individual's duties and responsibilities. In addition, the outcome(s) of this conference may serve the district as the basis for identifying immediate and long-range staff development needs. Following this conference, an *Annual Evaluation Report* will be prepared and presented to the individual teacher (Form included with policy). The teacher shall be provided a copy of the report, and will sign an original indicating receipt of a copy.

IV. Criteria for Evaluation

In evaluating a teacher's overall performance, the listing of Performance Areas for Teacher Evaluation are to be considered significant (See form included with policy). These criteria are divided into four (4) major categories, each containing several substatements which further define the tasks and expectations in that area. Separate criteria will be developed for guidance counselors, social workers, school psychologists and other support personnel as deemed appropriate.

The criteria used for evaluation are neither restrictive nor limiting and their purview may be modified to best suit individual circumstances.

V. Evaluation Reports

    A. *Annual Evaluation Report*

        1. *Annual Evaluation Reports* will be completed by designated administrative/supervisory personnel on forms provided by the district for such purposes.

        2. An *Annual Evaluation Report* covering the performance of Regular Substitute and Probationary personnel will be submitted by

the principal to the Personnel Office no later than *June 1,* of the school year.

3. An *Annual Evaluation Report* covering the performance of part-time and tenured personnel will be submitted by the principal to the Personnel Office *no later than June 15,* of the school year.

4. In any case where a teacher has multiple building assignments, the principal of the building where the teacher spends the greatest portion of time will be responsible for the *Annual Evaluation Report.*

B. *Tenure Report*

1. Teachers in the final year of their probationary period shall be recommended by the principal for tenure or for discontinued service in a *Tenure Report* submitted to the Personnel Office. This report will include a description of strengths and weaknesses, and an assessment of overall performance in each individual's area of responsibility, based upon a review of the full probation period.

2. In those cases where the known tenure eligibility date of an individual is *September 1,* the *Tenure Report* will be submitted to the Personnel Office *no later than April 1,* immediately preceding the September 1, tenure-eligibility date.

3. In those cases where the known tenure-eligibility date of an individual *is other than September 1,* the Tenure Report will be submitted to the Personnel Office *no later than ninety (90) calendar days* prior to the tenure eligibility date.

C. *Report Procedures*

1. Each teacher to be evaluated shall receive a copy of any evaluation report. The signature of the teacher to be evaluated will appear on the report to indicate the receipt of such report. The individual evaluated may submit a written response to any evaluation report.

2. Upon request, an individual shall be permitted to examine evaluation reports on file in the building or in the District Office.

Adopted 8/20/86

Harborfields Central School District, Greenlawn, New York

Appendix D

TEACHER INDUCTION PROGRAM

I. Planning and Organizing the Teacher Induction Program

    1. Describe the size, composition, responsibilities and working conditions of the district induction council(s), Identify the induction coordinator and council members by:

The thirteen (13) members of the East Stroudsburg Area School District Induction Council are: (1) Superintendent, (Ex-Officio), (2) Assistant Superintendent for Administration and Personnel, (Committee Co-Chairperson) (3) Assistant Superintendent for Curriculum and Instruction (Committee Co-Chairperson), (4) Grades 6–8 Intermediate Principal (5) Grades K–5 Elementary Principal (6) Grade 2 Teacher#1 Elementary School, Grade 1 Teacher #2 Elementary School, (8) Grade 4 Teacher #3 Elementary School, (9) Grade 6 Teacher, #4 Elementary School, (10) Grade 7–8 Reading Teacher, Junior High School (11) Grade 7–8 Spanish Teacher, Junior High School, (12) Grade 9–12 Business Teacher, Senior High School, (13) Grade 9–12 Social Studies Teacher, Senior High School

    2. In compliance with Act 178 and guidelines provided by the Pennsylvania Department of Education, the East Stroudsburg Area School District chose its committee through successive balloting by all professional staff. Initially, any professional staff could nominate any other professional staff member to this committee. At an earlier meeting with central staff administration, the local education association advisory committee agreed on the makeup of the committee (i.e., one (1) representative from each elementary school and two (2) representatives from the junior high school and two (2) representatives from the senior high school). In addition, the committee includes one (1) elementary school principal, one (1) secondary school principal, and two (2) central office administrators. The district induction coordinators were elected by the committee at its organization meeting.

    3. Provide a description of how mentor teacher(s) and mentor teams were selected and how they function.

      A. Mentor

        1. Qualifications:

Permanent certification

    Five (5) years of teaching experience

    Assigned to the same building as the inductee

    Assigned to the same department as the inductee

Matching planning time

One inductee per mentor

Such alternatives to the above as are mutually agreeable to the

221

members of the Induction Team (specific alternative: Tenured
teachers with a minimum of two (2) years of experience in this
district.

2. Initial Selection Procedure

Separate lists of names submitted by administrators and teachers

Names appearing on both lists will form a pool from which mentors
will be selected by the building principal

Participation in this program by mentor is voluntary

3. Subsequent Procedure

Mentor pool will be carried over from previous year

Additional nominations made annually or as need dictates

B. Building Induction Team

1. Membership

Building principal

Mentor(s)

Inductee(s)

Resource personnel (as needed)

C. Role of the Mentor

1. Acts as a resource person to the inductee:

Offers advice, help and assistance to the inductee on all matters
relating to the teaching process

Establishes a supportive relationship with inductees

Works with the new teacher on routine building matters, paperwork,
etc.

2. Arranges to give feedback to inductee during the regular workday

3. Sets regular schedule of formal meetings with inductee(s)

4. Keeps a log of all meetings on prescribed log form (Form included
herein)

D. Role of the Building Induction Team

1. In relation to inductee:

Sees that inductee(s) concerns are being met

Provides support and assistance for the inductee and the mentor in
meeting the program's goals

Introduces inductee to resource personnel

2. In relation to overall program:

Sees that inductee's concerns are being met/as hired

Provides support and assistance for the inductee and the mentor in
meeting their combined goals

Introduces inductee to resource personnel

Reports program progress to the District Council.

3. Other Information Regarding Mentors

All new teachers (experienced and inexperienced) joining the faculty
at East Stroudsburg Area School District after the start of the school
year shall be provided with a mentor when the major portion of the
school year (i.e., one semester or more) is yet to be completed.

The building principal will make a determination regarding the need for formally assigning a mentor for experienced teachers who join the East Stroudsburg Area School District.

The selection of a mentor and the pairing of the mentor and the inductee shall be the responsibility of the building principal

4. A universal needs assessment survey is administered annually for purposes of establishing needs and priorities for Act 178 programs, this induction program and for locally sponsored inservice and staff development program (Copy of survey form included with program). In addition, an end-of-the cycle survey was conducted (Spring 1990) to solicit feedback from participants in the first 2-year induction cycle.

II. Program Content

1. Goals/Objectives

The major goal of this plan is to facilitate and provide support for new teachers in the East Stroudsburg Area School District and to insure an orderly and successful passage of the staff member through the initial year of teaching in the district.

This plan includes service to:

1. The first year teacher
2. The experienced teacher new to the district
3. The long-term substitute teacher

The specific objectives of this plan are to provide:

1. Meaningful training in classroom management and organization
2. Meaningful training for the induction in instructional skills and district expectations as they relate to clinical supervision, curriculum and instruction
3. Opportunity to develop an understanding of the school community, parents and students
4. A support system for the inductee through the utilization of a qualified mentor
5. A formal structure through which the inductee will become familiar with district policies, procedures and resources
6. Identify the general topics to be covered in your TIP and include a brief description of how each topic will be addressed, and
7. Indicate how you intend to include the results of research on effective teaching to cover such topics as:

Effective classroom management

Instructional delivery techniques

School/community relations

Professional communications

Other topics as appropriate

TOPICS/ACTIVITIES FOR INDUCTEES

Strand I—All first-year teachers and all teachers whose Instructional I Certificate was issued on or after 6/1/87. Optional for all others as individual needs dictate. Classroom Management Skills/Instructional Delivery Skills

1. First day procedures (opening of school)
2. Motivating students
3. Assessing/evaluating students' work
4. Classroom management skills
5. Individual differences: remedial, accelerated and other special needs students
6. Classroom discipline
7. Instructional delivery skills
8. Designing a lesson
9. Opportunity to observe other teachers in the district
10. Other related matters of importance to the inductee

Developing Relations with Children, Families, Colleagues and the Community (To be addressed in building induction team meetings during September and October and one-to-one meetings with mentor as needed.)

1. PTO/PTA Organizations
2. Home-school communication procedures
3. Parent/teacher conference procedures
4. Community resources/agencies
5. Teacher/pupil relationships
6. Collegial relationships

Strand II—Required for all teacher new to this district, regardless of previous experience. Building Policies and Procedures (To be addressed in building induction team meetings with mentor as needed).

1. Materials acquisition
2. Attendance procedures
3. Schedule
4. Extra duties
5. Emergency phone numbers
6. Record keeping/lesson planning
7. Textbooks/resource materials
8. Field trip procedures
9. Library and Media Center Services
10. Pupil Support Services: Guidance Program, Health Service Program Homebound Instruction Program, Psychological Services
11. Extra-curricular activities
12. TELLS (State minimum competency tests)
13. Right-to-know training (video)
14. Other topics as appropriate

District Policies and Procedures (To be addressed in August preservice session: *First Induction Session*

1. Overview of New Teacher Induction Program
2. District philosophy
3. Contractual review
4. Professional interests/communications: staff development, professional organizations, certification and induction (state regulations)
5. Discipline policy
6. Grading and retention policy
7. Curriculum guides/planned course documents
8. Federal Programs
9. Right-To-Know (general information)
10. Other topics as appropriate

Note: *A Second Induction Session* will be held each school year for the purpose of filling in gaps as shown by the Continuing Needs Assessment survey to be administered to inductees at the close of the first quarter of the school year.

Human resources and fiscal support for program Training sessions (i.e., First Induction Session and Second Induction Session) will be developed by the committee and implemented by the central office administrative staff. Department Chairperson and Coordinator will also be available for these sessions as well as local university and or Intermediate Unit staff.

Mentors are paid an annual stipend for each inductee for whom they are responsible. The stipend for 1990–1991 is $310; $325 for 1991–1992.

Approximately 20% of the budget of the Assistant Superintendent for Curriculum and Instruction is targeted for professional development programs. In addition, each building principal has limited funds for teaching and administrative staff attendance conference. Each secondary department chairperson has $100.00 per person in his/her department for conference attendance. Additional compensation is provided for professional staff for curriculum work.

The East Stroudsburg Area School District grants reimbursement for graduate course work taken beyond that required for permanent certification at the rate of $100 per credit hour for up to eighteen (18) credit hours per year.

Teacher salary increments are made for multiples of six (6) credits in accordance and with the salary schedule and the contract with teachers. Such increments are made effective upon the date of completion of the appropriate credits and the submission of an official transcript.

Create a timeline for the implementation of the content of the TIP. This should include starting and ending dates for specific activities. (See also Checklist of Activities.)

Several evaluation devices will be used: (copies of each included with program)

The Continuing Needs Assessment Survey (Administered to inductees at the close of the first quarter.)

Survey of inductees who completed the program in the previous two (2) years.

(Administered March 1st.)

Program evaluation form. (Administered to Administrators, Mentors and Inductees in June.)

Several documents will record the inductees participation and completion of the TIP.

The Checklist of Activities

The Mentor's Meeting Log

The Certificate of Completion

Aggregate listing of inductees completing the program for each year

Approved 5/17/90

East Stroudsburg Area School District

Appendix E

DRUG AND ALCOHOL POLICY

I. PREFACE

A. The East Stroudsburg Area School District Board of Education, Administration and staff believe in the individual value and potention of each member of the school community. We recognize that chemical abuse and dependency impair the ability of individuals to develop their full potential. We also recognize that problems created by chemical abuse and dependency have an adverse effect on the ability of all members of the school community to achieve personal and district goals. Our policy is based on the belief that chemical dependency is a life-threatening illness that affects individuals in all areas of their lives. It is also our belief that chemical dependency is a treatable illness.

B. This policy is the result of a coordinated effort involving all members of the school-community to effectively respond to the use and abuse of chemicals in the East Stroudsburg Area School District.

II. STATEMENT OF POLICY

A. Through the use of a revised curriculum, classroom activities, community input, support and resources, a strong and consistent administrative and faculty effort, and rehabilitative and disciplinary procedures, the East Stroudsburg Area School District Administration and staff will work to educate, prevent and intervene in the use and abuse of all drug, alcohol, and mood-altering substances by the entire student population.

B. All School District personnel recognize that the responsibility of the student for his or her actions increases with age. Therefore, at the elementary level, an investigation into the nature of the offense shall be considered *prior* to the implementation of this policy.

C. As an extension of this policy, the following rules, regulations and guidelines shall be used by all school district personnel when responding to drug, mood-altering substance, and alcohol-related situations.

III. DEFINITION OF TERMS

A. *Assessment* — An evaluation with recommendations by a professional drug and alcohol counselor from a local agency. The assessment can be done at the agency or at school.

B. *Confiscation* — The search for and/or seizure of any drug/alcohol or mood-altering substance by school employees.

C. *Cooperative Behavior* — The willingness of a student to work with staff and school personnel in a reasonable and helpful manner, complying with the requests and recommendations of the staff and school personnel.

227

D. *Distributing* — Delivering, selling, passing, sharing, or giving any alcohol, drug or mood-altering substance, as defined by this policy, from one person to another or to aide therein.

E. *Drug/Alcohol Counselor* — An educational specialist or guidance counselor with expertise in the area of chemical abuse and dependency.

F. *Drug/Alcohol and Mood-Altering Substance* — Any alcohol or malt beverage, any drug listed in Act 64 (1972) as a controlled substance, chemical, abused substance or medication for which a prescription is required under the law and/or any substance which is intended to alter mood. Examples include, but are not limited to, beer, wine, liquor, marijuana, hashish, chemical solvents, glue, look-alike substances, and any capsules or pills not registered with the nurse, annotated within the student's health record and then given in accordance with the school district's policy for the administration of medication to students in school.

G. *Drug Paraphernalia* — Any utensil or item which, in the school's reasonable judgment, is commonly associated with the use of drugs, alcohol, or mood-altering substances. Examples include, but are not limited to: roach clips, pipes and bowls.

H. *Possession* — The act of holding on their person, among their possessions, or under their control, without any attempt to distribute, any alcohol, drug, or mood-altering substance, as defined by this policy.

I. *School Property* — Not only actual buildings, facilities and ground on the school campus, but also including any facility being used for a school function, school bus stop, school parking area, and routes traveled to and from school by any means.

J. *School-Sponsored Activity* — Any activity which the School District has approved, either during or after school hours.

K. *Core Team* — This is a multi-disciplinary team composed of school personnel (teachers, administrators, nurses, counselors). This team will be trained to understand and work on the issues of adolescent chemical use and abuse, death, suicide, and teenage pregnancy. The team will be involved in the identification and referral process of students coming to their attention through the procedures outlined in this policy.

L. *Uncooperative Behavior* — Resistance or refusal, either verbal, physical or passive, on the part of the student to comply with the reasonable request or recommendations of school personnel. Defiance, assault, deceit and flight shall constitute examples of uncooperative behavior. Uncooperative behavior shall also include the refusal to comply with the recommendations of a licensed drug and alcohol facility.

IV. RULES AND REGULATIONS

A student who, on school grounds, during a school session, or anywhere at a school-sponsored activity, is under the influence of alcohol, drugs, or mood-altering substances or possesses, uses, dispenses, sells, or aids in the procurement of alcohol, narcotics, restricted drugs, mood-altering substances, or any substance purported to be a restricted substance or over-the-counter drug shall be subject to discipline pursuant to the provision and procedures outlined in East Stroudsburg Area School District's Discipline Code (Policy #5114).

V. SCHOOL GUIDELINES

A. As an integral part of the East Stroudsburg Area School District Drug and Alcohol Prevention Program, these guidelines represent one component in a district-wide effort to respond effectively to drug, mood-altering substance, and alcohol-related situations that may occur on school property or at school-sponsored activities.

B. The guidelines are intended to provide a consistent minimum disciplinary means to respond to drug, mood-altering substance, and alcohol-related events.

C. The East Stroudsburg Area School District will provide a safe and healthy environment for students with due consideration for their legal rights and responsibilities.

D. The Board reserves the right to use any extraordinary measures deemed necessary to control substance abuse, even if the same is not provided for specifically in any rule or regulation enumerated herein.

RECOMMENDED GUIDELINES FOR RE-ENTRY TO SCHOOL AFTER TREATMENT FOR DRUG AND ALCOHOL ABUSE

1. The school will receive from the treatment center pertinent information regarding their requirements for a student in After-Care prior to formal administrators' conference.

2. A conference will be held with the administrator, parent/guardian, Core Team, and/or counselor and returning pupil from treatment center/agency.

3. The Core Team will be available to facilitate the transition of the After-Care Program in the school.

4. Teachers will report the student's progress to the Core Team for at least a 90-day period. Parents will be requested to share information with the Core Team.

5. The Core Team will monitor the Student Support/After-Care Program.

6. The involved agency will notify the school of student's progress and After-Care attendance and program.

PROCEDURE FOR HANDLING OF A CONFISCATED CHEMICAL SUBSTANCE

1. Any confiscated substance will be placed in an envelope or appropriate container (A witness be present.)

2. The following information will be noted on the outside of the envelope/container:
    a. Name of school
    b. Date and time
    c. Description and number of contents (i.e., leafy material, pill, capsule)
    d. Signature of both parties (administrator/designee and witness)

3. The envelope/container will be sealed, using tape.

4. The appropriate law enforcement agency will be called by the administrator to come for the substance: East Stroudsburg Boro Police.... 421-5500 or Pennsylvania State Police ... 839-7701.

5. The official receiving the substance will be asked to open it in the presence of the school administrator/designee and witness.

6. The official receiving the substance will be asked to sign and date the envelope/container. A copy will be retained by the school.

PROCEDURE FOR CONDUCTING A SEARCH IN SCHOOL

1. The primary purpose for all school searches is for the protection of the health, safety and welfare of students and faculty and for the protection of school property and the educational process.

2. The basis for all school searches will be reasonable suspicion or reasonable cause to believe that there may be a danger to the student being searched, other students, faculty, school property or the educational process.

3. Voluntary disclosure of the suspected property, or consent to make the search will be sought before commencing an involuntary search.

4. Warrantless searches will be conducted only upon the basis of reasonable suspicion that the student is concealing something, possession of which is either in violation of the law or of school rules.

5. School searches will be conducted out of concern for the school population under the doctrine of in loco parentis.

6. All school lockers are the property of the School District. Any locker and the contents within may be searched without the consent of the student.

7. All personal property in the possession, or under the control, of the student may be subject to search.

8. The search will be conducted by the school administrator or his designee in the presence of another staff member. Whenever possible, the student whose property or locker is being searched shall be requested to be present. However, in a situation involving the likelihood of a clear and present danger or the removal of the drug or substance being sought, the search may be conducted in the absence of the student.

Appendix F

MORAL AND ETHICAL VALUES

The following statements of premises and beliefs are for the use of teaching staff members in carrying out their responsibilities in this school system. Each teacher is expected to identify ways in which he/she can most effectively implement these moral and ethical values in his/her work with pupils and the other staff members of our schools.

1. INSTILLING IN OTHERS A DESIRE FOR EXCELLENCE IN WORK, MANNERS AND ACHIEVEMENT, because the responsibilities and duties of a citizen in our democracy demand intelligent and active participation in the institutions of our society.

2. STRESSING THE VALUES OF INTELLECTUAL HONESTY AND RESPECT FOR TRUTH, because freedom depends upon the existence and practice of these values as demonstrated in the lives and associations of our people.

3. PRACTICING RESPECT AND THOUGHTFULNESS OF OTHERS, because the dignity and worth of each individual is preserved and enriched in our associations with one another. In a democracy, law and order at all levels of society come about through mutual respect and concern for others and the institutions they represent.

4. RAISING EACH PUPIL'S SENSE OF VALUES AND STANDARDS OF BEHAVIOR, because of our aim to raise the level of civilization among our people as they live, learn and work at home and throughout the world.

5. HELPING PUPILS EXERCISE SELF-DISCIPLINE, SELF-DIRECTION, AND SELF-EVALUATION IN THEIR LIVES, because these practices promote orderliness and regulation in our lives, collectively and individually. Also, a continuous self-evaluation give us measures of the degree to which we are reaching the goals in our lives.

6. EXERCISING RESPECT FOR ALL FORMS OF DULY AND DEMOCRATICALLY CONSTITUTED AUTHORITY, because law and order come by in such a way, is the best guarantee of peace and harmonious relations in our society.

7. DEVELOPING A SENSE OF RESPONSIBILITY AND INDEPENDENCE IN OUR BEHAVIOR, because the effective discharge of an individual's citizenship in a democracy is a personal and a private matter as well as social. Our hope in teaching pupils to think is that these pupils will be able to make intelligent, independent choices.

8. UNDERSTANDING AND SHOWING BY OUR ACTIONS THAT PRIVILEGES CARRY RESPONSIBILITIES, because it is through carrying out the

231

responsibilities of active and effective citizenship which come the privileges of life, liberty, and the pursuit of happiness and our freedoms.

9. DEMONSTRATING PATRIOTISM AND APPRECIATION FOR FREEDOM IN OUR COUNTRY, because in such a way we help in the transmission of our democratic heritage and freedoms.

10. INCREASING OUR ABILITY TO RECOGNIZE AND APPRECIATE RIGHT FROM WRONG AND JUSTICE FROM INJUSTICE, because of our concern for the total welfare of self and others. This ability must increase if we are to grow in awareness of the needs of others and skill in helping meet these needs.

11. SHOWING RESPECT AND APPRECIATION FOR PERSONAL AND PUBLIC PROPERTY, because the safety and preservation of the general welfare of our people depends upon this respect.

12. EXERCISING TOLERANCE AS WE STRIVE FOR UNDERSTANDING OF OTHERS' IDEAS AND BELIEFS, because the integrity and self-esteem of each human personality is dependent upon this toleration and respect. The interdependence of peoples in this world demands our efforts to understand these peoples and their contribution to civilization.

13. DEMONSTRATING DEPENDABILITY AND CONSCIENTIOUSNESS IN ACCEPTING AND DISCHARGING ONE'S RESPONSIBILITY AT WORK, because the quality of our work and the leadership we give through our vocation makes our citizenship more meaningful. Democratic living is based upon the contribution each person makes to getting the job done.

14. EXHIBITING A WILLINGNESS TO STRIVE TO REACH THE MAXIMUM IN HELPING OTHERS, because our goal of helping all children become all that they are capable of becoming demands a dedication where those engaged in teaching perform tasks of helping children learn to their maximum potential. The very existence of differences among individuals necessitates that we exhaust all resources at our disposal in helping others.

15. STRIVING FOR CONSISTENCY, FIRMNESS AND UNDERSTANDING IN DISCIPLINARY DEALING WITH PUPILS, because acceptable and desirable behavior takes on additional meaning as we act in this direction. Self-discipline in pupils is encouraged and strengthened as we exercise consistency and firmness in the way we discipline and manage these pupils.

16. INSTILLING A FEELING OF PRIDE IN SELF, SCHOOL AND COMMUNITY, because these attitudes are responsible for making school and community a healthier, safer and more enjoyable place in which to live.

17. UNDERSTANDING AND APPRECIATING THAT THE DEVELOPMENT OF ATTITUDES IS MORE IMPORTANT THAN THE SETTING OF RULES, because such a positive approach to our responsibility in being effective citizens promotes the general welfare far more than a concern for setting rules to govern every aspect of our life. In a democracy, where the people make the rules, it is more important that we work in building attitudes rather than simply being followers of rules.

18. STRIVING TO DEVELOP MUTUAL COURTESY AND RESPECT BETWEEN TEACHERS AND PUPILS, because we learn more in this democratic

way of living. Interaction between teachers and pupils is necessary for effective learning. It is fallacious to think that we get respect simply because we are adults. We must learn respect from pupils as we earn respect from our adult peers. Effective teaching is dependent upon this principle in any situation.

19. HELPING PUPILS APPRECIATE THEIR EDUCATION AND THE SCHOOL, because where there is interest and enjoyment, the potential for more learning to take place is greater.

20. WORKING TOWARD DEVELOPING AND PROMOTING GOOD HUMAN QUALITIES AND RELATIONS, because these efforts on the part of everyone contribute to the harmony, functioning and general welfare of our society.

21. STRIVING TO BUILD MUTUAL RESPECT BETWEEN ALL MEMBERS OF THE SCHOOL TEACHING STAFF, because this is one of the characteristic features of a true profession.

22. STRIVING FOR CONSISTENCY IN PRACTICING ACCEPTABLE AND DESIRABLE BEHAVIOR DESCRIBED IN THE FOREGOING, because we teach by example of our lives. The development of behavior and character among pupils is strengthened as teachers consistently practice these desirable standards of behavior. Common understanding and appreciation among the staff as to what constitutes desirable and acceptable standards of behavior, and a concerted effort on the part of the teaching staff to promote these standards, is a vital force in the character education of our pupils.

GLOSSARY

Ability. Inherent or learned capacity, aptitude, skill, or knowledge that enables a person to perform successfully on his or her job.

Absenteeism. The often deliberate practice or habitual condition of being away from work lasting for one or several days or work periods. Its rate is usually estimated by the percentage of working days the employee reports to and spends in work.

Abstract. A summary or condensation of contents, basic methods, conclusions, suggestions or other related information in a single document or report.

Accommodation. An act or process by which individuals or groups attempt to adjust or modify their attitudes, values, roles, or behavior patterns in order to internalize or otherwise come to common terms with the various aspects of an organizational or social environment.

Accountability. The requirement that organization members to whom responsibility and authority are delegated be held answerable for results.

Achievement test. An examination that measures the extent to which a person has acquired certain information or mastered certain skills, usually as a result of specific instruction.

Action research. The method through which organizational development change agents learn what improvements are needed and how the organization can best be aided in making improvements.

Activate. To organize or make operative a particular task or purpose.

Activity. The tasks or actions taken to secure a result. They usually are inputs rather than outputs, usually are means rather than ends. Plans often are activity-oriented, but in plans all activities are prioritized and aimed toward a desired result.

Adaptability. A personal habit, quality, or ability to realize and make use of one's potentials within existing environmental or social conditions, or opportunities.

Adaptive behavior. Any behavior pattern that helps the individual to adjust to the demands of his or her environment and, thereby, satisfy his or her various physical, psychological, or social needs.

Ad hoc committee. A special committee created to work toward and accomplish a particular task or purpose.

Administrative. Pertaining to the techniques or functions of managing public affairs or services.

Administrative analysis. A systematic investigation of the causes and possible solutions of administrative and managerial problems within the framework of the scientific method, research, management science, and creative thinking.

235

Administrative control. The process of influencing organizational forces, activities, or events by management, in order to make sure that the objectives which have been set and tasks which have been assigned are carried out according to the requirements of organizational plans, standards, policies, or programs. A continuous job of planning, evaluating, organizing, regulating, verifying, restraining, analyzing, and synchronizing.

Administrative discretion. Authority, freedom, and power delegated to an official in discerning and making independent decisions on problems within his or her area of responsibility.

Administrative hearing. An adjudicative proceeding of administrative or regulatory agencies concerning the violations of the rules and regulations of these agencies. It is usually held in public, and the decisions may be appealed.

Administrative organization. The over-all administrative structure, usually consisting of line, staff, and auxiliary agencies or departments through which the management and control of operations and personnel is accomplished.

Administrative policy. A statement of a rule, judgement, or decision which, by defining and outlining the goals and objectives of an organization, can guide and regulate organizational policies and methods.

Administrative system. The method, process or result of producing or interrelating administrative information through the application of conventional and/or electronic communication devices.

Administrator. An official who is authorized and accountable for carrying out the purpose or provisions of law, rule, or policy; a functionary.

Admonition. An advice, warning, or reprimand, given orally by a supervisor to a subordinate about his or her area of responsibility. It carries with it an implied penalty or sanction.

Alienation. A psycho-social process that is characterized by a tendency of an individual to become apathetic toward and estranged from those around him or her.

Antisocial. Pertaining to impulsive and hostile attitudes and actions toward existing moral codes, social norms, institutions or relationships; an antisocial person has difficulties in being with, being with, and in forming close personal ties with other people.

Appropriation. An authorization granted by a legislative body to make expenditures and to incur obligations for specific purposes.

Aptitude. A combination of native and acquired abilities and other characteristics which can be regarded as predictive of a person's ability to become proficient in a line of activity with a given amount of training.

Arbitration. A process of reaching a settlement in organizational disputes by bringing in a third, ideally neutral, party to make decisions after hearing both sides of such dispute.

Ascribed status. A status which an employee has outside of the job hierarchy, usually as a result of kinship, associations or professional reputation or membership. It often effects his relationship with others on the job.

Asocial. Pertaining to unawareness or indifference toward and avoidance of existing moral codes, social norms or relationships.

Atypical. Differing or deviating from a norm, standard, or characteristics in a given pattern or situation.

Authoritorian Leadership. Absolute leadership where by the person vested with authority sets the goals, plans, and determines all policy, assigns functions, prescribes the procedures, directs, checks, judges, and corrects the work in great detail.

Authoritarian Personality. A personality which is characterized by a number of interrelated and measurable anti-democratic attitudes, among which conventionality, intellectual rigidity, ethnocentrism, anxiety, submission, conservatism, and a generally calculating orientation toward people seem to predominate.

Autistic thinking. A type of irrational thinking which is characterized by fantasies, daydreaming, reveries; or irrational adjustive reactions. It is usually being influenced by strong emotional and self-centered needs.

Aversive stimulus. A stimulus which, when applied after the occurence of a response, will decrease the probability of occurrence of such response in the future.

Batch processing. A conventional approach to processing whereby a number of information units are accumulated, sorted, and grouped according to simularity, and processed as a batch during the same computer run.

Budgets. Statements of financial resources set aside for specific activities in a given period of time.

Bureaucracy. Any large complex organization system which tends to organize and administer its functions and activities through excessive reliance on (1) centralization of power and authority; (2) specialization and specific spheres of competence; (3) professionalization; (4) minutely graded hierarchy of officials, each of whom is responsible to a superior; (5) rigid rules and regulations; (6) routine (red tape); (7) formal, written communications, and; (8) records.

Censorship. The process of examining ideas with the purpose of correcting or eliminating them before they are published or expressed through any of the various media of communication.

Centralization. The extent to which authority is concentrated at the top of the organization.

Change agent. The individual leading or guiding the process of a change in an organizational situation.

Coalition. Usually, a temporary process or condition of combining persons, groups, or organizations for the purpose of increasing their effectiveness in influencing or controlling others.

Code of ethics. A statement or set of statements of ideal moral and professional standards and behavior, established by a professional or government organization to guide the conduct of its members.

Cognitive structure. An aspect of personality that is characterized by the values, beliefs, knowledge, or attitudes an individual has about his or her environment.

Collaborative management. Management through power sharing and subordinate participation; the opposite of hierarchial imposition of authority.

Collective bargaining. The process of negotiating and administering agreements between labor and management concerning wages, working conditions, and other aspects of the work environment.

Communication network. A set of channels within an organization or group through which communication travels.

Community. Any locality or region in which people who are living in close proximity and having formed some sort of social, economic, and legal institutions and organizations can, through their relationship with these institutions and organizations, satisfy most of their needs.

Computer. A high-speed electronic device which is capable of (1) performing arithmetic and/or logical operations; (2) making decisions; (3) check its own correctness; (4) communicate and report results, and; (5) store results for future availability.

Concept. A general idea or image of an object or group of objects on which theories or models may be constructed; it is more inclusive than definition.

Conceptual skill. The mental ability to guide and coordinate the organization's activities through the comprehension of the organization as a whole and an understanding of the interdependence of its part.

Constant dollars. Dollar amounts that have been adjusted by means of cost indexes to eliminate inflationary factors and allow direct comparison across years.

Consumer Price Index. A monthly measure, compiled by the Bureau of Labor Statistics, of changes in the price of goods and services consumed by urban families and individuals. The index includes a group of about 300 goods and services, ranging from food to automobiles, and from rent to haircuts, normally purchased by urban wage earners.

Controlling. Controlling means that principals attempt to assure that the school is moving toward its goals.

Cooperation. Working together to accomplish shared goals.

Cooperative learning. The instructional use of small groups so that students work together to maximize their own and each other's learning.

Cooptation. A process of establishing or maintaining the power of an organization through the selection and absorption of new leaders from the lower levels into the policy-making levels of the organization by those already in power; a formal or informal sharing of power.

Criterion. A standard, norm, measurement, or value by which a judgement or evaluation of quantities, qualities, performance, or other related factors can be made.

Culture. A complex entity of all explicit and implicit ideas, values, customs, institutions, beliefs, attitudes, habits, cor related behavior patterns which are learned from and practiced by means of communication and social contact between people in a certain area or period.

Current dollars. Dollar amounts that have not been adjusted to compensate for inflation.

Curriculum. A statement of non-random events.

Curricular unity. Another term for the optimization of work in schools.

Decentralization. The delegation of power and authority from higher to lower levels of the organization, often accomplished by the creation of small, self-contained organizational units.

Decision making. The process of identifying and selecting a course of action to solve a specific problem.

Delegation. The act of assigning formal authority and responsibility for completion of specific activities to a subordinate.

Demographics. The study of populations, the size and characteristics of groups of people.

Discipline. The process or result of conditioning, directing, or improving individual or group attitudes and behavior in the organization through leadership, motivation, guidance, training and/or the maintenance and application of formal authority, sanctions, rules, and regulations. Also, a condition of voluntary conformity to organizational policies and procedures.

Distributive leadership. A term referring to a process of delegating leadership functions and roles to, or sharing it with members of a group.

Dysfunctional conflict. Any conflict that results in decreased efficiency and greater factionalism within the organization.

Education. A set of experiences through which children (and adults) pass.

Effective leadership. Leadership that produces movement in the long-term best interests of the group(s).

Effectiveness. The ability to determine appropriate objectives: doing the right things.

Efficacy. The ability to make a positive difference in students' lives.

Environment. Any or all of the natural and man-made elements or conditions which are capable of influencing the development of personality, character, attitudes, social behavior of, and the interaction among individuals and groups.

Ethos. The value-orientation, characteristics, and generally, the way of life of a given group.

External environment. The environment outside the organization.

Feedback. The information and data required by each manager to (1) write effective objectives and plans, (2) monitor their progress while they are being carried out, and (3) measure accomplishment after the action is completed.

Formalization. Attainment of organizational objectives through uniform procedures which are established and legitimized by top management.

Function. All or any identifiable segment of an organization's mission or purpose regardless of the manner in which it is performed.

Functional organization. Originated by. F.W. Taylor, this term now refers to a type of organization in which the direction and management of work is divided according to specialized functions or duties, rather than to pure line or staff areas of responsibilities.

Goal. When distinguished from objectives, is usually defined as a longer-term broader statement of intent. Often referred to as a sense of direction.

Goal congruence. A harmonious relationship between the goals of a group (organization) and the goals of its members.

Grievance. An employee's expressed feeling about a real or perceived injury, injustice, or mistreatment in connection with his or her employment conditions and relationships which is brought to the attention of management.

Horizontal compatibility. When objectives and plans are blended and balanced with those of the principal's associates across the school.

Human relations. A management practice (or program) which, through the use of psychological and sociological theories and methods of group dynamics, and its relations to the organization as a human system, attempts to integrate employees into the organization in such a manner as to increase production, cooperation, harmony and good employee relationships.

Human resource planning. Planning for the future personnel needs of an organization, taking into account both internal activities and factors in the external environment.

Induction and orientation. Activities intended to ease an individual's entrance into an organization through introducing the individual to the organization and providing information on the organization.

Inflation. An upward movement in general price levels that results in a decline of purchasing power.

Innovation. Any creative and risk-taking process by which new ideas, values, standards, methods, or procedures are conceived, developed, introduced, and/or followed up for the purpose of meeting certain existing or possible future needs.

Input. The actions or methods taken to secure the output.

Instruction. Teaching directed by curriculum.

Instructional transactions. Instructional algorithms, patterns of learning interactions, usually far more complex than a single display and a single response, which have been designed to enable the learner to acquire a certain kind of knowledge or skill.

Joint objective. An end result requiring action by two or more administrators.

Leadership. The process of moving a group (or groups) in some direction through mostly noncoercive means.

Line organization. The simplest type of organizational hierarchy in which formal authority, communication, and control flows directly in a shortest possible line, from the top executive to the various subordinate managers, supervisors, or related officers in complete charge of particular operations, until the level of execution is reached.

Management. Getting things done through other people. The process of planning, organizing, leading, and controlling the efforts of organization members and of using all other organizational resources to achieve stated organizational goals.

Management ability. Working with and through individuals and groups to accomplish organizational goals.

Management by objectives (MBO). A formal set of procedures that establishes and reviews progress toward common goals for principals and teachers.

Mediation. An attempt or process of calling in a third-party in a dispute to help negotiate and reconcile differences by finding and suggesting some acceptable means by which that dispute may mutually be settled.

Mentors. Individuals who pass on the benefits of their knowledge to other individuals who require assistance and are usually less experienced.

Mission. The reason or purpose for the organization's existence. Can be applied to an entire organization or a unit of it.

Motivation. Stimulating or being stimulated toward having a positive attitude or behavior toward an idea, person, group or work environment.

Mutual goal setting. An employee evaluation system which consists of a series of discussions between a supervisor and his or her subordinate whereby the objectives and goals of future performance are established and/or reviewed.

Objective. The specific end result expected from a principal and the time at which it will be achieved, the what, when, and who.

Objectives. The targeted goals of an organization toward which resources and efforts are channeled.

Organization. A rational, legimiate, and ideally dynamic relationship of people, formally coordinated through specialization, authority, hierarchy, division of labor, communication, and standard procedures toward the accomplishment of certain goals, objectives, or some common, mutually agreed purposes.

Organization chart. A simplified graphic presentation of the formal interrelationships of the various structural and functional units of an organization in terms of their (1) purposes and objectives; (2) channels of formal communication; (3) lines or levels of formal authority, control and coordination, and; (4) tasks, processes, activities and their location.

Organizational conflict. Disagreement between individuals or groups within the organization stemming from the need to share scarce resources or engage in interdependent work activities, or from differing statuses, goals, or cultures.

Organizational culture. The set of important understandings, such as norms, values, attitudes, and beliefs, shared by organizational members.

Organizational design. The determination of the organizational structure that is most appropriate for the strategy, people, technology, and tasks of the organization.

Organizational goals. The purpose, mission, and objectives that are the reason for an organization's existence and that form the basis of its strategy.

Orientation. A form of training process by which new employees are acquainted, guided and adjusted to established and approved organizational policies, rules, methods, procedures, benefits, duties, activities and responsibilities in terms of personnel and environmental relationships.

Output. The end results being sought.

Paradigm. A representative model, pattern or example of an idea, theory or experiment.

Participative action. An action of applying group dynamics to work situations by managers in order to involve the greatest number of employees in problem-solving or decision-making processes which may effect them.

Performance appraisal. The process of evaluating an individual's performance by comparing it to existing standards or objectives.

Plan. The how to, the steps or ways and means by which the objective is to be achieved, often termed programming an objective.

Planning. Planning implies that principals think through their goals and actions in advance.

Policy. A standing plan that establishes general guidelines for decision making.

Procedure. A standing plan of detailed guidelines for handling organizational actions that occur regularly.

Process. The combination of several methods, procedures and operations required to accomplish a stated goal or objective of an organization.

Profession. A society-oriented occupation that is characterized by extensive specialized training, high social status and power, codes of ethics and institutionalization.

Projects. The smaller and separate portions of programs.

Public interest. An ambiguous term referring to ideas, activities, services, programs or qualities, which are perceived to be beneficial to the majority of the members of a community.

Public relations. All activities, methods, attitudes and functions of management aimed at the identification, evaluation and influencing of the opinions and interests of any person or group toward the organization.

Pupil/teacher ratio. Student enrollment, for a given period of time, divided by the number representing the total fulltime equivalency of classroom teaching assignments serving these pupils during the same period.

Reliability. In statistics, the degree to which a test is consistent in measuring what it is designed to measure.

Retraining. A management method and process of preparing employees already with the organization for new skills which are created by various internal (organizational) or external (economic, social, technological, etc.) needs.

School. A workplace to house non-random events.

School climate. The social system and culture of the school, including the organizational structure of the school and values and expectations within it.

School leadership. The structuring of experiences of children and adolescents to bring about desired outcomes and doing what is required to enable that structuring take place.

School learning climate. The school learning climate refers to the norms and attitudes of the staff and students that influence learning in the school.

Scientific management. The application of scientific principles and methods to the investigation and analysis of organizational activities.

Single-use plans. Detailed courses of action that probably will not be repeated in the same form in the future.

Situational variables. All changeable ideas, elements, traits, characteristics or processes which exist in the physical or social environment of organizations.

Social climate. The sum of all group forces and patterns which effect or influence the attitudes and behavior patterns of its members.

Standardized test. An examination for which there is data on reliability and validity, administered and scored according to specific instructions, and capable of being interpreted in terms of adequate norms.

Strategic planning. The activity formulation by the administration of an organization's objectives and the definition of strategies for achieving them.

Stretch. The degree by which an objective requires the principal to achieve above average effort or above routine as usual level.

Supervision. The function and activity of making sure that the objectives of the organization are carried out according to plans and policies which are designated and handed down from management.

Synergy. Joint work toward a common goal.

Syntality. The sum of all traits, attitudes, abilities, interests, drives, behavior patterns, activities or tendencies of the individual members of a group by which that group can consistently be defined and recognized. Syntality is to group as personality is to the individual.

Target period. The period of time covered by the objective, the date by which the result must be achieved.

Transaction skill. The structure of a transaction identifying the interactions, parameters, and knowledge representation needed for a given class of transactions.

Urbanization. A social, political, economic and cultural process of (1) concentrating people in metropolitan or urban communities, and; (2) involving them in a way of life that is characteristic of such communities.

Validity. Correctness. It is a degree to which a test actually measures the qualities, criteria, predictions or correlatins which it is intended to measure.

Vertical communication. Any communication that moves up or down the lines of responsibility.

Vertical compatibility. When objectives and plans are blended and balanced with those of associates above and below the principal.

Work design. Any document that directs teaching.

BIBLIOGRAPHY

Achilles, C.M.: *Forcast: Stormy Weather Ahead in Educational Administration.* Issues in Education, 2: 2, Fall 1984, pp. 127–135.

Adler, M. J.: *The Paideia Proposal.* New York, Macmillan, 1982.

Albert, K. J.: *Handbook of Business Problem Solving.* New York, McGraw-Hill, 1980.

Allen, M.: The principal's role in developing accountability. *Thrust, 17,* 1988, pp. 17–19.

Ambrosie, Frank: The case for collaborative, versus negotiated decision making. *NASSP Bulletin,* 1989.

American Youth: A Statistical Snapshot. Washington, Commission on Youth and America's Future, June 1987.

A Nation at Risk: The Imperative for Educational Reform. Washington, U.S. Government Printing Office, April, 1983.

A Nation Prepared: Teachers for the 21st Century. Hyattsville, Carnegie Forum on Education and Economy, May 1986.

A New Look at Empowerment. Arlington, American Association of School Administrators, 1990.

Angus, L.: School leadership and educational reform. Paper presented at the annual meeting of the American Educational Research Association, April 1988.

An Imperiled Generation: Saving Urban Schools. Princeton, The Carnegie Foundation, 1988.

Aplin, N. O. and Daresh, J. C.: The superintendent as an educational leader. *Planning and Changing. 15:* 4, Winter 1984, pp. 209–218.

Applebaum, Richard P.: Empowering teachers: do principals have the power?" *Phi Delta Kappan, 70:* December 1988, p. 313.

Aquila, F. D. and Galovic, J.: The principal as change agent: encouraging teachers to adopt change. *NASSP Bulletin, 72:* 50, March 1988.

Armstrong, John D.: A change of leaders: a case study in instructional leadership. *NASSP Bulletin 72:* 510, October 1988, pp. 11–16.

Armstrong, M. and Lorentzen, J. F.: *Handbook of Personnel Management Practice.* Englewood Cliffs, Prentice Hall, 1982, p. 3.

Arnn, John W., Jr. and Mangieri, John N.: Effective leadership for effective schools: a survey of principal attitudes. *NASSP Bulletin, 72:* 505, February 1988, pp. 1–7.

Avila, Linda: Just what is instructional leadership anyway?" *NASSP Bulletin, 74:* 525, April 1990, pp. 52–57.

Bader, Lois A.: Communicating with teachers honestly. *Phi Delta Kappan, 70:* 8, April 1989, p. 626.

246 *The Principal*

Bailey, Gerald D. and Adams, William F.: Leadership strategies for nonbureaucratic leadership, *NASSP, 74:* 524, March 1990, pp. 21–28.

Baily, W. J., Filos, R. and Kelly, B.: Exemplary principals and stress, how do they cope? *NASSP Bulletin, 71,* 1987, pp. 77–81.

Baldridge, J. Victor and Deal, Terrence: *The Dynamics of Organizational Change in Education.* Berkeley, McCutchan, 1983.

Bailey, Gerald D.: *How to Improve Curriculum Leadership, Twelve Tenets.* Reston, National Association of Secondary School Principals. January 1990.

Barker, Bruce O.: Planning, using the new technology in classrooms. *NASSP Bulletin, 74:* 529, November 1990, p. 31.

Barnett, B. and Long C.: Peer-assisted leadership: principals learning from each other. *Phi Delta Kappan,* May 1986, pp. 672–674.

Barr, A.: Wisconsin studies of the measurement and prediction of teacher effectiveness: a summary of investigations. *Journal of Experimental Education, 30:* 1961, pp. 1–156.

Behling, Herman E. Jr. and Champion, Robly H.: *The Principal as Instructional Leader. Lutherville,* Instructional Improvement Institute, 1986.

Bendiner, Robert.: *The Politics of Schools.* New York, Harper & Row, 1969.

Bennett, William, J.: *American Education: Making It Work.* Washington, U.S. Government Printing Office, 1988.

Bennis, Warren: Leadership transforms vision into action. *Industrial Week,* May 1982.

Bennis, Warren: Transformative power and leadership. In *Leadership and Organization Culture.* edited by Thomas J. Sergiovanni and John E. Corbally, Urbana-Champaign, University of Illinois Press, 1984, pp. 64–71.

Bennis, Warren: *Changing Organizations.* New York, McGraw-Hill, 1966.

Bennis, W. and Nanus, B.: Leaders: *The Strategies for Taking Charge.* New York, Harper and Row, 1985.

Benoit, Bob and Braun, Joseph A.: Prototypes: the mentor as an expert coach: a model for rural school districts. *Phi Delta Kappan, 70:* 7, February 1989, p. 488.

Berman, Jill: The managerial behavior of female high school principals: implications for training. Paper presented at the annual meeting of the American Educational Research Association, New York, March 1982.

Blake, R. R., Houton, J. S., Barnes, L. B. and Greiner, L. E.: Breakthrough in organization development. *Harvard Business Review, 42:* 1964, pp. 133–135.

Blanchard, Robert D.: How to create a positive atmosphere in your school. *Principal, 70:* 3, January 1991, pp. 47–48.

Blanche, J. A.: One district's response to the reform movement. *NASSP Bulletin, 72:* Fall 1988, pp. 108–109.

Blase, J. J.: The micropolitical orientation of teachers toward closed school principals. *Education and Urban Society, 23:* 1991, pp. 356–378.

Blumberg, Arthur: The craft of school administration and some other rambling thoughts. *Educational Administration Quarterly, 20:* 4, Fall 1984, pp. 24–40.

Blumberg, Arthur and Greenfield, William. *The Effective Principal: Perspectives on School Leadership.* Boston, Allyn and Bacon, 1980.

Bolton, D.: *Evaluating Administrative Personnel in School Systems.* New York, Teachers College Press, 1980.

Bookbinder, R. M. et al.: *Critical Issues in Education: A Guide for School Administrators.* Englewood Cliffs, Prentice Hall, 1972.

Bossert, Steven et al.: *The Instructional Management Role of the Principal: A Preliminary Review and Conceptualization.* San Francisco, Far West Laboratory for Educational Research and Development, 1982.

Bowles, S. and Gintis, H.: *Schooling in Capitalist America: Educational Reform and the Contradictions of Economic Life.* New York, Basic, 1976.

Boyan, E. L.: Follow the leader: commentary on research in educational administration. *Educational Research, 10:* 2, February 1981, pp. 6–21.

Boyer, E. L.: *High School: A Report on Secondary Education in America.* New York, Harper & Row, 1983.

Bradford, David L. and Cohen Allan R.: *Managing for Excellence: A Guide to Developing High Performance in Contemporary Organizations.* New York, John Wiley, 1984.

Bradley, Larry G. and Vrettas, Arthur T.: Strategic planning and the secondary principal: the key approach to success. *NAASP Bulletin.* March 1990, pp. 30–37.

Brookover, Wilbur et al.: *Creating Effective Schools.* Holmes Beach, Learning Publications, 1982.

Bryk, Anthony S. and Thum, Yeog Meng: *The Effects of High School Organization on Dropping Out.* New Brunswick, Center for Policy Research in Education, February 1989.

Burns, James MacGregor: *Leadership.* New York, Harper and Row, 1978.

Button, H. W.: Doctrines of administration: a brief history. *Educational Administration Quarterly, 2:* 3, Autumn 1966, pp. 216–24.

Buttram, J. L.: Effective teacher evaluation procedures. *Education Leadership.* April 1987, pp. 5–6.

Byars, Lloyd L. and Rue, Leslie W.: *Human Resource Management.* 2nd Ed. Homewood, Richard D. Irwin, 1987.

Byrne, David R. et. al.: *The Senior High School Principalship.* Volume I. The National Survey. Reston, National Association of Secondary Principals, 1978.

Calabrese, R. L.: The principal: an agent for reducing teacher stress. *NASSP Bulletin, 71:* 1987, pp. 66–70.

Caldwell, M.: *Status Report on the Virginia Beginning Teacher Assistance Program.* Charlottesville, University of Virginia Press, 1986.

Caldwell, William, and Lutz, Frank W.: The measurement of principal rule administration behavior and its relationship to educational leadership. *Educational Administration Quarterly, 14:* Spring 1978, pp. 63–79.

Campbell, J. P.: Personnel training and development. *Annual Review of Psychology,* 1971.

Campbell, Roald F. and Gregg, Russell: *Administrative Behavior in Education.* New York, Harper and Brothers, 1957, p. 367.

Carter, Carolyn J. and Klotz, Jack: What principals must know before assuming the role of instructional leader. *NASSP Bulletin, 74:* 525, April 1990, pp. 36–42.

Challenges for School Leaders. Arlington, American Association of School Administrators, 1988.

Challenge to Urban Education: Results in the Making, A Report of the Council of the Great City Schools, Washington, The Council of the Great City Schools, 1987.

Changing of the old ways. *Journal of Research and Development, 22:* 2, Winter, 1989, pp. 7–12.

Clark, W. and Houser, H.: Supervisor's role under Theory Z. *Supervisory Management,* May 1984.

Cline, H. D. and Richardson, M. D.: The reform of school administrator preparation: the Kentucky principal's internship model. Paper presented at the Annual Meeting of the National Council of Professors of Educational Administration. Kalamazoo, August 1988.

Clinton, Bill.: Who will manage the schools? *Phi Delta Kappan, 68:* 4, November 1986, pp. 208–10.

Clune, W. H. and White, P. A.: *School-Based Management: Institutional Variation, Implementation, and Issues for Further Research.* New Brunswick, Center for Policy Research in Education, 1988.

Clinton, B.: *Speaking of Leadership.* Denver, Educational Commission of the States, July 1987.

Coleman, J. et al.: *Equality of Educational Opportunity.* Washington, U.S. Government Printing Office, 1966.

Collins, Eliza G. C.: Executive Success: *Making It in Management.* New York, John Wiley, 1983.

Concerns in Education: Some Popular Assertions About School Administrators: Are They Myths or Realities? Arlington, Educational Research Service, 1988.

Cook, William J.: *The Urgency of Change: America's Schools in Transition.* New York, Underdog, 1988.

Crowson, Robert L. and Porter-Gehrie, Cynthia.: The discretionary behavior of principals in large-city schools. *Educational Administration Quarterly, 16:* Winter 1980, pp. 45–69.

Cuban, L.: Effective schools: a friendly but cautionary note. *Phi Delta Kappan, 64:* 10, 1983, pp. 695–696.

Cunard, Robert F.: Sharing instructional leadership: a view to strengthening the principal's position. *NAASP Bulletin, 74:* 525, April 1990, pp. 30–35.

Cusick, P.: *The Egalitarian Ideal and the American High School.* New York, Longman, 1983.

Dale, Ernest: *Planning and Developing the Company Organization Structure.* New York, American Management Association, 1955, p. 14.

Daresh, J. C.: *The Practicum in Preparing Educational Administrators: A Status Report.* Paper presented at the annual meeting of the Eastern Educational Research Association. Boston, February 1987.

David, J., Purkey, S. and White, P.: Restructuring in progress: lessons from pioneering districts. Paper prepared for the National Governors' Association, Washington, 1988.

Davies, Don: The emerging third force in education. *Inequalities in Education, 15:* 5, November 1973.

Deal, T. E. and Kennedy, A. A.: *Corporate Culture.* Reading, Addison-Wesley, 1982.

Developing a vision statement, some considerations for principals. *NASSP Bulletin, 74:* 523, Fall 1990, pp. 6–12.

Developing Leaders for Restructuring Schools: New Habits of Mind and Heart. Washington, DC: Superintendent of Documents, U.S. Printing Office, 1991.

Dewey, John: *Democracy and Education.* New York, Macmillan, 1916.

Donmoyer, Robert and Wagstaff, Juanita Garcia: Principals can be effective managers and instructional leaders. *NAASP Bulletin, 74:* 525, April 1990, pp. 20–29.

Drake, Thelbert L. and Roe, William H.: *The Principalship.* New York, Macmillan, 1986, pp. 14–15.

Dropouts in America: *Enough Is Known for Action.* Washington, Institute for Educational Leadership, 1987.

Drucker, Peter: *Managing in Turbulent Times.* New York, Harper and Row, 1980.

Drucker, Peter: *The New Realities.* New York, Harper and Row, 1989.

Duke, D. and Stiggins, R.: Evaluating the performance of principals: a descriptive study. *Educational Administration Quarterly, 21:* 4, 1985, pp. 71–78.

Dyer, L.: Bringing human resources into the strategy formulation process. *Human Resources Management, 22:* 1983, pp. 257–273.

Ebermeier, H.: *Diagnostic Assessment of School and Principal Effectiveness: Technical Manual.* Topeka, KanLEAD Educational Consortium, 1990.

Edmonds, R.: Effective schools for the urban poor. *Educational Leadership, 37:* 1979.

Eisner, Jane: Good schools have quality principals. In The Journalism Research Fellows Report: *What Makes an Effective School,* edited by D. Brindage, Washington, Institute for Educational Leadership, 1979.

Elam, Stanley M.: The 22nd annual Gallup Poll of the public's attitudes toward the public schools. *Phi Delta Kappan,* September 1990.

Ellett, C. D., Capie, W. and Johnson, C. E.: Assessing teacher performance. *Educational Leadership. 38:* 3, 1980, pp. 219–220.

Elmore, R. F.: Early experience in restructuring schools: voices from the field. *Realities in Education Series,* Washington, National Governors Association, 1987.

Ely, Donald P. et al.: *Trends and Issues in Educational Technology.* Washington, Office of Educational Research and Improvement, 1989.

Empowering leadership. *Teachers College Record, 91:* Fall 1989, pp. 81–96.

Empowering teachers: do principals have the power? *Phi Delta Kappan, 70:* 4, December 1988, pp. 313–316.

English, Fenwick: *Developing Total Curriculum Quality Control:* responding to the challenge of HSPT. Trenton, State Department of Education. 1986.

English, Fenwick: *Getting the Most from the New Jersey HSPT: A Practical Guide to Resolving Design and Delivery Problems in Schools.* Trenton, State Department of Education. 1985.

Erickson, D. A.: Research on educational administration: the state-of-the-art. *Educational Researcher, 8:* March 1979, pp. 9–14.

Featherstone, Helen: Repeating a grade: does it help? *Harvard Education Letter,* March 1986.

Finn, Chester E., Jr.: Teacher unions and school quality: potential allies or inevitable foes? *Phi Delta Kappan,* January 1985.

Fombrun, Charles J., Tichy Noel M. and Devanna, Mary Anne: *Strategic Human Resource Planning.* New York, John Wiley, 1984.

Foskett, J. M.: *The Normative World of the Elementary School Principal.* Eugene, Center for the Advanced Study of Educational Administration, 1967.

Fray, L. and Lindberg, R.: *How to Develop the Strategic Plan, 2nd. ed.* New York, American Management Association Extension Institute, 1987.

Frymier, J.: Bureaucracy and the neutering of teachers. *Phi Delta Kappan, 69:* 1, September 1987, pp. 9–14.

Fullan, Michael G.: Staff development, innovation, and institutional development, Alexandria, *Changing School Culture Through Staff Development,* ASCD, 1990, pp. 3–25.

Gainey, Donald D.: Teacher evaluation and supervision for school improvement: myth or reality, *NASSP Bulletin, 74:* 524, March 1990, pp. 14–19.

Gardner, John W.: The tasks of leadership. *NASSP Bulletin, 72:* 510, October 1988, p. 77.

Garfield, Charles: *Peak Performers: The New Heroes of American Business.* New York, William Morris, 1986.

Geisert, Gene: Participatory management: panacea or hoax? *Educational Leadership, 46:* 3, November 1988, pp. 56–59.

Genck, F. H.: Improving performance. *The School Administrator.* January 1982, pp. 14–15.

Gideonse, H., Holm, D. and Westheimer, R.: *School Site Budgeting: Abstracting the Literature.* A project for the Educational Panel of the Cincinnatus Association, 1981.

Ginsberg, R.: Worthy goal unlikely reality: the principal as instructional leader. *NAASP Bulletin, 72:* April 1988, pp. 76–82.

Glickman, C.: Good and/or effective schools: what do we want?" *Phi Delta Kappan, 68:* 8, 1981, pp. 622–24.

Goldhammer, Keith: Evolution in the profession? *Education Administration Quarterly, 19:* 3, Summer 1983, pp. 249–272.

Goldhammer, Keith et al.: *Issues and Problems in Contemporary Educational Administration.* Eugene, The Center for the Advanced Study of Educational Administration, 1967, p. 1.

Goldman, Connie and O'Shea, Cindy: A culture for change. *Educational Leadership,* May 1990, pp. 41–43.

Goodlad, J. I.: Educational leadership toward the third era. *Educational Leadership, 35:* 1978, pp. 322–31.

Goodlad, J. I.: *The School As Workplace: Staff Development.* Chicago, National Society for the Study of Education, 1983, p. 45.

Goodlad, J. I.: *A Place Called School.* New York, McGraw-Hill, 1984.

Gorton, Richard A.: *School Leadership and Administration: Important Concepts, Case Studies and Simulations, 3rd ed.* Springfield, William C. Brown, 1987.

Gorton, Richard A.: *School Administration and Supervision: Important Issue, Concepts, and Case Studies. 2nd ed.* Dubuque, William C. Brown, 1983.

Gorton, Richard A.: *School Administration and Supervision: Leadership Challenges and Opportunities.* 2nd ed. Dubuque, William C. Brown, 1983.

Gorton, Richard A. and McIntyre, Kenneth E.: *The Senior High School Principalship. Volume II. The Effective Principal.* Reston, National Association of Secondary School Principals, 1978.

Greenfield, William D.: Empirical research on school principals: the state of the art. Paper presented at the annual meeting of the American Educational Research Association, New York, March 1982.

Greenfield, William D.: *Instructional Leadership: Concepts, Issues, and Controversies.* Boston, Allyn and Bacon, 1987.

Greenfield, William D.: Research on school principals: an analysis. *The Effective Principal.* Washington, National Association of Secondary Principals, 1982.

Patterns of organization change. *Harvard Business Review, 45:* 1967, pp. 119–128.

Gregg, Russell T.: *Administrative Behavior in Education.* New York, Harper and Row, 1957. p. 296.

Griffith, D. E.: *Educational Administration: Reform PDQ or RIP.* Tempe, University Council for Educational Administration. Occasional Paper #8312, 1988.

Griffiths, Daniel E.: *Human Relations in School Administration.* New York, Appleton-Century-Crofts, 1956, pp. 96–121.

Gross, N. and Herriot, R. E.: *Staff Leadership in Public Schools: A Sociological Inquiry.* New York, Wiley, 1965.

Grove, Andrew S.: Everybody is a manager. *The City College Alumnus, 86:* 1, Winter 1991, pp. 8–10.

Gulick, Luther and Urwick, L. (Eds.): *Papers on the Science of Administration.* New York, Institute for Public Administration, 1937.

Guthrie, James W.: School-based management: the next needed education reform. *Phi Delta Kappan, 68:* 4, December 1986, pp. 305–309.

Gutknecht, Douglas B. and Miller, Janet R.: *The Organizational and Human Resources Sourcebook.* New York, University Press of America, 1986.

Hahn, Andrew and Danzberger, Jacqueline: *Dropouts in America: Enough is Known for Action.* Washington, The Institute for Educational Leadership Publications, 1987.

Haimann, Theo and Hilgert, Raymond L.: *Supervision: Concepts and Practices of Management.* Cincinnati, South-Western, 1987.

Hale-Benson, J.: *Black Children: Their Roots, Culture, and Learning Styles, rev. ed.* Baltimore, The Johns Hopkins University Press, 1986.

Hallinger, P. and Murphy, J.: Assessing the instructional leadership behavior of principals. The *Elementary School Journal, 86:* 2, 1985, pp. 217–248.

Hallinger, P., Murphy, J., Weil, M., Mesa, R. and Mitman, A.: School effectiveness: identifying the specific practices and behaviors of principals. *NASSP Bulletin, 67:* 463, 1983, pp. 83–91.

Hard, Shirley M. et al.: *Taking Charge of Change.* Alexandria, Association for Supervision and Curriculum Development, 1987.

Hardler, Harry: Administrators need training too. *Thrust for Educational Leadership, 16:* 7, May–June 1987, pp. 8–9.

Harris, B. M. et al.: *Personnel Administration in Education: Leadership for Instructional Improvement.* Boston, Allyn and Bacon, 1979.

Harris, George W. and Dawes, Ruth A. H.: *The Business Management Tasks of the School Principalship.* Springfield, Charles C Thomas, 1988.

Hatley, Richard V. and Pennington, Buddy R.: Role conflict resolution behavior of high school principals. *Educational Administration Quarterly, 11:* Autumn 1975, pp. 67–84.

Heisler, W. J. and Houck, John W.: *A Matter of Dignity.* London, University of Notre Dame, 1977.

Hemphill, J. K. et al.: *Administrative Performance and Personality.* New York, Teachers College Press, 1962.

Henderson, Richard I.: *Performance Appraisal.* Reston, Reston Publishing, 1984.

Heneman, H. G. et al.: *Managing Personnel and Human Resources.* Homewood, Dow Jones-Irwin, 1981.

Hershey, Paul W.: Selecting and developing educational leaders: a search for excellence. *NASSP Bulletin, 70:* 486, January 1986, pp. 1–2.

Hickman, C. R. and Silva, M. A.: *Creating Excellence: Managing Corporate Culture, Strategy, and Change in the New Age.* New York, New American Library, 1984.

Hofstede, G.: *Culture's Consequences: International Differences in Work-Related Values.* Beverly Hills, Sage, 1980.

Honoring the best in education research. *School Administrator, 47:* 3, March 1990, pp. 30–31.

Howell, B.: Profile of the principalship. *Educational Leadership, 38:* 4, January 1981, pp. 333–336.

Hoy, W. and Miskel, C.: *Education Administration: Theory Research and Practice.* New York, Random House, 1987.

Hughes, L. W. and Ubben, G. C.: *The Elementary Principal's Handbook.* Newton, Allyn and Bacon, 1984.

Inducting Principals. Alexandria, VA: National Association of Elementary Principals, 1989.

Irwin, C. C.: Model describes how principals can achieve quality instruction. *NAASP Bulletin,* September 1985.

Jencks, C. et al.: *Inequality: A Reassessment of the Effect of Family and Schooling in America.* New York, Basic, 1972.

Jensen, A.: How much can we boost scholastic achievement? *Harvard Education Review, 1:* 1969.

Joyce, Bruce R.: *The Structure of School Improvement.* New York, Longman, 1983.

Joyce, Bruce and Showers, Beverly: *Student Achievement Through Staff Development.* White Plains, Longman, 1988.

Joyce, Bruce: *Changing School Culture Through Staff Development:* 1990 Yearbook. Alexandria, Association for Supervision and Curriculum Development, 1990.

Kampol, Barry and Weisz, Eva: The effective principal and curriculum, a focus on leadership. *NAASP Bulletin, 74:* 525, April 1990, pp. 15–19.

Kanter, Rosabeth Moss: Power failure in management circuits. *Harvard Business Review, 57:* 4, July–August 1979, pp. 65–75.

Katz, D. and Kahn, R. L.: *The Social Psychology of Organization.* New York, John Wiley and Sons, 1966.

Katz, Robert L.: Skills of an effective administrator. *Harvard Business Review, 33:* I, January–February 1955, pp. 33–42.

Keefe, James W.: The critical questions of instructional leadership. *NAASP Bulletin, 71:* 498, April 1987, pp. 49–56.

Keefe, James W. and Jenkins, John M.: *Instructional Leadership Handbook.* Reston, National Association of Secondary School Principals, 1984.

Kimbrough, Ralph B. and Nunnery, Michael Y.: *Educational Administration: An Introduction.* New York, Macmillan, 1976.

Knezevich, S.: *The American School Superintendent.* Washington, The American Association of School Administrators, 1975.

Knezevich, Stephen J.: *Administration of Public Education.* New York, Harper and Row, 1969.

Knight, P.: The practice of school-based curriculum development. *Journal of Curriculum Studies, I:* 1984, pp. 37–48.

Knoll, Marcia K.: *Elementary Principal's Survival Guide.* Englewood Cliffs, Prentice Hall, 1988.

Kojimoto, C: The kid's eye view of effective principals. *Educational Leadership, I:* 1987, pp. 69–74.

Kolb, David A., Rubin, Irwin M. and McIntyre, James M.: Organizational Psychology: *An Experiential Approach to Organizational Behavior, 4th ed.* Englewood Cliffs, Prentice Hall, 1984, p. 102.

Kouzes, James M. and Posner, Larry Z.: *The Leadership Challenge.* San Francisco, Jossey-Bass, 1987.

Kowalski, T. J.: Barriers to preparing effective principals. *Illinois School Research and Development, 23:* 1, Fall 1986, pp. 1–7.

Krajewski, R. J. and Shuman, R. B.: *The Beginning Teacher: A Practical Guide to Problem Solving.* Washington, NEA, 1979.

Krug, F.: The principal's impact on student achievement. Doctoral dissertation, San Francisco State University, 1986.

Kuhn, Robert Lawrence: *Handbook for Creative and Innovative Managers.* New York, McGraw-Hill, 1988.

Kyle, Regina M. J. (Ed.): *Reaching for Excellence.* Washington, National Institute of Education, 1985.

Langlois, Donald E. and Colarusso, Mary Rita: Improving teacher evaluation. *The Education Digest, 54:* 13, 1988.

Latham, G. and Wexley, K.: *Increasing Productivity Through Performance Appraisal.* Menlo Park, Addison Wesley, 1981.

Leaders for America's Schools. Tempe, University Council for Educational Administration, 1987.

Leadership: maintaining vision in a complex arena. *NASSP Bulletin, 74:* 523, February 1990, p. 4.

Lefkowitz, Bernard: Tough Change: *Growing Up on Your Own in America.* New York, Free, 1987.

Leithwood, Kenneth A.: *The Principal's Role in Teacher Development.* Alexandria, Association for Curriculum and Supervision Development, 1990, pp. 71–90.

Levin, Henry M. and Hopfenberg, Wendy S.: Don't remediate: accelerate! *Principal, 70:* 3, January 1991, pp. 11–13.

Levine, D. and Lezotte, L.: *Unusually Effective Schools.* Madison, National Center for Effective School Research and Development, 1990.

Lewellen, James R.: Effective leadership: key components. *NASSP Bulletin, 74:* 524, March 1990, pp. 5–12.

Lewin, Kurt: *Field Theory in Social Sciences.* New York, Harper and Row, 1951.

Lewis, Anne: *Restructuring America's Schools.* Arlington, AASA, 1989.

Lewis, Anne C.: Partnerships: *Connecting School and Community.* Arlington, American Association of School Administrators, 1986.

Lewis, James, Jr.: *Achieving Excellence in Our Schools . . . By Taking Lessons from America's Best-Run Companies.* Westbury, Wilkerson, 1985.

Lezotte, Lawrence W. and Brancroft, Beverly A.: *School Improvement Based on Effective Schools Research.* Washington, National Institute of Education, 1985.

Licata, Joseph W. and Ellett, Chad D.: LEAD program provides support, development for new principals. *NAASP Bulletin, 74:* 525, April 1990, pp. 5–11.

Lieberman, A.: Teachers and principals: turf, tension, and new tasks. *Phi Delta Kappan, 69:* 9, May 1988, pp. 648–653.

Likert, Rensis: *New Patterns in Management.* New York, McGraw-Hill, 1961, p. 20.

Lindelow, J.: School based management. In *School Leadership:* Handbook for Survival, S. C. Smith, et al. (Eds.), Columbia, National Committee for Citizens in Education, 1981.

Lipham, J. M. and Francke, D. C.: Non-verbal behavior of administrators. *Educational Administration Quarterly, 2:* Spring 1966, pp. 101–09.

Lippitt, G. L. and Schmidt, W. T.: Crisis in developing organizations. *Harvard Business Review, 25:* 6, November–December 1967, pp. 102–112.

Logan, Joseph F.: Ready, set, empower! Superintendents can sow the seeds for growth. *School Administrator, 146:* 1, 1989, pp. 20–22.

Lomotey, K.: Black principals in black elementary schools: school leadership and school success. Doctoral dissertation, Stanford University, 1985.

Lomotey, K.: Cultural diversity in the school: implications for principals. *NASSP Bulletin, 73:* 521, December 1989, pp. 81–88.

Madsen, K. B.: *Modern Theories of Motivation.* New York, Wiley, 1974, p. 301.

Mager, P. and Pipe, P.: *Analyzing Performance Problems.* Belmont, Lear, Siegler, Fearson, 1978, pp. 11–16.

Mahon, J. Patrick.: Is the equal access issue settled? *Journal of Law and Education, 19:* 4, Fall 1990, pp. 543–547.

Mangier, John N. and Arnn, John W. Jr.: Excellent schools: the leadership functions of principals. *American Educator, 21:* 3, 1985.

Marburger, C.: *One School at a Time: School Based Management a Process for Change.* Columbia, National Committee for Citizens in Education, 1985.

Martin, W. J. and Willower, D. J.: The managerial behavior of high school principals. *Educational Administration Quarterly, 17:* 1981, pp. 69–70.

Maslow, Abraham H.: *Motivation and Personality.* New York, Harper and Row, 1970.

McCleary, L. E. and Hensley, S. P.: *Secondary School Administration: Theoretical Basis for Professional Practice.* New York, Dodd, Mead, 1965, p. 287.

McConkey, Dale D.: *MBO for Nonprofit Organizations.* New York, American Management Association, 1975.

McCune, Shirley D.: *Guide to Strategic Planning for Educators.* Alexandria, Association for Supervision and Curriculum Development, 1986.

McCurdy, J.: *The Role of the Principal in Effective Schools: Problems and Solutions.* Arlington, American Association of School Administrators, 1983.

McDaniel, T. R.: What's your P. Q. (principal quotient)? a quiz on improving instruction. *Phi Delta Kappan, 63:* 1982, pp. 464–68.

McLaughlin, Milbrey W. et al.: Constructing a personalized school environment. *Phi Delta Kappan, 72:* 3, November 1990, pp. 230–235.

McLaughlin, Milbrey W. and Pfeifer R. Scott: *Teacher Evaluation: Improvement, Accountability, and Effective Learning.* New York, Teachers College Press, 1988.

McGregor, Douglas: *The Human Side of Enterprise.* New York, McGraw-Hill, 1960, p. 15.

Meadows, B. J.: The rewards and risks of shared leadership. *Phi Delta Kappan, 71:* 7, March 1990, pp. 545–48.

Medley, Donald M., Coker, Homer and Soar, Robert S.: *Measurement-Based Evaluation of Teacher Performance: An Empirical Approach.* New York, Longman, 1984.

Meyer, John W.: Organizations as ideological systems. In *Leadership and Organization Culture,* edited by T. J. Sergiovanni and J. E. Corbally, Urbana-Champaign, University of Illinois Press, 1984.

Miklos, E.: *Educational Leadership in Schools.* Geelong, Australia, Deokin University, 1980.

Miklos, E.: Evolution in administrator preparation programs. *Educational Administration Quarterly, 19:* 3, Summer 1983, pp. 153–177.

Miskel, Cecil G.: Principals' attitudes toward work and co-workers, situational factors, perceived effectiveness, and innovative effort. *Educational Administration Quarterly, 13:* Spring 1977, pp. 51–70.

Miskel, Cecil G.: Principals' perceived effectiveness, innovation effort, and the school situation. *Educational Administration Quarterly, 13:* Winter 1977, pp. 31–46.

Models of shared leadership: evolving structure and relationships. *Urban Review, 20:* 4, Winter 1988, pp. 229–45.

Mondy, R. Wayne and Noe, Robert M. III.: Personnel: *The Management of Human Resources, 2nd ed.* Boston, Allyn and Bacon, 1984.

Morphet, Edgar L., Johns, Rose L. and Reller, Theodore L.: *Educational Organization and Administration.* Englewood Cliffs, Prentice Hall, 1967.

Morris, V., Crowson, R. L., Hurwitz, E. Jr., and Porter-Gehrie, C.: The urban principal: middle manager in the educational bureaucracy. *Phi Delta Kappan, 63:* June 1982, pp. 689–692.

Morris, Van Cleve et al.: *Principals in Action: The Reality of Managing Schools.* Columbus, Merrill, 1984.

Morris, Van Cleve et al.: *The Urban Principal: Discretionary Decision-Making in a Large*

Educational Organization. University of Illinois at Chicago Circle, March 20, 1981.

Murphy, J., Hallinger, P. and Peterson, K.: Supervising and evaluating principals in effective school districts. *Educational Leadership, 42:* October 1985, pp. 79–82.

Murphy, Joseph: Instructional leadership: focus on curriculum responsibilities. *NASSP Bulletin, 74:* 525, April 1990, pp. 1–4.

Naisbett, John: *Megatrends: Ten New Directions Transforming Our Lives.* New York, Warner, 1982.

Nickerson, N. C. and Davis, D. E.: *Critical Issues in School Administration.* Chicago, Rand McNally, 1968, p. 17.

Nickerson, Neal and Mook, Amy: School and community relations: another aspect of instructional leadership. *NAASP Bulletin, 72:* 510, October 1988, pp. 44–47.

Niehouse, O. L.: Leadership concepts for the principal: a practical approach. *NAASP Bulletin, 72:* 62, January 1988, pp. 50–52.

Norris, Cynthia J.: Developing visionary leaders for tomorrow's schools. Reston, *NASSP Bulletin, 74:* 526, May 1990, pp. 6–10.

Norris, Cynthia J. and Achilles, Charles M.: *Intuitive Leadership: A New Dimension for Educational Leadership.* Planning and Changing, Summer 1987.

Notar, E. E.: What do new principals say about their university training and its relationship to their jobs. *National Forum of Applied Educational Research Journal, 1:* 2, Volume 1, 1988–1989, pp. 14–18.

Nunnery, M. Y.: Reform of K–12 educational administrator preparation: some basic questions. *Journal of Research and Development in Education, 15:* 2, 1982, pp. 44–52.

Oliva, Peter F. *Supervision for Today's Schools, 3rd ed.* New York, Longman, 1988.

Otto, C. P. and Glaser, R. P.: How to prepare and present a training forecast. *Training and Development Journal, 24:* 3, 1970, pp. 24–29.

Ovard, Glen F.: Leadership: maintaining vision in a complex area. *NASSP Bulletin, 74:* 523, February 1990, 1–4.

Parker, B.: School based management: improve education by giving parents, principals more control of your schools. *The American School Board Journal, 7:* 1979, pp. 20–24.

Participative management is a double-edged sword. *Training, 26:* January, 1989, pp. 52–57.

Patterson, Jerry L. et al.: *Productive School Systems for a Nonrational World.* Alexandria, Association for Supervision and Curriculum Development, 1986.

Pellicer, L. O.: Providing instructional leadership: a principal challenge. *NASSP Bulletin, 66,* 458, October 1982, pp. 61–70.

Pellicer, L. O. et al.: *High School Leaders and Their Schools.* Reston, NASSP, 1988.

Personnel evaluation: premises, realities, and constraints. *NASSP Bulletin, 72:* 512, December 1988, pp. 84–87.

Personnel Research: A Symposium Report. *Public Personnel Management, 18:* 2, Summer 1989, pp. 109–92.

Peters, T. *A Passion for Excellence.* New York, Random House, 1980.

Peters, Thomas J. and Austen, Nancy: *A Passion for Excellence: The Leadership Difference.* New York, Random House, 1985.

Peters, T. J. and Waterman, R. H.: *In Search of Excellence: Lessons from America's Best-Run Companies.* New York, Harper and Row, 1982.

Peterson, Kent D.: *Making Sense of Principals' Work.* Paper presented at the annual meeting of the American Educational Research Association in Los Angeles, April 1981.

Pharis, William L., and Zachariya, Sally Banks: *The Elementary School Principalship in 1978: A Research Study.* Arlington, National Association of Elementary School Principals, 1979.

Pierce, L. C.: *Decentralization and Educational Reform in Florida.* Paper presented at the AERSA, Toronto, 1978.

Pierce, P. R.: *The Origin and Development of the Public School Principalship.* Chicago, University of Chicago Press, 1935.

Pitner, N.: The study of administrator effects and effectiveness. *Handbook of Research in Educational Administration,* New York, Longman, 1988, pp. 99–122.

Ploghoft, Milton E. and Perkins, Claude G.: Instructional leadership: is the principal prepared? *NAASP Bulletin, 72:* 510, October 1988, pp. 23–27.

Powers, D. and Powers, M.: *Making Participatory Management Work.* San Francisco, Jossey-Bass, 1983.

Pryor, Fred: The Energetic Manager. Englewood Cliffs, Prentice Hall, 1987.

Raven, John: *Competence in Modern Society.* London, H. K. Lewis, 1984.

Ravitch, Diane: *A good school. The American Scholar,* 53: 4, 1984.

Ravitch, Diane: *The Revisionists Revised: A Critique of the Radical Attack on the Schools.* New York, Basic, 1978.

Redick, M.: The staff as decision makers. *Thrust, 17:* 14, May–June 1988.

Reilly, David H.: The principalship: the need for a new approach. *Education, 104:* 3, Spring 1984, pp. 242–47.

Report Card on School Reform: *The Teachers Speak.* Princeton, Carnegie Foundation for the Advancement of Teaching, 1988.

Revelle, Penelope and Revelle, Charles: *The Environment: Issues and Choices for Society.* Boston, Willard Grant, 1984.

Rist, M. C.: Here's what empowerment will mean for your schools. *Executive Educator, VII:* 8, August 1989, pp. 16–19.

Robbins, Stephen P.: *Organization Theory: The Structure and Design of Organizations.* Englewood Cliffs, Prentice Hall, 1983.

Roe, W. H. and Drake, T. L.: *The Principalship.* New York, Macmillan, 1974.

Rogus, Joseph F.: Developing a vision statement, some considerations for principals. *NASSP Bulletin, 74:* 523, February 1990, pp. 6–12.

Rogus, Joseph F.: Instructional leadership: an informal approach. *NAASP Bulletin, 72:* 510, October 1988, pp. 17–22.

Rosenholtz, S. J.: Education reform strategies: will they increase teacher commitment?" American *Journal of Education, 4:* 1987, pp. 534–562.

Rutherford, W. L., Hord, S. M. and Thurber, J. C.: *Preparing Principals for Leadership Roles in School Improvement.* Education and Urban Society, 17: November 1984, pp. 29–48.

Russell, J. S., Mazzarella, J. A., White, T. and Maurer, S.: *Linking the Behaviors and*

Activities of Secondary School Principals to School Effectiveness: A Focus on Effective and Ineffective Behaviors. Eugene, Center for Educational Policy and Management, 1985.

Salley, C. et al.: What principals do: a preliminary occupational analysis. *The Principal in Metropolitan Schools,* edited by D. A. Erickson and T. L. Reller. Berkeley, McCutchan, 1979.

Sarason, S.: *The Culture of the School and the Problem of Change.* Boston, Allyn and Bacon, 1971.

Schaefer, R.: *School as a Center of Inquiry.* John Dewey Society Lecture No. 9, New York, Harper and Row, 1967.

School Leadership Preparation: *A Preface for Action.* Washington, American Association of Colleges for Teacher Education, 1988.

Schuman, David and Olufs, Dick W. III.: *Public Administration in the United States.* Lexington, D. C. Heath, 1988.

Sergiovanni, Thomas J.: *The Principalship: A Reflective Practice Perspective.* Boston, Allyn and Bacon, 1987.

Sergiovanni, Thomas J. et al.: *Educational Governance and Administration.* 2nd ed. Englewood Cliffs, Prentice Hall, 1987.

Shanker, Albert: *Staff Development and the Restructured School.* Alexandria, ASCD, 1990, pp. 91–103.

Shibles, Mark R.: *School Leadership Preparation: A Preface for Action.* AACTE, Summer 1988, pp. 1–18.

Shockley, W.: A debate challenge: geneticity is 80 percent for white identical twins' I.Q.s. *Phi Delta Kappan, 6:* 1972.

Shoemaker, J. and Fraser, H.: What principals can do: some implications from studies of effective schooling. *Phi Delta Kappan, 63:* 1981, pp. 178–182.

Shulik, J. P.: Project IMPACT in elementary schools. *Educational Leadership, 45:* 41, April 1988.

Shulman, L.: Knowledge and teaching: foundations of the new reform. *Harvard Educational Review, 57:* 1987, pp. 1–22.

Silver, Paula F.: Principals' conceptual ability in relations to situation and behavior. *Educational Administration Quarterly, II:* Autumn 1975, pp. 49–66.

Site-based management: creating a vision and mission statement. *NASSP Bulletin, 73:* 519, October 1989, pp. 79–83.

Simon, Herbert A.: *Administrative Behavior.* New York, Macmillan, 1951.

Sizer, T. R.: *Horace's Compromise: The Dilemma of the American High School.* Boston, Houghton-Mifflin, 1984.

Slater, Robert O.: How does leadership affect teaching and learning? *The School Administrator, 45:* 3, March 1988, pp. 13–20.

Smith, John K.: Educational leadership: a moral and practical activity. *The NAASP Bulletin, 72:* 510, October 1988, pp. 1–10.

Smith, Stuart C. and Scott, James L.: *The Collaborative School: A Work Environment for Effective Instruction.* Eugene, Clearinghouse on Educational Management, 1990.

Snyder, K. J. and Johnson, W. L.: Retraining principals for productive school management. *Educational Research Quarterly., 9:* 3, 1985, pp. 19–28.

Staff Relations in School Administration. Washington, American Association of School Administrators, 1955.

Stimson, Terry D., Applebaum, Richard P.: Empowering teachers: do principals have the power? *Phi Delta Kappan, 70:* 4, December 1988, pp. 313–16.

Stone, Jesse: *Lessons from the Business Literature.* Andover, The Regional Laboratory for Educational Improvement of the Northeast and Islands, 1991.

Stoner, James A. F. and Wankel, Charles: *Management, 3rd ed* Englewood Cliffs, Prentice Hall, 1986.

Stoops, Emery. Rafferty, Max and Johnson, Russell E.: Handbook of Educational Administration: *A Guide for the Practitioner,* Boston, Allyn and Bacon, 1975.

Stronge, James H.: Managing for productive schools: the principal's role in contemporary education, *NASSP Bulletin, 74:* 524, March 1990, pp. 1–5.

Strother, Deborah Burnett: Peer coaching for teachers: opening classroom doors. *Phi Delta Kappan, 70:* 10, June 1989, p. 824.

Sudlow, Robert E.: *What is an Effective School?* Washington, National Institute of Education, 1985.

Supervision in the age of teacher empowerment. *Educational Leadership. 46:* 8, May, 1989, pp. 27–29.

Tanner, Daniel and Tanner, Laurel: *Curriculum Development: Theory Into Practice, 2nd ed* New York, Macmillan, 1980.

Tanner, Daniel and Tanner, Laurel: *Supervision in Education: Problems and Practices.* New York, Macmillan, 1987.

Taylor, Arthur and Valentine, Barbara: *What Research Says About Effective Schools.* Washington, National Institute of Education, December 1985.

Taylor, Frederick: *Scientific Management.* New York, Harper and Row, 1911.

Teacher Development in Schools: *A Report of the Ford Foundation.* New York, Academy for Educational Development, 1985.

Teacher participation in management of school systems. *Teachers College Record, 90:* 2, Winter 1988, pp. 259–80.

The assessment center process for selecting school leaders. *School Organization, 9:* 1989. pp. 103–13.

The Importance of Being Pluralistic: Improving the Preparation of School Administrators. Notes on Reform No. 6. Charlottesville, National Policy Board for Educational Administration, December 1989.

Theory based decision making: a survival tool for principals. *NASSP Bulletin, 73:* 518, September 1989, pp. 17–21.

The principal as curriculum supervisor. *Principal, 69:* 3, January 1990, pp. 6–9.

The Principal as Instructional Leader: A Research Synthesis. Monograph Series Paper No. 1. Springfield, Illinois State Board of Education, 1986.

The process of school improvement: some practical messages from research. *School Organization, 9:* 1989, Volume 9, pp. 53–64.

Thompson, Rosemary A.: Strategies for crisis management in the schools. *NASSP Bulletin, 74:* 4, February 1990, pp. 54–58.

Time for Results: The Governor's 1991 Report on Education. Washington, National Governor's Association Center for Policy Research and Analysis, August 1986.

Tomorrow's Teachers: A Report of the Holmes Group. Lansing, The Holmes Group, April 1986.

Turn to your teachers for curriculum improvement. Educational Leadership, 11: 4, April 1989, 37.

Uttal, B.: The corporate culture vultures. *Fortune,* October 17, 1983, pp. 66–72.

Valentine, Jerry W.: *The Audit of Principal Effectiveness: A Process for Self-Improvement.* Washington, Department of Education, April 1989.

Valentine, Jerry W. and Bowman, Michael L.: *Principal Effectiveness in National Recognition Schools, A Research Project Summary Report.* Washington, Department of Education, July 1989.

Valentine, Jerry et al.: *The Middle Level Principalship: A Survey of Middle Level Principals and Programs.* Reston, National Association of Secondary Principals, 1982, vol. I.

Walcott, H.: *The Man in the Principal's Office.* New York, Holt, Rinehart and Winston, 1973.

Walker, D.: *The Effective Administrator.* San Francisco, Jossey-Bass, 1979.

Ward, James G. and Hildebrand, Alexandria: Will legislative mandates for instructional leadership improve the schools? *NAASP Bulletin, 72:* 510, October 1988, pp. 48–51.

Wasden, F. D. et. al. Preparing principals in a school-university partnership. *Principal, 67:* 1, September 1987, pp. 16–18.

Webb, L. D. et al.: *Personnel Administration in Education.* Columbus, Merrill, 1986.

Webster, W. E.: The high-performing educational manager. *Phi Delta Kappa Fastbacks, 273:* 1988, pp. 6–34.

Wehlage, Gary et al.: *Reducing the Risk: Schools as Communities of Support.* New York, Falmer, 1989.

Weick, K. E.: Educational organizations as loosely coupled systems. *American Science Quarterly,* March 1976.

Weinstein, Donald F.: *Administrator's Guide to Curriculum Mapping.* Englewood Cliffs, Prentice Hall, 1986.

Weisbord, Marvin R.: *Productive Workplace.* San Francisco, Jossey-Bass, 1987.

What Next? *More Leverage for Teachers?* Denver, Education Commission of the States, July 1986.

White, P. A.: *Resource Materials on School Based Management.* New Brunswick, Center for Policy Research in Education, 1988.

Whitehead, Alfred North: *The Aims of Education and Other Essays.* New York, Macmillan, 1929.

Who Will Teach Our Children? Sacramento, California Commission on the Teaching Profession, November 1985.

Wiles, Kindall: *Supervision for Better Schools.* New York, Prentice Hall, 1950, p. 133.

Willie, C. V.: *Effective Education: A Minority Policy Perspective.* New York, Greenwood, 1987.

Willower, D. J.: Micropolitics and the sociology of school organizations. *Education and Urban Society, 23:* 1991, pp. 442–454.

Wise, A. E.: The two conflicting trends in school reform: legislated learning revisited. *Phi Delta Kappan, 69:* 5, 1985, pp. 328–333.

Wise, A. E. et al.: *Teacher Evaluation: A Study of Effective Practices.* Santa Monica, Rand Corporation, June 1984.

Wolcott, H. F.: *The Man in the Principal's Office: An Ethnography.* New York, Holt, Rinehart and Winston, 1973.

INDEX